ABOUT THE EDITOR

Joseph Mersand, Ph.D., has devoted himself throughout his long career as a teacher to the theatre and its literature. He has written and edited books about the drama over a period of twenty years. Among these are *The American Drama, 1930-1940; The Play's the Thing*, and *The American Drama Since 1930*. Dr. Mersand was chairman of the Editorial Committee of the National Council of Teachers of English, which authorized the publication of *Guide to Play Selection*, a standard work.

For ten years Dr. Mersand served as chairman of the English and Speech Departments at Long Island City High School in New York City. Highly regarded in his field, he has been an instructor at Cornell University; Queens College; Teachers College, Columbia University; Syracuse University; and New York University. He is a past president of the National Council of Teachers of English and is chairman emeritus of the English department at Jamaica High School in New York City.

THREE PLAYS ABOUT BUSINESS IN AMERICA

THE ADDING MACHINE
by Elmer L. Rice

BEGGAR ON HORSEBACK
by George S. Kaufman and Marc Connelly

ALL MY SONS
by Arthur Miller

Edited and with Introductions by Joseph Mersand

WASHINGTON SQUARE PRESS
POCKET BOOKS • NEW YORK

THREE PLAYS ABOUT BUSINESS IN AMERICA

WASHINGTON SQUARE PRESS edition published October, 1964
6th printing ....November, 1973

Published by
POCKET BOOKS, a division of Simon & Schuster, Inc.,
630 Fifth Avenue, New York, N.Y.

L

WASHINGTON SQUARE PRESS editions are distributed in the
U.S. by Simon & Schuster, Inc., 630 Fifth Avenue, New York,
N.Y. 10020, and in Canada by Simon & Schuster of Canada, Ltd.,
Richmond Hill, Ontario, Canada.

Contents

THE ADDING MACHINE

by Elmer L. Rice

Introduction

Today it is more than forty years since Elmer Rice's *The Adding Machine* was produced by the Theatre Guild. Yet the play remains perhaps the best exemplar of its genre, that of the expressionistic drama. Also, the delineation of the effects of the dull routine of daily living and working is as effective in the 1960's as it was in the 1920's. Whereas Mr. Zero was thrown out of his job because his boss was planning to install an adding machine, today many thousands are thrown out of semiskilled and unskilled jobs by the introduction of automation.

The Adding Machine has fascinated critics and audiences for four decades, and it is still produced in many community and college theatres. Hardly any study of the American drama fails to refer to this play as the forerunner of an important movement in art in its various forms.

John Gassner in his *Masters of the Drama* declares:

The Adding Machine, written in the heyday of expressionism, in 1923, was one of the most original plays of the American stage. His stylized portrait of the morons produced by mechanization of culture and labor in the person of Mr. Zero, for whom Heaven is too immoral, was nothing short of brilliant. Here Rice triumphed as an ironist and as an observer.[1]

Writing only a few days after its première, Ludwig Lewisohn expressed what many of the critics of the time felt:

Examine this play scene by scene, symbol by symbol.

---

[1] *Masters of the Drama*, p. 684.

The structure stands. There are no holes in its roof. It
gives you the pleasure of both poetry and science, the
warm beauty of life and love, the icy delight of mathe-
matics. . . . Here is an American drama with no loose
ends or ragged edges or silly last-act compromises, re-
tractions, reconciliations. The work, on its own ground,
in its own mood, is honest, finished, sound.[2]

Sooner or later, in a discussion of *The Adding Machine*, the
meaning of expressionism comes up. Perhaps Philip Moeller,
who directed the play for the Theatre Guild, and who had to
do so according to the intentions of the author, defines the
meaning of the expressionistic mode in his introduction to
the Samuel French edition of the play.

The "expressionist" school is concerned with the difference between interpreting a character from the objective
and subjective point of view. Now if "expressionism" is
objective seeing, as all observation must be, it is *subjective* projection; that is, all the half-understood "hinter-
land" thoughts, all the yearnings and unknown suppres-
sions of the mind, are exposed, so to speak, in spite of
the character, just as an X-ray exposes the inner structure
of a thing as against its outer, more obvious and seeming
form.[3]

If a great play is to stand the test of time it must have uni-
versality of appeal. *The Adding Machine* was produced not
only in America, but also in England, Argentina, Austria,
France, Germany, Holland, Hungary, Japan, Mexico, Norway,
and elsewhere. The new generation of readers, as was the old,
will be intrigued by the dialogue which reveals not only the
drab external lives of the characters but their inner thoughts
as well. Long before Eugene O'Neill's asides in *Strange Inter-
lude*, Elmer Rice had used them in Scene II of *The Adding
Machine*.

---

[2] From *The Nation*, April 14, 1923, as quoted by Joseph T. Shipley, *Guide
to Great Plays*, p. 543.
[3] Foreword to *The Adding Machine*, pp. vii-x.

Today's readers will admire what Edmond M. Gagey called "this merciless satire of the white-collar drudge slave to his job and victim of the very system he champions." [4]

Likewise, the structure, the stage design, and the sound effects merit study as one of the early examples in American drama in which the dramatic conventions of the early 1900's were successfully broken, and a newer, fresher spirit entered our playhouses. In a career that has spanned half a century, Elmer Rice has written nothing finer than this comparatively early play.

Elmer L. Rice

Certain writers have become associated with particular areas, rural and urban, which always influence their books: e.g., Thomas Hardy with Wessex, Arnold Bennett with the English pottery district, Ben Hecht with Chicago, Mary E. W. Freeman with New England, Arthur Schnitzler with prewar Vienna. Elmer Rice is the interpreter of New York. His novel *Imperial City* (1937) is the most complete picture of the metropolis ever attempted, and there have been many attempts.

Of his numerous plays about New York, Rice's *Street Scene* is probably the most convincing. However, Rice has not confined himself to writing about Manhattan. *Between Two Worlds* (1934) takes place on an Atlantic liner on its way to Europe. *Judgment Day* (1934) is laid in an unnamed European country, though it is obviously a dramatization of the trial of Dimitrov for the burning of the German Reichstag. *The Left Bank* (1931) has Paris as its setting. Yet critics will agree that Rice has been most successful when he has described New York and its inhabitants, in *Street Scene* (1929), in *Counsellor-at-Law* (1931), and in his various other plays about the law.

Rice's study of law may explain his qualities as a playwright. From almost his first play to the most recent, he has exhibited a passionate hatred for injustice, which at times

[4] *Revolution in American Drama*, p. 151.

worked to the detriment of his dramaturgy. He has always been admired for his marvelously accurate observation of small, though vital details. New Yorkers experienced many pleasures in *Street Scene* and in *Counsellor-at-Law* that were denied to visitors: The New York audiences could more easily recognize characters by the appropriateness of their speech, their dress, and their mannerisms.

Elmer Rice's plays abound in many small cameos of portraiture. *Street Scene* has more than forty characters, most of whom are sharply delineated and clearly differentiated. *Counsellor-at-Law* and *We, the People* also have large casts that require full-length roles, not mere walk-on parts.

Equally apparent throughout his plays is his awareness and dislike of the materialistic aspects of contemporary American civilization. In one of his early plays, *The Subway*, which was not produced until *Street Scene* had become a hit, he describes the wearying effects of daily office routine upon a sensitive young girl. *The Adding Machine* (1923), produced by the Theatre Guild and later revived by the Phoenix Theatre, is an allegory of a young man's experiences in a business civilization that has little respect for individual personalities.

As long as Rice confined himself to demonstrating the tragic implications of industrialization and commercialism, critics were willing to accept him. They had the precedents of John Galsworthy in *Justice*, of Shaw and his imitators, of the young dramatists of the twenties, and of O'Neill in *Beyond the Horizon*.

But Rice, after the great success of *Counsellor-at-Law*, with its assortment of sharp portraits in a metropolitan law office, next tried to present his vision of the disintegrating effect of the Depression in *We, the People*. The critics abandoned him. They had expected another series of portraits, not a passionate outburst against prejudiced judges, company unions, unscrupulous employers, and other unpleasant features of Big Business.

The following year, Rice's anger at the persecution in Nazi Germany led him to portray in *Judgment Day* the Reichstag Fire trials, in which such characters as Göring, Hitler, and

Van der Lubbe appeared. The New York critics were even
more dissatisfied. While granting that Rice was within his
rights as a dramatist to be angry with the Nazis, they denied
him the privilege of using the stage as a soapbox against
naziism. Here, they said, was a melodramatic harangue, not
a play. Rice, accustomed to unfavorable criticism, went
ahead with the presentation of another play that same year.
This time the critics' disapproval proved too much, and
Between Two Worlds closed quickly.

In 1936, his refusal to compromise with his principles
caused him to resign his position as New York City Director
of the Federal Theatre Project because the government had
refused to permit the first edition of "The Living Newspaper"
to include mention of Mussolini and Haile Selassie.

One may admire a man's courage in undauntedly facing
his adversaries and still consider him an ineffective dramatist.
This seems to have been the critics' attitude. However, Rice
knew as well as any man in the theatre that many plays have
become successes even after their universal condemnation by
the reviewers.

One explanation for the lukewarm reception of Rice's later
plays might be that New York audiences were not prepared
for them. Only two years after *We, the People,* Clifford Odets'
Waiting for Lefty made its astonishing appearance. The Theatre Union, born in 1933, could offer such tendentious dramas
as *Peace on Earth, Stevedore, The Black Pit,* and *Sailors of
Cattaro.* Rice's was that pioneering effort which seems always
destined to fail because of its strangeness.

Today, in reading the early dramatic study of the American
Depression, *We, the People,* one cannot help admitting the
courage of its author. Rice, in 1931, had won great popular
and critical success with *Counsellor-at-Law.* Perhaps only the
appearance of *Of Thee I Sing* in the same season took the
Pulitzer Prize out of his hands. He knew enough of New York
(his novel *Imperial City* has enough plot for ten plays) to
have produced another genre painting. Yet he chose to write
We, the People—something entirely different. Time will tell

whether Rice lost himself as a dramatist while he found himself as a campaigner for social justice.

Rice has great gifts for comedy but he does not resort to comedy simply because it is easier for audiences to accept than grim drama. When comedy appears in his plays, it usually derives from the characters. The mother of Mr. Simon, the district leader, and the gum-chewing stenographer of *Counsellor-at-Law;* the Italian janitor, and the Russian Socialist of *Street Scene*—these are characters comic because they are human, and their verisimilitude provokes the laughter of recognition, a frequent experience in the theatre.

Has Elmer Rice made any distinguished contributions to American drama, or is he but another successful dramatist popular for the moment, earning only a paragraph in the history of American drama in the twentieth century? Rice has revealed certain gifts of characterization, which leads one to believe that his reputation will depend on the permanence of these characters. In the theatre, one easily comes under their spell and is quite willing to believe in their existence. Rice knows the souls of several people and can describe many more. Thus, his portrait of Simon, the counsellor-at-law, is probably his masterpiece. Having worked in law offices and knowing, as well as did any practicing dramatist, the personality of the Jewish professional man whose parents were humble immigrants, Rice naturally excels in this characterization. The mother of Simon, with her pride in her son's prominence and her repeated use of the expression, "I've got plenty of time," is a living portrait. Not many playwrights have succeeded in creating such characters.

With the dramatist's keen eye for the revealing detail, Rice can create a character merely by giving him a distinctive walk. Thus, in *Counsellor-at-Law,* one of the secretaries had a gait the like of which had not been seen on the stage before. She walked as if all the world's weight of weariness and unappreciated excellence were locked up in her heart. Whenever she appeared, the audience was amused. It may have been a dramatic trick, but it was an effective one.

Next in importance among Rice's significant contributions

is his skill in interpreting New York life. One of the favorite topics of conversation among playgoers when *Street Scene* was the hit of the town was the exact location of the street described. Some disputants went so far as to photograph three-story houses that they were certain had been the models for the one in the play. Only Rice's statement that his setting was a generalization of the many brownstone houses in Manhattan put an end to the discussion. The zeal of the debaters was an indication of that "willing suspension of disbelief" that Coleridge said was so necessary for complete enjoyment of the theatre. Very few stage pictures of daily life in New York City can compare with *Street Scene*.

Elmer Rice probably prefers to be judged, however, as a dramatist of social justice. To be sure, he is in a great company, which includes George Bernard Shaw, Gerhart Hauptmann, and Sean O'Casey, to mention but a few of the most distinguished in the field.

The doctrine of Alexandre Dumas *fils* that art should be for man's sake could be said to motivate such writers. They do not measure out their emotions to be sure that their indignation does not overbalance their sense of the dramatic. Sometimes, as was the case with Galsworthy, whose temperament was controlled, the indignation of the playwright is communicated to the spectator subtly without being stated explicitly in the play. It is ridiculous, of course, to chastise Rice because his temperament is unlike Galsworthy's and hence frequently causes him to overstate, when the restrained Englishman might have used understatement.

It is to Rice's credit that he refused to curry popular approval by continuing to turn out realistic portraits simply because they had been successful. What elevates Rice to the higher category of American dramatists is his refusal to limit himself to one proved type of play. Like O'Neill, who constantly experimented with new forms, Rice used different techniques. In *The Adding Machine* he tried expressionism at a time when it was the last word in Continental drama. In *We, the People*, Rice took the spectators into his confidence, particularly in the last act when he made the audience the jury before which his hero is tried.

Rice is a brave fighter who uses the stage as his vehicle. He is not a propagandist preaching universal unionization or revolution as a solution for the economic ills of our time. He preaches *against* rather than *for*. He is opposed to oppression, whether in Nazi Germany, in a midwestern American town, or in czarist Russia. He is alive to the beauties of the world, one of which—young love—is tenderly portrayed in several of his plays. He has written about the ugliness of our impersonal business society, which makes possible such tragedies as those he describes in *The Adding Machine*, *Street Scene*, and *We, the People*.

With the exception of *Dream Girl* (1945), Elmer Rice's later plays have not won the critical or popular acclaim that greeted *On Trial* (1914), *The Adding Machine* (1923), and *Street Scene* (1929). He is one of the few living playwrights whose dramatic career spans almost five decades. Most critics will agree that in these years he has made three noteworthy contributions to American drama. In *On Trial* he successfully used for the first time on the stage the flashback technique of the movies. In *The Adding Machine* he wrote the first American Expressionist play. In *Street Scene* he presented the most realistic picture of New York City on the contemporary stage. In 1947, *Street Scene* was produced as an exciting musical, with music by Kurt Weill and lyrics by Langston Hughes. It has taken its place among the dozen or so serious musicals of the American theatre.

Elmer Rice may be admired for the skill with which he has employed a wide variety of styles, ranging from stark realism in *Street Scene* through expressionism in *The Adding Machine* to fantasy in *Dream Girl*. He has frequently been an advocate of liberal causes and freedom of expression. He is one of the few survivors of that exciting group of dramatists who came on the scene in the twenties and who did so much to raise the American drama from its low level in the early part of the century to its present-day leadership in world theatre. As an example of the expressionistic drama of the twenties, *The*

Adding Machine stands head and shoulders above the count-less others that crowded the Broadway stage in the bountiful days of the boom era. It well deserves inclusion in the ANTA Series of Distinguished Plays.

JOSEPH MERSAND

FURTHER READING

Dickinson, Thomas H. *Playwrights of the New American Theatre*. New York: Macmillan, 1925, pp. 317-19.

Flexner, Eleanor. *American Playwrights, 1918–1938*. New York: Simon and Schuster, 1938, p. 285.

Gagey, Edmond M. *Revolution in American Drama*. New York: Columbia University Press, 1947——, p. 151.

Gassner, John. *Masters of the Drama* (3rd ed.). New York: Dover, 1954, p. 684.

Hewitt, Barnard. *Theatre U.S.A., 1668–1957*. New York: McGraw-Hill, 1959, pp. 351-53.

Krutch, Joseph Wood. *The American Drama Since 1918*. New York: Random House, 1939, pp. 230-33.

Kunitz, Stanley J., and Haycraft, Howard. *Twentieth Century Authors*. New York: H. W. Wilson, 1942, pp. 1166-67.

Kunitz, Stanley J. *Twentieth Century Authors: First Supplement*. New York: H. W. Wilson, 1955, pp. 826-27.

Mantle, Burns. *American Playwrights of Today*. New York: Dodd, Mead, 1929, pp. 175-80.

——. *Contemporary American Playwrights*. New York: Dodd, Mead, 1938, pp. 54-61.

Moeller, Philip. Foreword to *The Adding Machine*. New York: Samuel French, 1956, pp. vii-x.

Morehouse, Ward. *Matinee Tomorrow*. New York: Whittlesey House, 1949, p. 224.

Moses, Montrose J. *Representative American Dramas*. Boston: Little, Brown, 1941, pp. 575-80.

Quinn, Arthur Hobson. *A History of the American Drama from the Civil War to the Present Day*. New York: F. S. Crofts, 1936, vol. 2, p. 110.

Roberts, Vera Mowry. *On Stage*. New York: Harper and Row, 1962, pp. 451, 472.

Shipley, Joseph T. *Guide to Great Plays*. Washington: Public Affairs Press, 1956, pp. 541-43.

Short, Ernest. *Introducing the Theatre*. London: Eyre and Spottiswoode, 1949, pp. 158, 169-71, 248.

THE ADDING MACHINE

Cast of Characters

MR. ZERO

MRS. ZERO

MESSRS. ONE, TWO, THREE, FOUR, FIVE, SIX,
and their respective wives

DAISY DIANA DOROTHEA DEVORE

THE BOSS

POLICEMAN

TWO ATTENDANTS

JUDY O'GRADY

A YOUNG MAN

SHRDLU

A HEAD

LIEUTENANT CHARLES

JOE

Scene One

(SCENE. A bedroom. A small room containing an "install-
ment plan" bed, dresser, and chairs. An ugly electric light
fixture over the bed with a single glaring naked lamp. One
small window with the shade drawn. The walls are papered
with sheets of foolscap covered with columns of figures.

MR. ZERO *is lying in the bed, facing the audience, his*
head and shoulders visible. He is thin, sallow, under-sized,
and partially bald. MRS. ZERO *is standing before the dresser*
arranging her hair for the night. She is forty-five, sharp-
featured, gray streaks in her hair. She is shapeless in her
long-sleeved cotton nightgown. She is wearing her shoes,
over which sag her ungartered stockings.)

MRS. ZERO *(As she takes down her hair).* I'm gettin' sick o'
them Westerns. All them cowboys ridin' around an' foolin'
with them ropes. I don't care nothin' about that. I'm sick of
'em. I don't see why they don't have more of them stories
like "For Love's Sweet Sake." I like them sweet little love
stories. They're nice an' wholesome. Mrs. Twelve was sayin'

to me only yesterday, "Mrs. Zero," says she, "what I like is one of them wholesome stories, with just a sweet, simple little love story." "You're right, Mrs. Twelve," I says. "That's what I like, too." They're showin' too many Westerns at the Rosebud. I'm gettin' sick of them. I think we'll start goin' to the Peter Stuyvesant. They got a good bill there Wednesday night. There's a Chubby Delano comedy called "Sea-Sick." Mrs. Twelve was tellin' me about it. She says it's a scream. They're havin' a picnic in the country and they sit Chubby next to an old maid with a great big mouth. So he gets sore an' when she ain't lookin' he goes and catches a frog and drops it in her clam chowder. An' when she goes to eat the chowder the frog jumps out of it an' right into her mouth. Talk about laugh! Mrs. Twelve was tellin' me she laughed so she nearly passed out. He sure can pull some funny ones. An' they got that big Grace Darling feature, "A Mother's Tears." She's sweet. But I don't like her clothes. There's no style to them. Mrs. Nine was tellin' me she read in *Picture-land* that she ain't livin' with her husband. He's her second, too. I don't know whether they're divorced or just separated. You wouldn't think it to see her on the screen. She looks so sweet and innocent. Maybe it ain't true. You can't believe all you read. They say some Pittsburgh millionaire is crazy about her and that's why she ain't livin' with her husband. Mrs. Seven was tellin' me her brother-in-law has a friend that used to go to school with Grace Darling. He says her name ain't Grace Darling at all. Her right name is Elizabeth Dugan, he says, an' all them stories about her gettin' five thousand a week is the bunk, he says. She's sweet, though. Mrs. Eight was tellin' me that "A Mother's Tears" is the best picture she ever made. "Don't miss it, Mrs. Zero," she says. "It's sweet," she says. "Just sweet and wholesome. Cry!" she says, "I nearly cried my eyes out." There's one part in it where this big bum of an Englishman—he's a married man, too—an' she's this little simple country girl. An' she nearly falls for him, too. But she's sittin' out in the garden, one day, and she looks up and there's her mother lookin' at her, right out of the clouds. So that night she locks the door of her room. An' sure enough, when everybody's in bed, along comes this big bum of an Englishman an' when she won't let him in what does he do but go an' kick open the door. "Don't miss it, Mrs. Zero," Mrs. Eight was tellin' me. It's at the Peter Stuyvesant Wednesday night, so don't be tellin' me you want to go to the Rosebud. The Eights seen it downtown at the Strand. They go downtown all the time. Just like us—nit! I guess by the time it gets to the Peter Stuyvesant all that part about kickin' in the door will be cut out. Just like they cut out that big cabaret scene in "The Price of Virtue." They sure are pullin' some rough stuff in the pictures nowadays. "It's no place for a young girl," I was tellin' Mrs. Eleven, only the other day. An' by the time they get uptown half of it is cut out. But you wouldn't go downtown —not if wild horses was to drag you. You can wait till they come uptown! Well, I don't want to wait, see? I want to see 'em when everybody else is seein' them an' not a month later. Now don't go tellin' me you ain't got the price. You could dig up the price all right, all right, if you wanted to. I notice you always got the price to go to the ball game. But when it comes to me havin' a good time then it's always: "I ain't got the price, I gotta start savin'." A fat lot you'll ever save! I got all I can do now makin' both ends meet an' you talkin' about savin'. *(She seats herself on a chair and begins removing her shoes and stockings.)* An' don't go pullin' that stuff about bein' tired. "I been workin' hard all day. Twice a day in the subway's enough for me." Tired! Where do you get that tired stuff, anyhow? What about me? Where do I come in? Scrubbin' floors an' cookin' your meals an' washin' your dirty clothes. An' you sittin' on a chair all day, just addin' figgers an' waitin' for five-thirty. There's no five-thirty for me. I don't wait for no whistle. I don't get no vacations neither. And what's more I don't get no pay envelope every Saturday night neither. I'd like to know where you'd be without me. An' what have I got to show for it?—slavin' my life away to give you a home. What's in it for me, I'd like to know? But it's my own fault, I guess. I was a fool for marryin' you. If I'd 'a' had any sense, I'd 'a' known what you were from the start. I wish I had it to do over again, I hope to tell you. You was goin' to do wonders, you was! You wasn't goin' to be a bookkeeper long—oh, no, not you. Wait till you got started—you was goin' to show 'em. There wasn't no job in the store that was too big for you. Well, I've been waitin'—waitin' for you to get started—see? It's been a good long wait, too. Twenty-five years! An' I ain't seen nothin' happen. Twenty-five years in the same job. Twenty-five years to-morrow! You're proud of it, ain't you? Twenty-five years in the same job an' never missed a day! That's somethin' to be proud of, ain't it? Sittin' for twenty-five years on the same chair, addin' up figures. What about bein' store-manager? I guess you forgot about that, didn't you? An' me at home here lookin' at the same four walls an' workin' my fingers to the bone to make both ends meet. Seven years since you got a raise! An' if you don't get one to-morrow, I'll bet a nickel you won't have the guts to go an' ask for one. I didn't pick much when I picked you, I'll tell the world. You ain't much to be proud of. (*She rises, goes to the window, and raises the shade. A few lighted windows are visible on the other side of the closed court. Looking out for a moment.*) She ain't walkin' around to-night, you can bet your sweet life on that. An' she won't be walkin' around any more nights, neither. Not in this house, anyhow. (*She turns away from the window.*) The dirty bum! The idea of her comin' to live in a house with respectable people. They should 'a' gave her six years, not six months. If I was the judge I'd of gave her life. A bum like that. (*She approaches the bed and stands there a moment.*) I guess you're sorry she's gone. I guess you'd like to sit home every night an' watch her goin's-on. You're somethin' to be proud of, you are! (*She stands on the bed and turns out the light. . . . A thin stream of moonlight filters in from the court. The two figures are dimly visible.* MRS. ZERO *gets into bed.*)

You'd better not start nothin' with women, if you know what's good for you. I've put up with a lot, but I won't put up with that. I've been slavin' away for twenty-five years, makin' a home for you an' nothin' to show for it. If you was any kind of a man you'd have a decent job by now an' I'd be gettin' some comfort out of life—instead of bein' just a slave, washin' pots an' standin' over the hot stove. I've stood it for twenty-five years an' I guess I'll have to stand it twenty-five more. But don't you go startin' nothin' with women—— *(She goes on talking as the curtain falls.)*

Scene Two

(SCENE. An office in a department store. Wood and glass partitions. In the middle of the room, two tall desks back to back. At one desk on a high stool is ZERO. *Opposite him at the other desk, also on a high stool, is* DAISY DIANA DOROTHEA DEVORE, *a plain, middle-aged woman. Both wear green eye shades and paper sleeve protectors. A pendent electric lamp throws light upon both desks.* DAISY *reads aloud figures from a pile of slips which lie before her. As she reads the figures,* ZERO *enters them upon a large square sheet of ruled paper which lies before him.)*

DAISY *(Reading aloud).* Three ninety-eight. Forty-two cents. A dollar fifty. A dollar fifty. A dollar twenty-five. Two dollars. Thirty-nine cents. Twenty-seven fifty.

ZERO *(Petulantly).* Speed it up a little, cancha?

DAISY. What's the rush? To-morrer's another day.

ZERO. Aw, you make me sick.

DAISY. An' you make me sicker.

ZERO. Go on. Go on. We're losin' time.

DAISY. Then quit bein' so bossy. *(She reads.)* Three dollars. Two sixty-nine. Eighty-one fifty. Forty dollars. Eight seventy-five. Who do you think you are, anyhow?

ZERO. Never mind who I think I am. You tend to your work.

DAISY. Aw, don't be givin' me so many orders. Sixty cents. Twenty-four cents. Seventy-five cents. A dollar fifty. Two fifty. One fifty. One fifty. Two fifty. I don't have to take it from you and what's more I won't.

ZERO. Aw, quit talkin'.

DAISY. I'll talk all I want. Three dollars. Fifty cents. Fifty cents. Seven dollars. Fifty cents. Two fifty. Three fifty.

22

Fifty cents. One fifty. Fifty cents. (*She goes bending over the slips and transferring them from one pile to another.* ZERO *bends over his desk, busily entering the figures.*)

ZERO (*Without looking up*). You make me sick. Always shootin' off your face about somethin'. Talk, talk, talk. Just like all the other women. Women make me sick.

DAISY (*Busily fingering the slips*). Who do you think you are, anyhow? Bossin' me around. I don't have to take it from you, and what's more I won't. (*They both attend closely to their work, neither looking up.*)

ZERO. Women make me sick. They're all alike. The judge gave her six months. I wonder what they do in the work-house. Peel potatoes. I'll bet she's sore at me. Maybe she'll try to kill me when she gets out. I better be careful. Hello. Girl Slays Betrayer. Jealous Wife Slays Rival. You can't tell what a woman's liable to do. I better be careful.

DAISY. I'm gettin' sick of it. Always pickin' on me about somethin'. Never a decent word out of you. Not even the time o' day.

ZERO. I guess she wouldn't have the nerve at that. Maybe she don't even know it's me. They didn't even put my name in the paper, the big bums. Maybe she's been in the work-house before. A bum like that. She didn't have nothin' on that one time—nothin' but a shirt. (*He glances up quickly, then bends over again.*) You make me sick. I'm sick of lookin' at your face.

DAISY. Gee, ain't that whistle ever goin' to blow? You didn't used to be like that. Not even good mornin' or good evenin'. I ain't done nothin' to you. It's the young girls. Goin' around without corsets.

ZERO. Your face is gettin' all yeller. Why don't you put some paint on it? She was puttin' on paint that time. On her cheeks and on her lips. And that blue stuff on her eyes. Just sittin' there in a shimmy puttin' on the paint. An' walkin' around the room with her legs all bare.

DAISY. I wish I was dead.

ZERO. I was a goddam fool to let the wife get on to me. She oughta get six months at that. The dirty bum. Livin' in a house with respectable people. She'd be livin' there yet, if the wife hadn't o' got on to me. Damn her!

DAISY. I wish I was dead.

ZERO. Maybe another one'll move in. Gee, that would be great. But the wife's got her eye on me now.

DAISY. I'm scared to do it, though.

ZERO. You oughta move into that room. It's cheaper than where you're livin' now. I better tell you about it. I don't mean to be always pickin' on you.

DAISY. Gas. The smell of it makes me sick. (ZERO *looks up and clears his throat.*)

DAISY (*Looking up, startled*). Whadja say?

ZERO. I didn't say nothin'.

DAISY. I thought you did.

ZERO. You thought wrong. (*They bend over their work again.*)

DAISY. A dollar sixty. A dollar fifty. Two ninety. One sixty-two.

ZERO. Why the hell should I tell you? Fat chance of you for-gettin' to pull down the shade!

DAISY. If I asked for carbolic they might get on to me.

ZERO. Your hair's gettin' gray. You don't wear them shirt waists any more with the low collars. When you'd bend down to pick somethin' up——

DAISY. I wish I knew what to ask for. Girl Takes Mercury After All-Night Party. Woman In Ten-Story Death Leap.

ZERO. I wonder where'll she go when she gets out. Gee, I'd like to make a date with her. Why didn't I go over there the night my wife went to Brooklyn? She never woulda found out.

DAISY. I seen Pauline Frederick do it once. Where could I get a pistol though?

ZERO. I guess I didn't have the nerve.

DAISY. I'll bet you'd be sorry then that you been so mean to me. How do I know, though? Maybe you wouldn't.

ZERO. Nerve! I got as much nerve as anybody. I'm on the level, that's all. I'm a married man and I'm on the level.

DAISY. Anyhow, why ain't I got a right to live? I'm as good

as anybody else. I'm too refined, I guess. That's the whole trouble.

ZERO. The time the wife had pneumonia I thought she was goin' to pass out. But she didn't. The doctor's bill was eighty-seven dollars. *(Looking up.)* Hey, wait a minute! Didn't you say eighty-seven dollars?

DAISY *(Looking up)*. What?

ZERO. Was the last you said eighty-seven dollars?

DAISY *(Consulting the slip)*. Forty-two fifty.

ZERO. Well, I made a mistake. Wait a minute. *(He busies himself with an eraser.)* All right. Shoot.

DAISY. Six dollars. Three fifteen. Two twenty-five. Sixty-five cents. A dollar twenty. You talk to me as if I was dirt.

ZERO. I wonder if I could kill the wife without anybody findin' out. In bed some night. With a pillow.

DAISY. I used to think you was stuck on me.

ZERO. I'd get found out, though. They always have ways.

DAISY. We used to be so nice and friendly together when I first came here. You used to talk to me then.

ZERO. Maybe she'll die soon. I noticed she was coughin' this mornin'.

DAISY. You used to tell me all kinds o' things. You were goin' to show them all. Just the same, you're still sittin' here.

ZERO. Then I could do what I damn please. Oh, boy!

DAISY. Maybe it ain't all your fault neither. Maybe if you'd had the right kind o' wife—somebody with a lot of common-sense, somebody refined—me!

ZERO. At that, I guess I'd get tired of bummin' around. A feller wants some place to hang his hat.

DAISY. I wish she would die.

ZERO. And when you start goin' with women you're liable to get into trouble. And lose your job maybe.

DAISY. Maybe you'd marry me.

ZERO. Gee, I wish I'd gone over there that night.

DAISY. Then I could quit workin'.

ZERO. Lots o' women would be glad to get me.

DAISY. You could look a long time before you'd find a sensible, refined girl like me.

ZERO. Yes, sir, they could look a long time before they'd find a steady meal-ticket like me.

DAISY. I guess I'd be too old to have any kids. They say it ain't safe after thirty-five.

ZERO. Maybe I'd marry you. You might be all right, at that.

DAISY. I wonder—if you don't want kids—whether—if there's any way——

ZERO *(Looking up)*. Hey! Hey! Can't you slow up? What do you think I am—a machine?

DAISY *(Looking up)*. Say, what do you want, anyhow? First it's too slow an' then it's too fast. I guess you don't know what you want.

ZERO. Well, never mind about that. Just you slow up.

DAISY. I'm gettin' sick o' this. I'm goin' to ask to be transferred.

ZERO. Go ahead. You can't make me mad.

DAISY. Aw, keep quiet. *(She reads.)* Two forty-five. A dollar twenty. A dollar fifty. Ninety cents. Sixty-three cents.

ZERO. Marry you! I guess not! You'd be as bad as the one I got.

DAISY. You wouldn't care if I did ask. I got a good mind to ask.

ZERO. I was a fool to get married.

DAISY. Then I'd never see you at all.

ZERO. What chance has a guy got with a woman tied around his neck?

DAISY. That time at the store picnic—the year your wife couldn't come—you were nice to me then.

ZERO. Twenty-five years holdin' down the same job!

DAISY. We were together all day—just sittin' around under the trees.

ZERO. I wonder if the boss remembers about it bein' twenty-five years.

DAISY. And comin' home that night—you sat next to me in the big delivery wagon.

ZERO. I got a hunch there's a big raise comin' to me.

DAISY. I wonder what it feels like to be really kissed. Men—dirty pigs! They want the bold ones.

ZERO. If he don't come across I'm goin' right up to the front office and tell him where he gets off.

DAISY. I wish I was dead.

ZERO. "Boss," I'll say, "I want to have a talk with you." "Sure," he'll say, "sit down. Have a Corona Corona." "No," I'll say, "I don't smoke." "How's that?" he'll say. "Well, boss," I'll say, "it's this way. Every time I feel like smokin' I just take a nickel and put it in the old sock. A penny saved is a penny earned, that's the way I look at it." "Damn sensible," he'll say. "You got a wise head on you, Zero."

DAISY. I can't stand the smell of gas. It makes me sick. You coulda kissed me if you wanted to.

ZERO. "Boss," I'll say, "I ain't quite satisfied. I been on the job twenty-five years now and if I'm gonna stay I gotta see a future ahead of me." "Zero," he'll say, "I'm glad you came in. I've had my eye on you, Zero. Nothin' gets by me." "Oh, I know that, boss," I'll say. That'll hand him a good laugh, that will. "You're a valuable man, Zero," he'll say, "and I want you right up here with me in the front office. You're done addin' figgers. Monday mornin' you move up here."

DAISY. Them kisses in the movies—them long ones—right on the mouth——

ZERO. I'll keep a-goin' right on up after that. I'll show some of them birds where they get off.

DAISY. That one the other night—"The Devil's Alibi"—he put his arms around her—and her head fell back and her eyes closed—like she was in a daze.

ZERO. Just give me about two years and I'll show them birds where they get off.

DAISY. I guess that's what it's like—a kinda daze—when I see them like that, I just seem to forget everything.

ZERO. Then me for a place in Jersey. And maybe a little Buick. No tin Lizzie for mine. Wait till I get started—I'll show 'em.

DAISY. I can see it now when I kinda half-close my eyes. The way her head fell back. And his mouth pressed right up against hers. Oh, Gawd! it must be grand! (There is a sudden shrill blast from a steam whistle.)

DAISY AND ZERO (Together). The whistle! (With great agility they get off their stools, remove their eye shades and sleeve *protectors and put them on the desks. Then each produces from behind the desk a hat—*ZERO, *a dusty derby,* DAISY, *a frowsy straw.* . . . DAISY *puts on her hat and turns toward* ZERO *as though she were about to speak to him. But he is busy cleaning his pen and pays no attention to her. She sighs and goes toward the door at the left.)*

ZERO *(Looking up).* G'night, Miss Devore.

(But she does not hear him and exits. ZERO *takes up his hat and goes left. The door at the right opens and the* BOSS *enters—middle-aged, stoutish, bald, well-dressed.)*

BOSS *(Calling).* Oh—er—Mister—er——— *(*ZERO *turns in surprise, sees who it is and trembles nervously.)*

ZERO *(Obsequiously).* Yes, sir. Do you want me, sir?

BOSS. Yes. Just come here a moment, will you?

ZERO. Yes, sir. Right away, sir. *(He fumbles his hat, picks it up, stumbles, recovers himself, and approaches the* BOSS, *every fibre quivering.)*

BOSS. Mister—er—er——

ZERO. Zero.

BOSS. Yes, Mr. Zero. I wanted to have a little talk with you.

ZERO *(With a nervous grin).* Yes sir, I been kinda expectin' it.

BOSS *(Staring at him).* Oh, have you?

ZERO. Yes, sir.

BOSS. How long have you been with us, Mister—er—Mister——

ZERO. Zero.

BOSS. Yes, Mister Zero.

ZERO. Twenty-five years to-day.

BOSS. Twenty-five years! That's a long time.

ZERO. Never missed a day.

BOSS. And you've been doing the same work all the time?

ZERO. Yes, sir. Right here at this desk.

BOSS. Then, in that case, a change probably won't be unwelcome to you.

ZERO. No, sir, it won't. And that's the truth.

BOSS. We've been planning a change in this department for some time.

ZERO. I kinda thought you had your eye on me.

BOSS. You were right. The fact is that my efficiency experts have recommended the installation of adding machines.

ZERO (*Staring at him*). Addin' machines?

BOSS. Yes, you've probably seen them. A mechanical device that adds automatically.

ZERO. Sure. I've seen them. Keys—and a handle that you pull. (*He goes through the motions in the air.*)

BOSS. That's it. They do the work in half the time and a high-school girl can operate them. Now, of course, I'm sorry to lose an old and faithful employee——

ZERO. Excuse me, but would you mind sayin' that again?

BOSS. I say I'm sorry to lose an employee who's been with me for so many years——

(*Soft music is heard—the sound of the mechanical player of a distant merry-go-round. The part of the floor upon which the desk and stools are standing begins to revolve very slowly.*)

BOSS. But, of course, in an organization like this, efficiency must be the first consideration——

(*The music becomes gradually louder and the revolutions more rapid.*)

BOSS. You will draw your salary for the full month. And I'll direct my secretary to give you a letter of recommendation——

ZERO. Wait a minute, boss. Let me get this right. You mean I'm canned?

BOSS (*Barely making himself heard above the increasing volume of sound*). I'm sorry—no other alternative—greatly regret —old employee—efficiency—economy—business—*business* —BUSINESS——

(His voice is drowned by the music. The platform is revolving rapidly now. ZERO *and the* BOSS *face each other. They are entirely motionless save for the* BOSS's *jaws, which open and close incessantly. But the words are inaudible. The music swells and swells. To it is added every off-stage effect of the theatre: the wind, the waves, the galloping horses, the locomotive whistle, the sleigh bells, the automobile siren, the glass-crash. New Year's Eve, Election Night, Armistice Day, and the Mardi-Gras. The noise is deafening, maddening, unendurable. Suddenly it culminates in a terrific peal of thunder. For an instant there is a flash of red and then everything is plunged into blackness.)*

(Curtain)

Scene Three

(SCENE. *The* ZERO *dining room. Entrance door at right. Doors to kitchen and bedroom at left. The walls, as in the first scene, are papered with foolscap sheets covered with columns of figures. In the middle of the room, upstage, a table set for two. Along each side wall, seven chairs are ranged in symmetrical rows.*

At the rise of the curtain MRS. ZERO *is seen seated at the table looking alternately at the entrance door and a clock on the wall. She wears a bungalow apron over her best dress.*

After a few moments, the entrance door opens and ZERO *enters. He hangs his hat on a rack behind the door and coming over to the table seats himself at the vacant place. His movements throughout are quiet and abstracted.*)

MRS. ZERO (*Breaking the silence*). Well, it was nice of you to come home. You're only an hour late and that ain't very much. The supper don't get very cold in an hour. An' of course the part about our havin' a lot of company to-night don't matter. (*They begin to eat.*)

Ain't you even got sense enough to come home on time? Didn't I tell you we're goin' to have a lot o' company to-night? Didn't you know the Ones are comin'? An' the Twos? An' the Threes? An' the Fours? An' the Fives? And the Sixes? Didn't I tell you to be home on time? I might as well talk to a stone wall. (*They eat for a few moments in silence.*)

I guess you musta had some important business to attend to. Like watchin' the score-board. Or was two kids havin' a fight an' you was the referee? You sure do have a lot of

31

business to attend to. It's a wonder you have time to come home at all. You gotta tough life, you have. Walk in, hang up your hat, an' put on the nose-bag. An' me in the hot kitchen all day, cookin' your supper an' waitin' for you to get good an' ready to come home! *(Again they eat in silence.)*

Maybe the boss kept you late to-night. Tellin' you what a big noise you are and how the store couldn't 'a' got along if you hadn't been pushin' a pen for twenty-five years. Where's the gold medal he pinned on you? Did some blind old lady take it away from you or did you leave it on the seat of the boss's limousine when he brought you home? *(Again a few moments of silence.)*

I'll bet he gave you a big raise, didn't he? Promoted you from the third floor to the fourth, maybe. Raise? A fat chance you got o' gettin' a raise. All they gotta do is put an ad in the paper. There's ten thousand like you layin' around the streets. You'll be holdin' down the same job at the end of another twenty-five years—if you ain't forgot how to add by that time.

(A noise is heard off-stage, a sharp clicking such as is made by the operation of the keys and levers of an adding machine. ZERO raises his head for a moment, but lowers it almost instantly.)

MRS. ZERO. There's the door-bell. The company's here already. And we ain't hardly finished supper. *(She rises.)*

But I'm goin' to clear off the table whether you're finished or not. If you want your supper, you got a right to be home on time. Not standin' around lookin' at score-boards. *(As she piles up the dishes, ZERO rises and goes toward the entrance door.)*

Wait a minute! Don't open the door yet. Do you want the company to see all the mess? An' go an' put on a clean collar. You got red ink all over it. (ZERO *goes toward bedroom door.)*

I should think after pushin' a pen for twenty-five years, you'd learn how to do it without gettin' ink on your collar.

(ZERO *exits to bedroom.* MRS. ZERO *takes dishes to kitchen talking as she goes.*)

I guess I can stay up all night now washin' dishes. You should worry! That's what a man's got a wife for, ain't it? Don't he buy her her clothes an' let her eat with him at the same table? An' all she's gotta do is cook the meals an' do the washin' an' scrub the floor, an' wash the dishes, when the company goes. But, believe me, you're goin' to sling a mean dish-towel when the company goes to-night!

(*While she is talking* ZERO *enters from bedroom. He wears a clean collar and is cramming the soiled one furtively into his pocket.* MRS. ZERO *enters from kitchen. She has removed her apron and carries a table cover which she spreads hastily over the table. The clicking noise is heard again.*)

MRS. ZERO. There's the bell again. Open the door, cancha?

(ZERO *goes to the entrance door and opens it. Six men and six women file into the room in a double column. The men are all shapes and sizes, but their dress is identical with that of* ZERO *in every detail. Each, however, wears a wig of a different color. The women are all dressed alike, too, except that the dress of each is of a different color.*)

MRS. ZERO (*Taking the first woman's hand*). How de do, Mrs. One.
MRS. ONE. How de do, Mrs. Zero.

(MRS. ZERO *repeats this formula with each woman in turn.* ZERO *does the same with the men except that he is silent throughout. The files now separate, each man taking a chair from the right wall and each woman one from the left wall. Each sex forms a circle with the chairs very close together. The men—all except* ZERO—*smoke cigars. The women munch chocolates.*)

SIX. Some rain we're havin'.

FIVE. Never saw the like of it.

FOUR. Worst in fourteen years, paper says.

THREE. Y'can't always go by the papers.

TWO. No, that's right, too.

ONE. We're liable to forget from year to year.

SIX. Yeh, come t' think, last year was pretty bad, too.

FIVE. An' how about two years ago?

FOUR. Still this year's pretty bad.

THREE. Yeh, no gettin' away from that.

TWO. Might be a whole lot worse.

ONE. Yeh, it's all the way you look at it. Some rain, though.

MRS. SIX. I like them little organdie dresses.

MRS. FIVE. Yeh, with a little lace trimmin' on the sleeves.

MRS. FOUR. Well, I like 'em plain myself.

MRS. THREE. Yeh, what I always say is the plainer the more refined.

MRS. TWO. Well, I don't think a little lace does any harm.

MRS. ONE. No, it kinda dresses it up.

MRS. ZERO. Well, I always say it's all a matter of taste.

MRS. SIX. I saw you at the Rosebud Movie Thursday night, Mr.
One.

ONE. Pretty punk show, I'll say.

TWO. They're gettin' worse all the time.

MRS. SIX. But who was the charming lady, Mr. One?

ONE. Now don't you go makin' trouble for me. That was my
sister.

MRS. FIVE. Oho! That's what they all say.

MRS. FOUR. Never mind! I'll bet Mrs. One knows what's what,
all right.

MRS. ONE. Oh, well, he can do what he likes—'slong as he be-
haves himself.

THREE. You're in luck at that, One. Fat chance I got of gettin'
away from the frau even with my sister.

MRS. THREE. You oughta be glad you got a good wife to look
after you.

THE OTHER WOMEN (*In unison*). That's right, Mrs. Three.

FIVE. I guess I know who wears the pants in your house,
Three.

MRS. ZERO. Never mind. I saw them holdin' hands at the movie the other night.

THREE. She musta been tryin' to get some money away from me.

MRS. THREE. Swell chance anybody'd have of gettin' any money away from you. *(General laughter.)*

FOUR. They sure are a loving couple.

MRS. TWO. Well, I think we oughta change the subject.

MRS. ONE. Yes, let's change the subject.

SIX *(Sotto voce)*. Did you hear the one about the travellin' salesman?

FIVE. It seems this guy was in a sleeper.

FOUR. Goin' from Albany to San Diego.

THREE. And in the next berth was an old maid.

TWO. With a wooden leg.

ONE. Well, along about midnight—— *(They all put their heads together and whisper.)*

MRS. SIX *(Sotto voce)*. Did you hear about the Sevens?

MRS. FIVE. They're gettin' a divorce.

MRS. FOUR. It's the second time for him.

MRS. THREE. They're two of a kind, if you ask me.

MRS. TWO. One's as bad as the other.

MRS. ONE. Worse.

MRS. ZERO. They say that she—— *(They all put their heads together and whisper.)*

SIX. I think this woman suffrage is the bunk.

FIVE. It sure is! Politics is a man's business.

FOUR. Woman's place is in the home.

THREE. That's it! Lookin' after the kids, 'stead of hangin' around the streets.

TWO. You hit the nail on the head that time.

ONE. The trouble is they don't know what they want.

MRS. SIX. Men sure get me tired.

MRS. FIVE. They sure are a lazy lot.

MRS. FOUR. And dirty.

MRS. THREE. Always grumblin' about somethin'.

MRS. TWO. When they're not lyin'!

MRS. ONE. Or messin' up the house.

MRS. ZERO. Well, believe me, I tell mine where he gets off.

SIX. Business conditions are sure bad.

FIVE. Never been worse.

FOUR. I don't know what we're comin' to.

THREE. I look for a big smash-up in about three months.

TWO. Wouldn't surprise me a bit.

ONE. We're sure headin' for trouble.

MRS. SIX. My aunt has gall-stones.

MRS. FIVE. My husband has bunions.

MRS. FOUR. My sister expects next month.

MRS. THREE. My cousin's husband has erysipelas.

MRS. TWO. My niece has St. Vitus's dance.

MRS. ONE. My boy has fits.

MRS. ZERO. I never felt better in my life. Knock wood!

SIX. Too damn much agitation, that's at the bottom of it.

FIVE. That's it! too damn many strikes.

FOUR. Foreign agitators, that's what it is.

THREE. They ought be run outa the country.

TWO. What the hell do they want, anyhow?

ONE. They don't know what they want, if you ask me.

SIX. America for the Americans is what I say!

ALL (*In unison*). That's it! Damn foreigners! Damn dagoes! Damn Catholics! Damn sheenies! Damn niggers! Jail 'em! shoot 'em! hang 'em! lynch 'em! burn 'em! (*They all rise.*)

ALL (*Sing in unison*). "My country 'tis of thee,
                              Sweet land of liberty!"

MRS. FOUR. Why so pensive, Mr. Zero?

ZERO (*Speaking for the first time*). I'm thinkin'.

MRS. FOUR. Well, be careful not to sprain your mind. (*Laughter.*)

MRS. ZERO. Look at the poor men all by themselves. We ain't very sociable.

ONE. Looks like we're neglectin' the ladies. (*The women cross the room and join the men, all chattering loudly. The door-bell rings.*)

MRS. ZERO. Sh! The door-bell! (*The volume of sound slowly diminishes. Again the door-bell.*)

ZERO (*Quietly*). I'll go. It's for me. (*They watch curiously as*

ZERO *goes to the door and opens it, admitting a policeman. There is a murmur of surprise and excitement.*)

POLICEMAN. I'm lookin' for Mr. Zero. (*They all point to* ZERO.)

ZERO. I've been expectin' you.

POLICEMAN. Come along!

ZERO. Just a minute. (*He puts his hand in his pocket.*)

POLICEMAN. What's he tryin' to pull? (*He draws a revolver.*) I got you covered.

ZERO. Sure, that's all right. I just want to give you somethin'. (*He takes the collar from his pocket and gives it to the policeman.*)

POLICEMAN (*Suspiciously*). What's that?

ZERO. The collar I wore.

POLICEMAN. What do I want it for?

ZERO. It's got blood-stains on it.

POLICEMAN (*Pocketing it*). All right, come along!

ZERO (*Turning to* MRS. ZERO). I gotta go with him. You'll have to dry the dishes yourself.

MRS. ZERO (*Rushing forward*). What are they takin' you for?

ZERO (*Calmly*). I killed the boss this afternoon.

(*Quick curtain as the policeman takes him off.*)

Scene Four

(SCENE. A court of justice. Three bare white walls without door or windows except for a single door in the right wall. At the right is a jury box in which are seated MESSRS. ONE, TWO, THREE, FOUR, FIVE, and SIX and their respective wives. On either side of the jury box stands a uniformed OFFICER. Opposite the jury box is a long, bare oak table piled high with law books. Behind the books ZERO is seated, his face buried in his hands. There is no other furniture in the room. A moment after the rise of the curtain, one of the officers rises and going around the table, taps ZERO on the shoulder. ZERO rises and accompanies the officer. The OFFICER escorts him to the great empty space in the middle of the court room, facing the jury. He motions to ZERO to stop, then points to the jury and resumes his place beside the jury box. ZERO stands there looking at the jury, bewildered and half afraid. The JURORS give no sign of having seen him. Throughout they sit with folded arms, staring stolidly before them.)

ZERO *(Beginning to speak; haltingly).* Sure I killed him. I ain't sayin' I didn't, am I? Sure I killed him. Them lawyers! They give me a good stiff pain, that's what they give me. Half the time I don't know what the hell they're talkin' about. Objection sustained. Objection over-ruled. What's the big idea, anyhow? You ain't heard me do any objectin', have you? Sure not! What's the idea of objectin'? You got a right to know. What I say is if one bird kills another bird, why you got a right to call him for it. That's what I say. I know all about that. I been on the jury, too. Them lawyers! Don't let 'em fill you full of bunk. All that bull about it bein' red

ink on the bill-file. Red ink nothin'! It was blood, see? I
want you to get that right. I killed him, see? Right through
the heart with the bill-file, see? I want you to get that right
—all of you. One, two, three, four, five, six, seven, eight,
nine, ten, eleven, twelve. Twelve of you. Six and six. That
makes twelve. I figgered it up often enough. Six and six
makes twelve. And five is seventeen. And eight is twenty-
five. And three is twenty-eight. Eight and carry two. Aw,
cut it out! Them damn figgers! I can't forget 'em. Twenty-
five years, see? Eight hours a day, exceptin' Sundays. And
July and August half-day Saturday. One week's vacation
with pay. And another week without pay if you want it.
Who the hell wants it? Layin' around the house listenin' to
the wife tellin' you where you get off. Nix! An' legal holi-
days. I nearly forgot them. New Year's, Washington's Birthday, Decoration Day, Fourth o' July, Labor Day, Election
Day, Thanksgivin', Christmas. Good Friday if you want it.
An' if you're a Jew, Young Kipper an' the other one—I
forget what they call it. The dirty sheenies—always gettin'
two to the other bird's one. An' when a holiday comes on
Sunday, you get Monday off. So that's fair enough. But
when the Fourth o' July comes on Saturday, why you're out
o' luck on account of Saturday bein' a half-day anyhow. Get
me? Twenty-five years—I'll tell you somethin' funny. Decoration Day an' the Fourth o' July are always on the same
day o' the week. Twenty-five years. Never missed a day,
and never more'n five minutes late. Look at my time card
if you don't believe me. Eight twenty-seven, eight thirty,
eight twenty-nine, eight twenty-seven, eight thirty-two.
Eight an' thirty-two's forty an'—— Goddam them figgers! I
can't forget 'em. They're funny things, them figgers. They
look like people sometimes. The eights, see? Two dots for
the eyes and a dot for the nose. An' a line. That's the mouth,
see? An' there's others remind you of other things—but I
can't talk about them, on account of there bein' ladies here.
Sure I killed him. Why didn't he shut up? If he'd only shut
up! Instead o' talkin' an' talkin' about how sorry he was an'
what a good guy I was an' this an' that. I felt like sayin'

to him: "For Christ's sake, shut up!" But I didn't have
the nerve, see? I didn't have the nerve to say that to
the boss. An' he went on talkin', sayin' how sorry he
was, see? He was standin' right close to me. An' his coat
only had two buttons on it. Two an' two makes four an'—
aw, can it! An' there was the bill-file on the desk. Right
where I could touch it. It ain't right to kill a guy. I know
that. When I read all about him in the paper an' about his
three kids I felt like a cheap skate, I tell you. They had the
kids' pictures in the paper, right next to mine. An' his wife,
too. Gee, it must be swell to have a wife like that. Some
guys sure is lucky. An' he left fifty thousand dollars just for
a rest-room for the girls in the store. He was a good guy, at
that. Fifty thousand. That's more'n twice as much as I'd
have if I saved every nickel I ever made. Let's see. Twenty-
five an' twenty-five an' twenty-five an'—aw, cut it out! An'
the ads had a big, black border around 'em; an' all it said
was that the store would be closed for three days on account
of the boss bein' dead. That nearly handed me a laugh, that
did. All them floor-walkers an' buyers an' high-muck-a-
mucks havin' me to thank for gettin' three days off. I hadn't
oughta killed him. I ain't sayin' nothin' about that. But I
thought he was goin' to give me a raise, see? On account
of bein' there twenty-five years. He never talked to me before, see? Except one mornin' we happened to come in the
store together and I held the door open for him and he said
"Thanks." Just like that, see? "Thanks!" That was the only
time he ever talked to me. An' when I seen him comin' up
to my desk, I didn't know where I got off. A big guy like
that comin' up to my desk. I felt like I was chokin' like and
all of a sudden I got a kind o' bad taste in my mouth like
when you get up in the mornin'. I didn't have no right to
kill him. The district attorney is right about that. He read
the law to you, right out o' the book. Killin' a bird—that's
wrong. But there was that girl, see? Six months they gave
her. It was a dirty trick tellin' the cops on her like that. I
shouldn't 'a' done that. But what was I gonna do? The wife
wouldn't let up on me. I hadda do it. She used to walk

around the room, just in her undershirt, see? Nothin' else
on. Just her undershirt. An' they gave her six months. That's
the last I'll ever see of her. Them birds—how do they get
away with it? Just grabbin' women, the way you see 'em do
in the pictures. I've seen lots I'd like to grab like that, but
I ain't got the nerve—in the subway an' on the street an' in
the store buyin' things. Pretty soft for them shoe-salesmen,
I'll say, lookin' at women's legs all day. Them lawyers! They
give me a pain, I tell you—a pain! Sayin' the same thing
over an' over again. I never said I didn't kill him. But that
ain't the same as bein' a regular murderer. What good
did it do me to kill him? I didn't make nothin' out of it.
Answer yes or no! Yes or no, me elbow! There's some things
you can't answer yes or no. Give me the once-over, you
guys. Do I look like a murderer? Do I? I never did no harm
to nobody. Ask the wife. She'll tell you. Ask anybody. I
never got into trouble. You wouldn't count that one time at
the Polo Grounds. That was just fun like. Everybody was
yellin', "Kill the empire! Kill the empire!" An' before I knew
what I was doin' I fired the pop bottle. It was on account
of everybody yellin' like that. Just in fun like, see? The
yeller dog! Callin' that one a strike—a mile away from the
plate. Anyhow, the bottle didn't hit him. An' when I seen
the cop comin' up the aisle, I beat it. That didn't hurt nobody. It was just in fun like, see? An' that time in the
subway. I was readin' about a lynchin', see? Down in
Georgia. They took the nigger an' they tied him to a tree.
An' they poured kerosene on him and lit a big fire under
him. The dirty nigger! Boy, I'd of liked to been there, with
a gat in each hand, pumpin' him full of lead. I was readin'
about it in the subway, see? Right at Times Square where
the big crowd gets on. An' all of a sudden this big nigger
steps right on my foot. It was lucky for him I didn't have
a gun on me. I'd of killed him sure, I guess. I guess he
couldn't help it all right on account of the crowd, but a
nigger's got no right to step on a white man's foot. I told
him where he got off all right. The dirty nigger. But that
didn't hurt nobody, either. I'm a pretty steady guy, you

gotta admit that. Twenty-five years in one job an' I never missed a day. Fifty-two weeks in a year. Fifty-two an' fifty-two an' fifty-two an'——They didn't have t' look for me, did they? I didn't try to run away, did I? Where was I goin' to run to! I wasn't thinkin' about it at all, see? I'll tell you what I was thinkin' about—how I was goin' to break it to the wife about bein' canned. He canned me after twenty-five years, see? Did the lawyers tell you about that? I forget. All that talk gives me a headache. Objection sustained. Objection over-ruled. Answer yes or no. It gives me a headache. And I can't get the figgers outta my head, neither. But that's what I was thinkin' about—how I was goin' t' break it to the wife about bein' canned. An' what Miss Devore would think when she heard about me killin' him. I bet she never thought I had the nerve to do it. I'd of married her if the wife had passed out. I'd be holdin' down my job yet, if he hadn't o' canned me. But he kept talkin' an' talkin'. An' there was the bill-file right where I could reach it. Do you get me? I'm just a regular guy like anybody else. Like you birds, now. (*For the first time the* JURORS *relax, looking indignantly at each other and whispering.*) Suppose you was me, now. Maybe you'd 'a' done the same thing. That's the way you oughta look at it, see? Suppose you was me——

THE JURORS (*Rising as one and shouting in unison*). GUILTY!

(ZERO *falls back, stunned for a moment by their vociferousness. The* JURORS *right-face in their places and file quickly out of the jury box and toward the door in a double column.*)

ZERO (*Recovering speech as the* JURORS *pass out at the door*). Wait a minute. Jest a minute. You don't get me right. Jest give me a chance an' I'll tell you how it was. I'm all mixed up, see? On account of them lawyers. And the figgers in my head. But I'm goin' to tell you how it was. I was there twenty-five years, see? An' they gave her six months, see? (*He goes on haranguing the empty jury box as the curtain falls.*)

Scene Five

NOTE:
This scene, which follows the court-room scene, was part
of the original script. It was omitted, however, when the
play was produced, and was performed for the first time
(in its present revised form) when the play was revived at
the Phoenix Theatre in New York in February, 1956.
———ELMER RICE

*(SCENE. In the middle of the stage is a large cage with
bars on all four sides. The bars are very far apart and the
interior of the cage is clearly visible. The floor of the cage
is about six feet above the level of the stage. A flight of
wooden steps lead up to it on the side facing the audience.*
ZERO *is discovered in the middle of the cage seated at a
table above which is suspended a single naked electric light.
Before him is an enormous platter of ham and eggs which he
eats voraciously with a large wooden spoon. He wears a
uniform of very broad black and white horizontal stripes.*

*A few moments after the rise of the curtain a man enters
at left, wearing the blue uniform and peaked cap of a* GUIDE.
He is followed by a miscellaneous crowd of MEN, WOMEN
and CHILDREN—*about a dozen in all.)*

THE GUIDE *(Stopping in front of the cage).* Now ladies and
gentlemen, if you'll kindly step right this way! *The crowd
straggles up and forms a loose semicircle around him.)*
Step right up, please. A little closer so's everybody can hear.
(They move up closer. ZERO *pays no attention whatever to
them.)* This, ladies and gentlemen, is a very in-ter-est-in'
specimen: the North American murderer, Genus—homo

43

sapiens, Habitat—North America. (*A titter of excitement.* THEY *all crowd up around the cage.*) Don't push. There's room for everybody.

A TALL LADY. Oh, how interesting!

A STOUT LADY (*Excitedly*). Look, Charley, he's eating!

CHARLEY (*Bored*). Yeh, I see him.

THE GUIDE (*Repeating by rote*). This specimen, ladies and gentlemen, exhibits the characteristics which are typical of his kind—

A SMALL BOY (*In a Little Lord Fauntleroy suit, whiningly*). Ma-ma!

HIS MOTHER. Be quiet, Eustace, or I'll take you right home.

THE GUIDE. He has the apposable thumbs, the large cranial capacity, and the highly developed prefrontal areas which distinguish him from all other species.

A YOUTH (*Who has been taking notes*). What areas did you say?

THE GUIDE (*Grumpily*). Pre-front-al areas. He learns by imitation and has a language which is said by some eminent philologists to bear many striking resemblances to English.

A BOY OF FOURTEEN. Pop, what's a philologist?

HIS FATHER. Keep quiet, can't you, and listen to what he's sayin'.

THE GUIDE. He thrives and breeds freely in captivity. This specimen was taken alive in his native haunts shortly after murdering his boss. (*Murmurs of great interest.*)

THE TALL LADY. Oh, how charming.

THE NOTE-TAKING YOUTH. What was that last? I didn't get it.

SEVERAL (*Helpfully*). Murdering his boss.

THE YOUTH. Oh—thanks.

THE GUIDE. He was tried, convicted, and sentenced in one hour, thirteen minutes, and twenty-four seconds, which sets a new record for this territory east of the Rockies and north of the Mason and Dixon line.

LITTLE LORD FAUNTLEROY (*Whiningly*). Ma-ma!

HIS MOTHER. Be quiet, Eustace, or Mama won't let you ride in the choo-choo.

THE GUIDE. Now take a good look at him, ladies and gents. It's his last day here. He's goin' to be executed at noon. (*Murmurs of interest.*)

THE TALL LADY. Oh, how lovely!

A MAN. What's he eating?

THE GUIDE. Ham and eggs.

THE STOUT LADY. He's quite a big eater, ain't he?

THE GUIDE. Oh, he don't always eat that much. You see we always try to make 'em feel good on their last day. So about a week in advance we let them order what they want to eat on their last day. They can have eight courses, and they can order anything they want—don't make no difference what it costs or how hard it is to get. Well, he couldn't make up his mind till last night and then he ordered eight courses of ham and eggs. (*They all push and stare.*)

THE BOY OF FOURTEEN. Look pop! He's eatin' with a spoon. Don't he know how to use a knife and fork?

THE GUIDE (*Overhearing him*). We don't dare trust him with a knife and fork, sonny. He might try to kill himself.

THE TALL LADY. Oh, how fascinating!

THE GUIDE (*Resuming his official tone*). And now friends if you'll kindly give me your kind attention for just a moment. (*He takes a bundle of folders from his pocket.*) I have a little souvenir folder, which I'm sure you'll all want to have. It contains twelve beautiful colored views, relating to the North American Murderer you have just been looking at. These include a picture of the murderer, a picture of the murderer's wife, the blood-stained weapon, the murderer at the age of six, the spot where the body was found, the little red school-house where he went to school, and his vine-covered boyhood home in southern Illinois, with his sweet-faced white-haired old mother plainly visible in the foreground. And many other interesting views. I'm now going to distribute these little folders for your examination. (*Sotto voce.*) Just pass them back, will you. (*In louder tones.*) Don't be afraid to look at them. You don't have to buy them if you don't want to. It don't cost anything to look at them. (*To the* NOTE-TAKING YOUTH *who is fumbling with a camera.*) Hey, there, young feller, no snapshots allowed. All right now, friends, if you'll just step this way. Keep close together and follow me. A lady lost her little boy here one time and by the time we found him, he was smoking cigarettes and hollering for a razor.

(Much laughter as they all follow him off left. ZERO finishes eating and pushes away his plate. As the crowd goes at left, MRS. ZERO enters at right. She is dressed in mourning garments. She carries a large parcel. She goes up the steps to the cage, opens the door, and enters. ZERO looks up and sees her.)

MRS. ZERO. Hello.

ZERO. Hello, I didn't think you were comin' again.

MRS. ZERO. Well, I thought I'd come again. Are you glad to see me?

ZERO. Sure. Sit down. *(She complies.)* You're all dolled up, ain't you?

MRS. ZERO. Yeh, don't you like it? *(She gets up and turns about like a mannequin.)*

ZERO. Gee. Some class.

MRS. ZERO. I always look good in black. There's some weight to this veil, though, I'll tell the world. I got a fierce headache.

ZERO. How much did all that set you back?

MRS. ZERO. Sixty-four dollars and twenty cents. And I gotta get a pin yet and some writin' paper—you know, with black around the edges.

ZERO. You'll be scrubbin' floors in about a year, if you go blowin' your coin like that.

MRS. ZERO. Well, I gotta do it right. It don't happen every day. *(She rises and takes up the parcel.)* I brought you somethin'.

ZERO *(Interested)*. Yeh, what?

MRS. ZERO *(Opening the parcel)*. You gotta guess.

ZERO. Er—er—gee, search me.

MRS. ZERO. Somethin' you like. *(She takes out a covered plate.)*

ZERO *(With increasing interest)*. Looks like somethin' to eat.

MRS. ZERO *(Nodding)*. Yeh. *(She takes off the top plate.)* Ham an' eggs!

ZERO *(Joyfully)*. Oh, boy! Just what I feel like eatin'! *(He takes up the wooden spoon and begins to eat avidly.)*

MRS. ZERO *(Pleased)*. Are they good?

ZERO *(His mouth full)*. Swell.

MRS. ZERO *(A little sadly)*. They're the last ones I'll ever make for you.

ZERO *(Busily eating)*. Uh-huh.

MRS. ZERO. I'll tell you somethin'—shall I?

ZERO. Sure.

MRS. ZERO *(Hesitantly)*. Well, all the while they were cookin' I was cryin'!

ZERO. Yeh? *(He leans over and pats her hand.)*

MRS. ZERO. I just couldn't help it. The thought of it just made me cry.

ZERO. Well—no use cryin' about it.

MRS. ZERO. I just couldn't help it.

ZERO. Maybe this time next year you'll be fryin' eggs for some other bird.

MRS. ZERO. Not on your life.

ZERO. You never can tell.

MRS. ZERO. Not me. Once is enough for me.

ZERO. I guess you're right at that. Still, I dunno. You might just happen to meet some guy—

MRS. ZERO. Well, if I do, there'll be time enough to think about it. No use borrowin' trouble.

ZERO. How do you like bein' alone in the house?

MRS. ZERO. Oh, it's all right.

ZERO. You got plenty room in the bed now, ain't you?

MRS. ZERO. Oh yeh. *(A brief pause.)* It's kinda lonesome though —you know, wakin' up in the mornin' and nobody around to talk to.

ZERO. Yeh, I know. It's the same with me.

MRS. ZERO. Not that we ever did much talkin'.

ZERO. Well, that ain't it. It's just the idea of havin' somebody there in case you want to talk.

MRS. ZERO. Yeh, that's it. *(Another brief pause.)* I guess maybe I use t' bawl you out quite a lot, didn't I?

ZERO. Oh well—no use talkin' about it now.

MRS. ZERO. We were always at it, weren't we?

ZERO. No more than any other married folks, I guess.

MRS. ZERO *(Dubiously)*. I dunno—

ZERO. I guess I gave you cause, all right.

MRS. ZERO. Well—I got my faults too.

ZERO. None of us are perfect.

MRS. ZERO. We got along all right, at that, didn't we?

ZERO. Sure! Better'n most.

MRS. ZERO. Remember them Sundays at the beach, in the old days?

ZERO. You bet. *(With a laugh.)* Remember that time I ducked you? Gee you was mad!

MRS. ZERO *(With a laugh)*. I didn't talk to you for a whole week.

ZERO *(Chuckling)*. Yeh, I remember.

MRS. ZERO. And the time I had pneumonia and you brought me them roses. Remember?

ZERO. Yeh, I remember. And when the doctor told me maybe you'd pass out, I nearly sat down and cried.

MRS. ZERO. Did you?

ZERO. I sure did.

MRS. ZERO. We had some pretty good times at that, didn't we?

ZERO. I'll say we did!

MRS. ZERO *(With a sudden soberness)*. It's all over now.

ZERO. All over is right. I ain't got much longer.

MRS. ZERO *(Rising and going over to him)*. Maybe—Maybe—if we had to do it over again, it would be different.

ZERO *(Taking her hand)*. Yeh. We live and learn.

MRS. ZERO *(Crying)*. If we only had another chance.

ZERO. It's too late now.

MRS. ZERO. It don't seem right, does it?

ZERO. It ain't right. But what can you do about it?

MRS. ZERO. Ain't there somethin'—somethin' I can do for you —before—

ZERO. No. Nothin'. Not a thing.

MRS. ZERO. Nothin' at all?

ZERO. No. I can't think of anything. (*Suddenly.*) You're takin' good care of that scrap-book, ain't you, with all the clippings in it?

MRS. ZERO. Oh, sure. I got it right on the parlor table. Right where everybody can see it.

ZERO (*Pleased*). It must be pretty near full, ain't it?

MRS. ZERO. All but three pages.

ZERO. Well, there'll be more tomorrow. Enough to fill it, maybe. Be sure to get them all, will you?

MRS. ZERO. I will. I ordered the papers already.

ZERO. Gee, I never thought I'd have a whole book full of clippings all about myself. (*Suddenly.*) Say, that's somethin' I'd like to ask you.

MRS. ZERO. What?

ZERO. Suppose you should get sick or be run over or somethin', what would happen to the book?

MRS. ZERO. Well, I kinda thought I'd leave it to little Beatrice Elizabeth.

ZERO. Who? Your sister's kid?

MRS. ZERO. Yeh.

ZERO. What would she want with it?

MRS. ZERO. Well, it's nice to have, ain't it? And I wouldn't know who else to give it to.

ZERO. Well, I don't want her to have it. That fresh little kid puttin' her dirty fingers all over it.

MRS. ZERO. She ain't fresh and she ain't dirty. She's a sweet little thing.

ZERO. I don't want her to have it.

MRS. ZERO. Who do you want to have it, then?

ZERO. Well, I kinda thought I'd like Miss Devore to have it.

MRS. ZERO. Miss Devore?

ZERO. Yeh. You know. Down at the store.

MRS. ZERO. Why should she have it?

ZERO. She'd take good care of it. And anyhow, I'd like her to have it.

MRS. ZERO. Oh, you would, would you?

ZERO. Yes.

MRS. ZERO. Well, she ain't goin' to have it. Miss Devore! Where does she come in, I'd like to know, when I got two sisters and a niece.

ZERO. I don't care nothin' about your sisters and your niece.

MRS. ZERO. Well, I do! And Miss Devore ain't goin' to get it. Now put that in your pipe and smoke it.

ZERO. What have you got to say about it? It's my book, ain't it?

MRS. ZERO. No, it ain't. It's mine now—or it will be tomorrow. And I'm goin' to do what I like with it.

ZERO. I should have given it to her in the first place—that's what I should have done.

MRS. ZERO. Oh, should you? And what about me? Am I your wife or ain't I?

ZERO. Why remind me of my troubles?

MRS. ZERO. So it's Miss Devore all of a sudden, is it? What's been goin' on, I'd like to know, between you and Miss Devore?

ZERO. Aw, tie a can to that!

MRS. ZERO. Why didn't you marry Miss Devore, if you think so much of her?

ZERO. I would if I'd of met her first.

MRS. ZERO *(Shrieking).* Ooh! A fine way to talk to me. After all I've done for you. You bum! You dirty bum! I won't stand for it! I won't stand for it! *(In a great rage she takes up the dishes and smashes them on the floor. Then, crying hysterically, she opens the cage door, bangs it behind her, comes down the steps, and goes off toward left.* ZERO *stands gazing ruefully after her for a moment, and then with a shrug and a sigh begins picking up the pieces of broken crockery.*

As MRS. ZERO *exits at left a door in the back of the cage opens and a* MAN *enters. He is dressed in a sky-blue padded silk dressing-gown which is fitted with innumerable pockets. Under this he wears a pink silk union-suit. His bare feet are in sandals. He wears a jaunty Panama hat with a red feather stuck in the brim. Wings are fastened to his sandals and to the shoulders of his dressing-gown.* ZERO, *who is busy picking up the broken crockery, does not notice him at first. The* MAN *takes a gold toothpick and begins carefully picking his teeth, waiting for* ZERO *to notice him.* ZERO *happens to look up and suddenly sees the* MAN. *He utters a cry of terror and shrinks into a corner of the cage, trembling with fear.)*

ZERO *(Hoarsely)*. Who are you?

MAN *(Calmly, as he pockets his toothpick)*. I'm the Fixer—from the Claim Department.

ZERO. Whaddya want?

FIXER. It's no use, Zero. There are no miracles.

ZERO. I don't know what you're talking about.

FIXER. Don't lie, Zero. *(Holding up his hand.)* And now that your course is run—now that the end is already in sight, you still believe that some thunderbolt, some fiery bush, some celestial apparition will intervene between you and extinction. But it's no use, Zero. You're done for.

ZERO *(Vehemently)*. It ain't right! It ain't fair! I ain't gettin' a square deal!

FIXER *(Wearily)*. They all say that, Zero. *(Mildly.)* Now just tell me why you're not getting a square deal.

ZERO. Well, that addin' machine. Was that a square deal—after twenty-five years?

FIXER. Certainly—from any point of view, except a sentimental one. *(Looking at his wristwatch.)* The machine is quicker, it never makes a mistake, it's always on time. It presents no problems of housing, traffic congestion, water supply, sanitation.

ZERO. It costs somethin' to buy them machines, I'll tell you that!

FIXER. Yes, you're right there. In one respect you have the advantage over the machine—the cost of manufacture. But we've learned from many years' experience, Zero, that the original cost is an inconsequential item compared to upkeep. Take the dinosaurs, for example. They literally ate themselves out of existence. I held out for them to the last.

They were damned picturesque—but when it came to a question of the nitrate supply, I simply had to yield. (*He begins to empty and clean his pipe.*) And so with you, Zero. It costs a lot to keep up all that delicate mechanism of eye and ear and hand and brain which you've never put to any use. We can't afford to maintain it in idleness—and so you've got to go. (*He puts the pipe in one of his pockets.*)

ZERO (*Falling to his knees, supplicatingly*). Gimme a chance, gimme another chance!

FIXER. What would you do if I gave you another chance?

ZERO. Well—first thing I'd go out and look for a job.

FIXER. Adding figures?

ZERO. Well—I ain't young enough to take up somethin' new. (*The* FIXER *takes out a police whistle and blows shrilly. Instantly two* GUARDS *enter.*)

FIXER. Put the skids under him boys, and make it snappy. (*He strolls away to the other side of the cage, and, taking a nail clipper from a pocket, begins to clip his nails as the* GUARDS *seize* ZERO.)

ZERO (*Struggling and shrieking*). No! No! Don't take me away! Don't kill me! Gimme a chance! Gimme another chance!

GUARD (*Soothingly*). Ah come on! Be a good fellow! It'll all be over in a minute!

ZERO. I don't want to die! I don't want to die! I want to live!

(*The* GUARDS *look at each other dubiously. Then one of them walks rather timidly over to the* FIXER, *who is busy with his nails.*)

GUARD (*Clearing his throat*). H'm!

FIXER (*Looking up*). Well?

GUARD (*Timidly*). He says he wants to live.

FIXER. No. He's no good.

GUARD (*Touching his cap, deferentially*). Yes sir!

(*He goes back to his companion and the two of them drag* ZERO *out at the back of the cage, still struggling and screaming. The* FIXER *puts away his nail clippers, yawns, then goes to the table and sits on the edge of it. From a pocket he takes an enormous pair of horn-rimmed spectacles. Then from another pocket he takes a folded newspaper, which he unfolds carefully. It is a colored comic supplement. He holds it up in front of him and becomes absorbed in it.*

A moment later the door at the back of the cage opens and a tall, brawny, bearded MAN *enters. He wears a red-flannel undershirt and carries a huge blood-stained axe. The* FIXER, *absorbed in the comic supplement, does not look up.)*

MAN *(Hoarsely).* O.K.

FIXER *(Looking up).* What?

MAN. O.K.

FIXER *(Nodding).* Oh, all right. *(The* MAN *bows deferentially and goes out at the back. The* FIXER *puts away his spectacles and folds the comic supplement carefully. As he folds the paper.)* That makes a total of 2137 black eyes for Jeff.

(He puts away the paper, turns out the electric light over his head, and leaves the cage by the front door. Then he takes a padlock from a pocket, attaches it to the door, and saunters off as the curtain falls.)

Scene Six

*(SCENE. A grave-yard in full moonlight. It is a second-rate grave-yard—no elaborate tombstones or monuments—just simple headstones and here and there a cross. At the back is an iron fence with a gate in the middle. At first no one is visible, but there are occasional sounds throughout: the hooting of an owl, the whistle of a distant whippoorwill, the croaking of a bull-frog, and the yowling of a serenading cat. After a few moments two figures appear outside the gate—a man and a woman. She pushes the gate and it opens with a rusty creak. The couple enter. They are now fully visible in the moonlight—*JUDY O'GRADY *and a* YOUNG MAN.*)*

JUDY *(Advancing).* Come on, this is the place.

YOUNG MAN *(Hanging back).* This! Why this here is a cemetery.

JUDY. Aw, quit yer kiddin'!

YOUNG MAN. You don't mean to say——

JUDY. What's the matter with this place?

YOUNG MAN. A cemetery!

JUDY. Sure. What of it?

YOUNG MAN. You must be crazy.

JUDY. This place is all right, I tell you. I been here lots o' times.

YOUNG MAN. Nix on this place for me!

JUDY. Ain't this place as good as another? Whaddya afraid of? They're all dead ones here! They don't bother you. *(With sudden interest.)* Oh, look, here's a new one.

YOUNG MAN. Come on out of here.

JUDY. Wait a minute. Let's see what it says. *(She kneels on a grave in the foreground and putting her face close to head-*

54

stone spells out the inscription.) z-e-r-o. Z-e-r-o. Zero! Say,
that's the guy——

YOUNG MAN. Zero? He's the guy killed his boss, ain't he?

JUDY. Yeh, that's him, all right. But what I'm thinkin' of is
that I went to the hoosegow on account of him.

YOUNG MAN. What for?

JUDY. You know, same old stuff. Tenement House Law. *(Minc-
ingly.)* Section blaa-blaa of the Penal Code. Third offense.
Six months.

YOUNG MAN. And this bird——

JUDY *(Contemptuously).* Him? He was mama's whitehaired
boy. We lived in the same house. Across the airshaft, see?
I used to see him lookin' in my window. I guess his wife
musta seen him, too. Anyhow, they went and turned the
bulls on me. And now I'm out and he's in. *(Suddenly.)* Say
—say—— *(She bursts into a peal of laughter.)*

YOUNG MAN *(Nervously).* What's so funny?

JUDY *(Rocking with laughter).* Say, wouldn't it be funny—if
if—— *(She explodes again.)* That would be a good joke on
him, all right. He can't do nothin' about it now, can he?

YOUNG MAN. Come on out of here. I don't like this place.

JUDY. Aw, you're a bum sport. What do you want to spoil my
joke for? *(A cat yammers mellifluously.)*

YOUNG MAN *(Half hysterically).* What's that?

JUDY. It's only the cats. They seem to like it here all right. But
come on if you're afraid. *(They go toward the gate. As they
go out.)* You nervous men sure are the limit.

(They go out through the gate. As they disappear ZERO'S
grave opens suddenly and his head appears.)

ZERO *(Looking about).* That's funny! I thought I heard her
talkin' and laughin'. But I don't see nobody. Anyhow, what
would she be doin' here? I guess I must 'a' been dreamin'.
But how could I be dreamin' when I ain't been asleep? *(He
looks about again.)* Well, no use goin' back. I can't sleep,
anyhow. I might as well walk around a little. *(He rises out
of the ground, very rigidly. He wears a full-dress suit of*

very antiquated cut and his hands are folded stiffly across his breast.)

ZERO *(Walking woodenly).* Gee! I'm stiff! *(He slowly walks a few steps, then stops.)* Gee, it's lonesome here! *(He shivers and walks on aimlessly.)* I should 'a' stayed where I was. But I thought I heard her laughin'. *(A loud sneeze is heard. ZERO stands motionless, quaking with terror. The sneeze is repeated.)*

ZERO *(Hoarsely).* What's that?

A MILD VOICE. It's all right. Nothing to be afraid of.

(From behind a headstone SHRDLU appears. He is dressed in a shabby and ill-fitting cutaway. He wears silver-rimmed spectacles and is smoking a cigarette.)

SHRDLU. I hope I didn't frighten you.

ZERO *(Still badly shaken).* No-o. It's all right. You see, I wasn't expectin' to see anybody.

SHRDLU. You're a newcomer, aren't you?

ZERO. Yeh, this is my first night. I couldn't seem to get to sleep.

SHRDLU. I can't sleep, either. Suppose we keep each other company, shall we?

ZERO *(Eagerly).* Yeh, that would be great. I been feelin' awful lonesome.

SHRDLU *(Nodding).* I know. Let's make ourselves comfortable. *(He seats himself easily on a grave. ZERO tries to follow his example but he is stiff in every joint and groans with pain.)*

ZERO. I'm kinda stiff.

SHRDLU. You mustn't mind the stiffness. It wears off in a few days. *(He seats himself on the grave beside ZERO and produces a package of cigarettes.)* Will you have a Camel?

ZERO. No, I don't smoke.

SHRDLU. I find it helps keep the mosquitoes away. *(He lights a cigarette.)*

SHRDLU *(Suddenly taking the cigarette out of his mouth).* Do you mind if I smoke, Mr.—Mr.——?

ZERO. No, go right ahead.

SHRDLU (*Replacing the cigarette*). Thank you. I didn't catch your name. (ZERO *does not reply.*)

SHRDLU (*Mildly*). I say I didn't catch your name.

ZERO. I heard you the first time. (*Hesitantly.*) I'm scared if I tell you who I am and what I done, you'll be off me.

SHRDLU (*Sadly*). No matter what your sins may be, they are as snow compared to mine.

ZERO. You got another guess comin'. (*He pauses dramatically.*) My name's Zero. I'm a murderer.

SHRDLU (*Nodding calmly*). Oh, yes, I remember reading about you, Mr. Zero.

ZERO (*A little piqued*). And you still think you're worse than me?

SHRDLU (*Throwing away his cigarette*). Oh, a thousand times worse, Mr. Zero—a million times worse.

ZERO. What did you do?

SHRDLU. I, too, am a murderer.

ZERO (*Looking at him in amazement*). Go on! You're kiddin' me!

SHRDLU. Every word I speak is the truth, Mr. Zero. I am the foulest, the most sinful of murderers! You only murdered your employer, Mr. Zero. But I—I murdered my mother. (*He covers his face with his hands and sobs.*)

ZERO (*Horrified*). The hell yer say!

SHRDLU (*Sobbing*). Yes, my mother!—my beloved mother!

ZERO (*Suddenly*). Say, you don't mean to say you're Mr. ——

SHRDLU (*Nodding*). Yes. (*He wipes his eyes, still quivering with emotion.*)

ZERO. I remember readin' about you in the papers.

SHRDLU. Yes, my guilt has been proclaimed to all the world. But that would be a trifle if only I could wash the stain of sin from my soul.

ZERO. I never heard of a guy killin' his mother before. What did you do it for?

SHRDLU. Because I have a sinful heart—there is no other reason.

ZERO. Did she always treat you square and all like that?

SHRDLU. She was a saint—a saint, I tell you. She cared for me
and watched over me as only a mother can.

ZERO. You mean to say you didn't have a scrap or nothin'?

SHRDLU. Never a harsh or an unkind word. Nothing except
loving care and good advice. From my infancy she devoted
herself to guiding me on the right path. She taught me to
be thrifty, to be devout, to be unselfish, to shun evil com-
panions and to shut my ears to all the temptations of the
flesh—in short, to become a virtuous, respectable, and God-
fearing man. (*He groans.*) But it was a hopeless task. At
fourteen I began to show evidence of my sinful nature.

ZERO (*Breathlessly*). You didn't kill anybody else, did you?

SHRDLU. No, thank God, there is only one murder on my soul.
But I ran away from home.

ZERO. You did!

SHRDLU. Yes. A companion lent me a profane book—the only
profane book I have ever read, I'm thankful to say. It was
called *Treasure Island*. Have you ever read it?

ZERO. No, I never was much on readin' books.

SHRDLU. It is a wicked book—a lurid tale of adventure. But it
kindled in my sinful heart a desire to go to sea. And so I
ran away from home.

ZERO. What did you do—get a job as a sailor?

SHRDLU. I never saw the sea—not to the day of my death.
Luckily, my mother's loving intuition warned her of my
intention and I was sent back home. She welcomed me
with open arms. Not an angry word, not a look of reproach.
But I could read the mute suffering in her eyes as we
prayed together all through the night.

ZERO (*Sympathetically*). Gee, that must 'a' been tough. Gee,
the mosquitoes are bad, ain't they? (*He tries awkwardly to
slap at them with his stiff hands.*)

SHRDLU (*Absorbed in his narrative*). I thought that experience
had cured me of evil and I began to think about a career.
I wanted to go in foreign missions at first, but we couldn't
bear the thought of the separation. So we finally decided
that I should become a proofreader.

ZERO. Say, slip me one o' them Camels, will you? I'm gettin' all bit up.

SHRDLU. Certainly. *(He hands* ZERO *cigarettes and matches.)*

ZERO *(Lighting up)*. Go ahead. I'm listenin'.

SHRDLU. By the time I was twenty I had a good job reading proof for a firm that printed catalogues. After a year they promoted me and let me specialize in shoe catalogues.

ZERO. Yeh? That must 'a' been a good job.

SHRDLU. It was a very good job. I was on the shoe catalogues for thirteen years. I'd been on them yet, if I hadn't—— *(He chokes back a sob.)*

ZERO. They oughta put a shot o' citronella in that embalmin'-fluid.

SHRDLU *(He sighs)*. We were so happy together. I had my steady job. And Sundays we would go to morning, afternoon, and evening service. It was an honest and moral mode of life.

ZERO. It sure was.

SHRDLU. Then came that fatal Sunday. Dr. Amaranth, our minister, was having dinner with us—one of the few pure spirits on earth. When he had finished saying grace, we had our soup. Everything was going along as usual—we were eating our soup and discussing the sermon, just like every other Sunday I could remember. Then came the leg of lamb—— *(He breaks off, then resumes in a choking voice.)* I see the whole scene before me so plainly—it never leaves me—Dr. Amaranth at my right, my mother at my left, the leg of lamb on the table in front of me and the cuckoo clock on the little shelf between the windows. *(He stops and wipes his eyes.)*

ZERO. Yeh, but what happened?

SHRDLU. Well, as I started to carve the lamb—— Did you ever carve a leg of lamb?

ZERO. No, corned beef was our speed.

SHRDLU. It's very difficult on account of the bone. And when there's gravy in the dish there's danger of spilling it. So Mother always used to hold the dish for me. She leaned forward, just as she always did, and I could see the gold locket around her neck. It had my picture in it and one of my baby curls. Well, I raised my knife to carve the leg of lamb—and instead I cut my mother's throat! *(He sobs.)*

ZERO. You must 'a' been crazy!

SHRDLU *(Raising his head, vehemently)*. No! Don't try to justify me. I wasn't crazy. They tried to prove at the trial that I was crazy. But Dr. Amaranth saw the truth! He saw it from the first! He knew that it was my sinful nature—and he told me what was in store for me.

ZERO *(Trying to be comforting)*. Well, your troubles are over now.

SHRDLU *(His voice rising)*. Over! Do you think this is the end?

ZERO. Sure. What more can they do to us?

SHRDLU *(His tones growing shriller and shriller)*. Do you think there can ever be any peace for such as we are—murderers, sinners? Don't you know what awaits us—flames, eternal flames!

ZERO *(Nervously)*. Keep your shirt on, Buddy—they wouldn't do that to us.

SHRDLU. There's no escape—no escape for us, I tell you. We're doomed! We're doomed to suffer unspeakable torments through all eternity. *(His voice rises higher and higher. A grave opens suddenly and a head appears.)*

THE HEAD. Hey, you birds! Can't you shut up and let a guy sleep? *(ZERO scrambles painfully to his feet.)*

ZERO *(To SHRDLU)*. Hey, put on the soft pedal.

SHRDLU *(Too wrought up to attend)*. It won't be long now! We'll receive our summons soon.

THE HEAD. Are you goin' to beat it or not? *(He calls into the grave)*. Hey, Bill, lend me your head a minute. *(A moment later his arm appears holding a skull.)*

ZERO *(Warningly)*. Look out! *(He seizes SHRDLU and drags him away just as THE HEAD throws the skull.)*

THE HEAD *(Disgustedly)*. Missed 'em. Damn old tabby cats! I'll get 'em next time. *(A prodigious yawn)*. Ho-hum! Me for the worms! *(THE HEAD disappears as the curtain falls.)*

Scene Seven

(SCENE. *A pleasant place. A scene of pastoral loveliness. A meadow dotted with fine old trees and carpeted with rich grass and field flowers. In the background are seen a number of tents fashioned of gay-striped silks and beyond gleams a meandering river. Clear air and a fleckless sky. Sweet distant music throughout.*

At the rise of the curtain, SHRDLU *is seen seated under a tree in the foreground in an attitude of deep dejection. His knees are drawn up and his head is buried in his arms. He is dressed as in the preceding scene.*

A few minutes later, ZERO *enters at right. He walks slowly and looks about him with an air of half-suspicious curiosity. He, too, is dressed as in the preceding scene. Suddenly he sees* SHRDLU *seated under the tree. He stands still and looks at him half fearfully. Then, seeing something familiar in him, goes closer.* SHRDLU *is unaware of his presence. At last* ZERO *recognizes him and grins in pleased surprise.*)

ZERO. Well, if it ain't——! (*He claps* SHRDLU *on the shoulder.*) Hello, Buddy! (SHRDLU *looks up slowly, then recognizing* ZERO, *he rises gravely and extends his hand courteously.*)

SHRDLU. How do you do, Mr. Zero? I'm very glad to see you again.

ZERO. Same here. I wasn't expectin' to see you, either. (*Looking about.*) This is a kinda nice place. I wouldn't mind restin' here a while.

SHRDLU. You may if you wish.

ZERO. I'm kinda tired. I ain't used to bein' outdoors. I ain't walked so much in years.

SHRDLU. Sit down here, under the tree.

ZERO. Do they let you sit on the grass?

SHRDLU. Oh, yes.

ZERO (*Seating himself*). Boy, this feels good. I'll tell the world my feet are sore. I ain't used to so much walkin'. Say, I wonder would it be all right if I took my shoes off; my feet are tired.

SHRDLU. Yes. Some of the people here go barefoot.

ZERO. Yeh? They sure must be nuts. But I'm goin' t' leave 'em off for a while. So long as it's all right. The grass feels nice and cool. (*He stretches out comfortably.*) Say, this is the life of Riley all right, all right. This sure is a nice place. What do they call this place, anyhow?

SHRDLU. The Elysian Fields.

ZERO. The which?

SHRDLU. The Elysian Fields.

ZERO (*Dubiously*). Oh! Well, it's a nice place, all right.

SHRDLU. They say that this is the most desirable of all places. Only the most favoured remain here.

ZERO. Yeh? Well, that let's me out, I guess. (*Suddenly.*) But what are you doin' here? I thought you'd be burned by now.

SHRDLU (*Sadly*). Mr. Zero, I am the most unhappy of men.

ZERO (*In mild astonishment*). Why, because you ain't bein' roasted alive?

SHRDLU (*Nodding*). Nothing is turning out as I expected. I saw everything so clearly—the flames, the tortures, an eternity of suffering as the just punishment for my unspeakable crime. And it has all turned out so differently.

ZERO. Well, that's pretty soft for you, ain't it?

SHRDLU (*Wailingly*). No, no, no! It's right and just that I should be punished. I could have endured it stoically. All through those endless ages of indescribable torment I should have exulted in the magnificence of divine justice. But this—this is maddening! What becomes of justice? What becomes of morality? What becomes of right and wrong? It's maddening—simply maddening! Oh, if Dr. Amaranth were only here to advise me! (*He buries his face and groans.*)

ZERO *(Trying to puzzle it out)*. You mean to say they ain't called you for cuttin' your mother's throat?

SHRDLU. No! It's terrible—terrible! I was prepared for anything—anything but this.

ZERO. Well, what did they say to you?

SHRDLU *(Looking up)*. Only that I was to come here and remain until I understood.

ZERO. I don't get it. What do they want you to understand?

SHRDLU *(Despairingly)*. I don't know—I don't know! If I only had an inkling of what they meant—— *(Interrupting him.)* Just listen quietly for a moment; do you hear anything? *(They are both silent, straining their ears.)*

ZERO *(At length)*. Nope.

SHRDLU. You don't hear any music? Do you?

ZERO. Music? No, I don't hear nothin'.

SHRDLU. The people here say that the music never stops.

ZERO. They're kiddin' you.

SHRDLU. Do you think so?

ZERO. Sure thing. There ain't a sound.

SHRDLU. Perhaps. They're capable of anything. But I haven't told you of the bitterest of my disappointments.

ZERO. Well, spill it. I'm gettin' used to hearin' bad news.

SHRDLU. When I came to this place, my first thought was to find my dear mother. I wanted to ask her forgiveness. And I wanted her to help me to understand.

ZERO. An' she couldn't do it?

SHRDLU *(With a deep groan)*. She's not here! Mr. Zero! Here where only the most favoured dwell, that wisest and purest of spirits is nowhere to be found. I don't understand it.

A WOMAN'S VOICE *(In the distance)*. Mr. Zero! Oh, Mr. Zero! *(ZERO raises his head and listens attentively.)*

SHRDLU *(Going on, unheedingly)*. If you were to see some of the people here—the things they do——

ZERO *(Interrupting)*. Wait a minute, will you? I think somebody's callin' me.

THE VOICE *(Somewhat nearer)*. Mr. Ze-ro! Oh! Mr. Ze-ro!

ZERO. Who the hell's that now? I wonder if the wife's on my

trail already. That would be swell, wouldn't it? An' I figured on her bein' good for another twenty years, anyhow.

THE VOICE *(Nearer).* Mr. Ze-ro! Yoo-hoo!

ZERO. No. That ain't her voice. *(Calling, savagely.)* Yoo-hoo. *(To* SHRDLU.*)* Ain't that always the way? Just when a guy is takin' life easy an' havin' a good time! *(He rises and looks off left.)* Here she comes, whoever she is. *(In sudden amazement.)* Well, I'll be——! Well, what do you know about that!

(He stands looking in wonderment, as DAISY DIANA DOROTHEA DEVORE *enters. She wears a much-beruffled white muslin dress which is a size too small and fifteen years too youthful for her. She is red-faced and breathless.)*

DAISY *(Panting).* Oh! I thought I'd never catch up to you. I've been followin' you for days—callin' an' callin'. Didn't you hear me?

ZERO. Not till just now. You look kinda winded.

DAISY. I sure am. I can't hardly catch my breath.

ZERO. Well, sit down an' take a load off your feet. *(He leads her to the tree. She sees* SHRDLU *for the first time and shrinks back a little.)*

ZERO. It's all right, he's a friend of mine. *(To* SHRDLU.*)* Buddy, I want you to meet my friend, Miss Devore.

SHRDLU *(Rising and extending his hand courteously).* How do you do, Miss Devore?

DAISY *(Self-consciously).* How do!

ZERO *(To* DAISY*).* He's a friend of mine. *(To* SHRDLU.*)* I guess you don't mind if she sits here a while an' cools off, do you?

SHRDLU. No, no, certainly not. *(They all seat themselves under the tree.* ZERO *and* DAISY *are a little self-conscious.* SHRDLU *gradually becomes absorbed in his own thoughts.)*

ZERO. I was just takin' a rest myself. I took my shoes off on account of my feet bein' so sore.

DAISY. Yeh, I'm kinda tired, too. *(Looking about.)* Say, ain't it pretty here, though?

ZERO. Yeh, it is at that.

DAISY. What do they call this place?

ZERO. Why—er—let's see. He was tellin' me just a minute ago. The—er—I don't know. Some kind o' fields. I forget now. (*To* SHRDLU.) Say, Buddy, what do they call this place again? (SHRDLU, *absorbed in his thoughts, does not hear him. To* DAISY.) He don't hear me. He's thinkin' again.

DAISY (*Sotto voce*). What's the matter with him?

ZERO. Why, he's the guy that murdered his mother—remember?

DAISY (*Interested*). Oh, yeh! Is that him?

ZERO. Yeh. An' he had it all figgered out how they was goin' t' roast him or somethin'. And now they ain't goin' to do nothin' to him an' it's kinda got his goat.

DAISY (*Sympathetically*). Poor feller!

ZERO. Yeh. He takes it kinda hard.

DAISY. He looks like a nice young feller.

ZERO. Well, you sure are good for sore eyes. I never expected to see you here.

DAISY. I thought maybe you'd be kinda surprised.

ZERO. Surprised is right. I thought you was alive an' kickin'. When did you pass out?

DAISY. Oh, right after you did—a coupla days.

ZERO (*Interested*). Yeh? What happened? Get hit by a truck or somethin'?

DAISY. No. (*Hesitantly.*) You see—it's this way. I blew out the gas.

ZERO (*Astonished*). Go on! What was the big idea?

DAISY (*Falteringly*). Oh, I don't know. You see, I lost my job.

ZERO. I'll bet you're sorry you did it now, ain't you?

DAISY (*With conviction*). No, I ain't sorry. Not a bit. (*Then hesitantly.*) Say, Mr. Zero, I been thinkin'—— (*She stops.*)

ZERO. What?

DAISY (*Plucking up courage*). I been thinkin' it would be kinda nice—if you an' me—if we could kinda talk things over.

ZERO. Yeh. Sure. What do you want to talk about?

DAISY. Well—I don't know—but you and me—we ain't really ever talked things over, have we?

ZERO. No, that's right, we ain't. Well, let's go to it.

DAISY. I was thinkin' if we could be alone—just the two of us, see?

ZERO. Oh, yeh! Yeh, I get you. (*He turns to* SHRDLU *and coughs loudly.* SHRDLU *does not stir.*)

ZERO (*To* DAISY). He's dead to the world. (*He turns to* SHRDLU.) Say, Buddy! (*No answer.*) Say, Buddy!

SHRDLU (*Looking up with a start*). Were you speaking to me?

ZERO. Yeh. How'd you guess it? I was thinkin' that maybe you'd like to walk around a little and look for your mother.

SHRDLU (*Shaking his head*). It's no use. I've looked everywhere. (*He relapses into thought again.*)

ZERO. Maybe over there they might know.

SHRDLU. No, no! I've searched everywhere. She's not here. (ZERO *and* DAISY *look at each other in despair.*)

ZERO. Listen, old shirt, my friend here and me—see?—we used to work in the same store. An' we got some things to talk over—business, see?—kinda confidential. So if it ain't askin' too much——

SHRDLU (*Springing to his feet*). Why, certainly! Excuse me! (*He bows politely to* DAISY *and walks off.* DAISY *and* ZERO *watch him until he has disappeared.*)

ZERO (*With a forced laugh*). He's a good guy at that. (*Now that they are alone, both are very self-conscious, and for a time they sit in silence.*)

DAISY (*Breaking the silence*). It sure is pretty here, ain't it?

ZERO. Sure is.

DAISY. Look at the flowers! Ain't they just perfect! Why, you'd think they was artificial, wouldn't you?

ZERO. Yeh, you would.

DAISY. And the smell of them. Like perfume.

ZERO. Yeh.

DAISY. I'm crazy about the country, ain't you?

ZERO. Yeh. It's nice for a change.

DAISY. Them store picnics—remember?

ZERO. You bet. They sure was fun.

DAISY. One time—I guess you don't remember—the two of us—me and you—we sat down on the grass together under a tree—just like we're doin' now.

ZERO. Sure I remember.

DAISY. Go on! I'll bet you don't.

ZERO. I'll bet I do. It was the year the wife didn't go.

DAISY *(Her face brightening)*. That's right! I didn't think you'd remember.

ZERO. An' comin' home we sat together in the truck.

DAISY *(Eagerly, rather shamefacedly)*. Yeh! There's somethin' I've always wanted to ask you.

ZERO. Well, why didn't you?

DAISY. I don't know. It didn't seem refined. But I'm goin' to ask you now, anyhow.

ZERO. Go ahead. Shoot.

DAISY *(Falteringly)*. Well—while we was comin' home—you put your arm up on the bench behind me—and I could feel your knee kinda pressin' against mine. *(She stops.)*

ZERO *(Becoming more and more interested)*. Yeh—well—what about it?

DAISY. What I wanted to ask you was—was it just kinda accidental?

ZERO *(With a laugh)*. Sure it was accidental. Accidental on purpose.

DAISY *(Eagerly)*. Do you mean it?

ZERO. Sure I mean it. You mean to say you didn't know it?

DAISY. No. I've been wantin' to ask you——

ZERO. Then why did you get sore at me?

DAISY. Sore? I wasn't sore! When was I sore?

ZERO. That night. Sure you was sore. If you wasn't sore why did you move away?

DAISY. Just to see if you meant it. I thought if you meant it you'd move up closer. An' then when you took your arm away I was sure you didn't mean it.

ZERO. An' I thought all the time you was sore. That's why I took my arm away. I thought if I moved up you'd holler and then I'd be in a jam, like you read in the paper all the time about guys gettin' pulled in for annoyin' women.

DAISY. An' I was wishin' you'd put your arm around me— just sittin' there wishin' all the way home.

ZERO. What do you know about that? That sure is hard luck,

that is. If I'd 'a' only knew! You know what I felt like doin'
—only I didn't have the nerve?

DAISY. What?

ZERO. I felt like kissin' you.

DAISY (*Fervently*). I wanted you to.

ZERO (*Astonished*). You would 'a' let me?

DAISY. I wanted you to! I wanted you to! Oh, why didn't you
—why didn't you?

ZERO. I didn't have the nerve. I sure was a dumbbell.

DAISY. I would 'a' let you all you wanted to. I wouldn't 'a'
cared. I know it would 'a' been wrong but I wouldn't 'a'
cared. I wasn't thinkin' about right an' wrong at all. I didn't
care—see? I just wanted you to kiss me.

ZERO (*Feelingly*). If I'd only knew. I wanted to do it, I swear
I did. But I didn't think you cared nothin' about me.

DAISY (*Passionately*). I never cared nothin' about nobody
else.

ZERO. Do you mean it—on the level? You ain't kiddin' me,
are you?

DAISY. No, I ain't kiddin'. I mean it. I'm tellin' you the truth.
I ain't never had the nerve to tell you before—but now I
don't care. It don't make no difference now. I mean it—
every word of it.

ZERO (*Dejectedly*). If I'd only knew it.

DAISY. Listen to me. There's somethin' else I want to tell you.
I may as well tell you everything now. It don't make no
difference now. About my blowin' out the gas—see? Do
you know why I done it?

ZERO. Yeh, you told me—on account o' bein' canned.

DAISY. I just told you that. That ain't the real reason. The real
reason is on account o' you.

ZERO. You mean to say on account o' me passin' out——?

DAISY. Yeh. That's it. I didn't want to go on livin'. What for?
What did I want to go on livin' for? I didn't have nothin'
to live for with you gone. I often thought of doin' it before.
But I never had the nerve. An' anyhow I didn't want to
leave you.

ZERO. An' me bawlin' you out, about readin' too fast an' readin' too slow.

DAISY *(Reproachfully)*. Why did you do it?

ZERO. I don't know, I swear I don't. I was always stuck on you. An' while I'd be addin' them figgers, I'd be thinkin' how if the wife died, you an' me could get married.

DAISY. I used to think o' that, too.

ZERO. An' then before I knew it, I was bawlin' you out.

DAISY. Them was the times I'd think o' blowin' out the gas. But I never did till you was gone. There wasn't nothin' to live for then. But it wasn't so easy to do, anyhow. I never could stand the smell o' gas. An' all the while I was gettin' ready, you know, stuffin' up all the cracks, the way you read about in the paper—I was thinkin' of you and hopin' that maybe I'd meet you again. An' I made up my mind if I ever did see you, I'd tell you.

ZERO *(Taking her hand)*. I'm sure glad you did. I'm sure glad. *(Ruefully.)* But it don't do much good now, does it?

DAISY. No, I guess it don't. *(Summoning courage.)* But there's one thing I'm goin' to ask you.

ZERO. What's that?

DAISY *(In a low voice)*. I want you to kiss me.

ZERO. You bet I will! *(He leans over and kisses her cheek.)*

DAISY. Not like that. I don't mean like that. I mean really kiss me. On the mouth. I ain't never been kissed like that. *(ZERO puts his arms about her and presses his lips to hers. A long embrace. At last they separate and sit side by side in silence.)*

DAISY *(Putting her hands to her cheeks)*. So that's what it's like. I didn't know it could be like that. I didn't know anythin' could be like that.

ZERO *(Fondling her hand)*. Your cheeks are red. They're all red. And your eyes are shinin'. I never seen your eyes shinin' like that before.

DAISY *(Holding up her hand)*. Listen—do you hear it? Do you hear the music?

ZERO. No, I don't hear nothin'!

DAISY. Yeh—music. Listen an' you'll hear it. *(They are both silent for a moment.)*

ZERO *(Excitedly)*. Yeh! I hear it! He said there was music, but I didn't hear it till just now.

DAISY. Ain't it grand?

ZERO. Swell! Say, do you know what?

DAISY. What?

ZERO. It makes me feel like dancin'.

DAISY. Yeh? Me, too.

ZERO *(Springing to his feet)*. Come on! Let's dance! *(He seizes her hands and tries to pull her up.)*

DAISY *(Resisting laughingly)*. I can't dance. I ain't danced in twenty years.

ZERO. That's nothin'. I ain't, neither. Come on! I feel just like a kid! *(He pulls her to her feet and seizes her about the waist.)*

DAISY. Wait a minute! Wait till I fix my skirt. *(She turns back her skirts and pins them above the ankles.)*

(ZERO seizes her about the waist. They dance clumsily but with gay abandon. DAISY's hair becomes loosened and tumbles over her shoulders. She lends herself more and more to the spirit of the dance. But ZERO soon begins to tire and dances with less and less zest.)

ZERO *(Stopping at last, panting for breath)*. Wait a minute! I'm all winded. *(He releases DAISY, but before he can turn away, she throws her arms about him and presses her lips to his.)*

ZERO *(Freeing himself)*. Wait a minute! Let me get my wind! *(He limps to the tree and seats himself under it, gasping for breath. DAISY looks after him, her spirits rather dampened.)*

ZERO. Whew! I sure am winded! I ain't used to dancin'. *(He takes off his collar and tie and opens the neckband of his shirt. DAISY sits under the tree near him, looking at him longingly. But he is busy catching his breath.)* Gee, my heart's goin' a mile a minute.

DAISY. Why don't you lay down an' rest? You could put your head on my lap.

ZERO. That ain't a bad idea. (*He stretches out, his head in* DAISY'S *lap.*)

DAISY (*Fondling his hair*). It was swell, wasn't it?

ZERO. Yeh. But you gotta be used to it.

DAISY. Just imagine if we could stay here all the time—you an' me together—wouldn't it be swell?

ZERO. Yeh. But there ain't a chance.

DAISY. Won't they let us stay?

ZERO. No. This place is only for the good ones.

DAISY. Well, we ain't so bad, are we?

ZERO. Go on! Me a murderer an' you committin' suicide. Anyway, they wouldn't stand for this—the way we been goin' on.

DAISY. I don't see why.

ZERO. You don't! You know it ain't right. Ain't I got a wife?

DAISY. Not any more you ain't. When you're dead that ends it. Don't they always say "until death do us part?"

ZERO. Well, maybe you're right about that, but they wouldn't stand for us here.

DAISY. It would be swell—the two of us together—we could make up for all them years.

ZERO. Yeh, I wish we could.

DAISY. We sure were fools. But I don't care. I've got you now. (*She kisses his forehead and cheeks and mouth.*)

ZERO. I'm sure crazy about you. I never saw you lookin' so pretty before, with your cheeks all red. An' your hair hangin' down. You got swell hair. (*He fondles and kisses her hair.*)

DAISY (*Ecstatically*). We got each other now, ain't we?

ZERO. Yeh. I'm crazy about you. Daisy! That's a pretty name. It's a flower, ain't it? Well—that's what you are—just a flower.

DAISY (*Happily*). We can always be together now, can't we?

ZERO. As long as they'll let us. I sure am crazy about you. (*Suddenly he sits upright.*) Watch your step!

DAISY (*Alarmed*). What's the matter?

ZERO (*Nervously*). He's comin' back.

DAISY. Oh, is that all? Well, what about it?

ZERO. You don't want him to see us layin' around like this, do you?

DAISY. I don't care if he does.

ZERO. Well, you oughta care. You don't want him to think you ain't a refined girl, do you? He's an awful moral bird, he is.

DAISY. I don't care nothin' about him. I don't care nothin' about anybody but you.

ZERO. Sure, I know. But we don't want people talkin' about us. You better fix your hair an' pull down your skirts. (DAISY *complies rather sadly. They are both silent as* SHRDLU *enters.*)

ZERO (*With feigned nonchalance*). Well, you got back all right, didn't you?

SHRDLU. I hope I haven't returned too soon.

ZERO. No, that's all right. We were just havin' a little talk. You know—about business an' things.

DAISY (*Boldly*). We were wishin' we could stay here all the time.

SHRDLU. You may if you like.

ZERO AND DAISY (*In astonishment*). What!

SHRDLU. Yes. Any one who likes may remain——

ZERO. But I thought you were tellin' me——

SHRDLU. Just as I told you, only the most favored do remain. But any one may.

ZERO. I don't get it. There's a catch in it somewheres.

DAISY. It don't matter as long as we can stay.

ZERO (*To* SHRDLU). We were thinkin' about gettin' married, see?

SHRDLU. You may or not, just as you like.

ZERO. You don't mean to say we could stay if we didn't, do you?

SHRDLU. Yes. They don't care.

ZERO. An' there's some here that ain't married?

SHRDLU. Yes.

ZERO (*To* DAISY). I don't know about this place, at that. They must be kind of a mixed crowd. ·

DAISY. It don't matter, so long as we got each other.

ZERO. Yeh, I know, but you don't want to mix with people that ain't respectable.

DAISY (*To* SHRDLU). Can we get married right away? I guess there must be a lot of ministers here, ain't there?

SHRDLU. Not as many as I had hoped to find. The two who seem most beloved are Dean Swift and the Abbé Rabelais. They are both much admired for some indecent tales which they have written.

ZERO (*Shocked*). What! Ministers writin' smutty stories! Say, what kind of a dump is this, anyway?

SHRDLU (*Despairingly*). I don't know, Mr. Zero. All these people here are so strange, so unlike the good people I've known. They seem to think of nothing but enjoyment or of wasting their time in profitless occupations. Some paint pictures from morning until night, or carve blocks of stone. Others write songs or put words together, day in and day out. Still others do nothing but lie under the trees and look at the sky. There are men who spend all their time reading books and women who think only of adorning themselves. And forever they are telling stories and laughing and singing and drinking and dancing. There are drunkards, thieves, vagabonds, blasphemers, adulterers. There is one——

ZERO. That's enough. I heard enough. (*He seats himself and begins putting on his shoes.*)

DAISY (*Anxiously*). What are you goin' to do?

ZERO. I'm goin' to beat it, that's what I'm goin' to do.

DAISY. You said you liked it here.

ZERO (*Looking at her in amazement*). Liked it! Say, you don't mean to say you want to stay here, do you, with a lot of rummies an' loafers an' bums?

DAISY. We don't have to bother with them. We can just sit here together an' look at the flowers an' listen to the music.

SHRDLU (*Eagerly*). Music! Did you hear music?

DAISY. Sure. Don't you hear it?

SHRDLU. No, they say it never stops. But I've never heard it.
ZERO (*Listening*). I thought I heard it before but I don't hear
    nothin' now. I guess I must 'a' been dreamin'. (*Looking
    about.*) What's the quickest way out of this place?
DAISY (*Pleadingly*). Won't you stay just a little longer?
ZERO. Didn't yer hear me say I'm goin'? Good-bye, Miss
    Devore. I'm goin' to beat it. (*He limps off at the right.*
    DAISY *follows him slowly.*)
DAISY (*To* SHRDLU). I won't ever see him again.
SHRDLU. Are you goin' to stay here?
DAISY. It don't make no difference now. Without him I might
    as well be alive.

(*She goes off right.* SHRDLU *watches her a moment, then
sighs and seating himself under the tree, buries his head on
his arm. Curtain falls.*)

Scene Eight

(SCENE. *Before the curtain rises the clicking of an adding machine is heard. The curtain rises upon an office similar in appearance to that in Scene Two except that there is a door in the back wall through which can be seen a glimpse of the corridor outside. In the middle of the room* ZERO *is seated completely absorbed in the operation of an adding machine. He presses the keys and pulls the lever with mechanical precision. He still wears his full-dress suit but he has added to it sleeve protectors and a green eye shade. A strip of white paper-tape flows steadily from the machine as* ZERO *operates. The room is filled with this tape— streamers, festoons, billows of it everywhere. It covers the floor and the furniture, it climbs the walls and chokes the doorways. A few moments later,* LIEUTENANT CHARLES *and* JOE *enter at the left.* LIEUTENANT CHARLES *is middle-aged and inclined to corpulence. He has an air of world-weariness. He is bare-footed, wears a Panama hat, and is dressed in bright red tights which are a very bad fit—too tight in some places, badly wrinkled in others.* JOE *is a youth with a smutty face dressed in dirty blue overalls.*)

CHARLES (*After contemplating* ZERO *for a few moments*). All right, Zero, cease firing.

ZERO (*Looking up, surprised*). Whaddja say?

CHARLES. I said stop punching that machine.

ZERO (*Bewildered*). Stop? (*He goes on working mechanically.*)

CHARLES (*Impatiently*). Yes. Can't you stop? Here, Joe, give me a hand. He can't stop.

JOE *and* CHARLES *each take one of* ZERO's *arms and with*

enormous effort detach him from the machine. He resists passively—mere inertia. Finally they succeed and swing him around on his stool. CHARLES *and* JOE *mop their foreheads.)*

ZERO (*Querulously*). What's the idea? Can't you lemme alone?

CHARLES (*Ignoring the question*). How long have you been here?

ZERO. Jes' twenty-five years. Three hundred months, ninety-one hundred and thirty-one days, one hundred thirty-six thousand——

CHARLES (*Impatiently*). That'll do! That'll do!

ZERO (*Proudly*). I ain't missed a day, not an hour, not a minute. Look at all I got done. (*He points to the maze of paper.*)

CHARLES. It's time to quit.

ZERO. Quit? Whaddya mean quit? I ain't goin' to quit!

CHARLES. You've got to.

ZERO. What for? What do I have to quit for?

CHARLES. It's time for you to go back.

ZERO. Go back where? Whaddya talkin' about?

CHARLES. Back to earth, you dub. Where do you think?

ZERO. Aw, go on, Cap, who are you kiddin'?

CHARLES. I'm not kidding anybody. And don't call me Cap. I'm a lieutenant.

ZERO. All right, Lieutenant, all right. But what's this you're tryin' to tell me about goin' back?

CHARLES. Your time's up, I'm telling you. You must be pretty thick. How many times do you want to be told a thing?

ZERO. This is the first time I heard about goin' back. Nobody ever said nothin' to me about it before.

CHARLES. You didn't think you were going to stay here forever, did you?

ZERO. Sure. Why not? I did my bit, didn't I? Forty-five years of it. Twenty-five years in the store. Then the boss canned me and I knocked him cold. I guess you ain't heard about that——

CHARLES (*Interrupting*). I know all about that. But what's that got to do with it?

ZERO. Well, I done my bit, didn't I? That oughta let me out.

CHARLES (*Jeeringly*). So you think you're all through, do you?

ZERO. Sure, I do. I did the best I could while I was there and then I passed out. And now I'm sittin' pretty here.

CHARLES. You've got a fine idea of the way they run things, you have. Do you think they're going to all of the trouble of making a soul just to use it once?

ZERO. Once is often enough, it seems to me.

CHARLES. It seems to you, does it? Well, who are you? And what do you know about it? Why, man, they use a soul over and over again—over and over until it's worn out.

ZERO. Nobody ever told me.

CHARLES. So you thought you were all through, did you? Well, that's a hot one, that is.

ZERO (*Sullenly*). How was I to know?

CHARLES. Use your brains! Where would we put them all? We're crowded enough as it is. Why, this place is nothing but a kind of repair and service station—a sort of cosmic laundry, you might say. We get the souls in here by the bushelful. Then we get busy and clean them up. And you ought to see some of them. The muck and the slime. Phoo! And as full of holes as a flour-sifter. But we fix them up. We disinfect them and give them a kerosene rub and mend the holes and back they go—practically as good as new.

ZERO. You mean to say I've been here before—before the last time, I mean?

CHARLES. Been here before! Why, you poor boob—you've been here thousands of times—fifty thousand, at least.

ZERO (*Suspiciously*). How is it I don't remember nothin' about it?

CHARLES. Well—that's partly because you're stupid. But it's mostly because that's the way they fix it. (*Musingly*.) They're funny that way—every now and then they'll do something white like that—when you'd least expect it. I guess economy's at the bottom of it, though. They figure that the souls would get worn out quicker if they remembered.

ZERO. And don't any of 'em remember?

CHARLES. Oh, some do. You see there's different types: there's the type that gets a little better each time it goes back—we just give them a wash and send them right through. Then there's another type—the type that gets a little worse each time. That's where you belong!

ZERO (*Offended*). Me? You mean to say I'm gettin' worse all the time?

CHARLES (*Nodding*). Yes. A little worse each time.

ZERO. Well—what was I when I started? Somethin' big?—A king or somethin'?

CHARLES (*Laughing derisively*). A king! That's a good one! I'll tell you what you were the first time—if you want to know so much—a monkey.

ZERO (*Shocked and offended*). A monkey!

CHARLES (*Nodding*). Yes, sir—just a hairy, chattering, long-tailed monkey.

ZERO. That musta been a long time ago.

CHARLES. Oh, not so long. A million years or so. Seems like yesterday to me.

ZERO. Then look here, whaddya mean by sayin' I'm gettin' worse all the time?

CHARLES. Just what I said. You weren't so bad as a monkey. Of course, you did just what all the other monkeys did, but still it kept you out in the open air. And you weren't women-shy—there was one little red-headed monkey——Well, never mind. Yes, sir, you weren't so bad then. But even in those days there must have been some bigger and brainier monkey that you kowtowed to. The mark of the slave was on you from the start.

ZERO (*Sullenly*). You ain't very particular about what you call people, are you?

CHARLES. You wanted the truth, didn't you? If there ever was a soul in the world that was labelled slave it's yours. Why, all the bosses and kings that there ever were have left their trademarks on your backside.

ZERO. It ain't fair, if you ask me.

CHARLES (*Shrugging his shoulders*). Don't tell me about it.

I don't make the rules. All I know is you've been getting worse—worse each time. Why, even six thousand years ago you weren't so bad. That was the time you were hauling stones for one of those big pyramids in a place they call Africa. Ever hear of the pyramids?

ZERO. Them big pointy things?

CHARLES (Nodding). That's it.

ZERO. I seen a picture of them in the movies.

CHARLES. Well, you helped build them. It was a long step down from the happy days in the jungle, but it was a good job—even though you didn't know what you were doing and your back was striped by the foreman's whip. But you've been going down, down. Two thousand years ago you were a Roman galley-slave. You were on one of the triremes that knocked the Carthaginian fleet for a goal. Again the whip. But you had muscles then—chest muscles, back muscles, biceps. (He feels ZERO's arm gingerly and turns away in disgust.) Phoo! A bunch of mush! (He notices that JOE has fallen asleep. Walking over, he kicks him in the shin.)

CHARLES. Wake up, you mutt! Where do you think you are! (He turns to ZERO again.) And then another thousand years and you were a serf—a lump of clay digging up other lumps of clay. You wore an iron collar then—white ones hadn't been invented yet. Another long step down. But where you dug, potatoes grew and that helped fatten the pigs. Which was something. And now—well, I don't want to rub it in——

ZERO. Rub it in is right! Seems to me I got a pretty healthy kick comin'. I ain't had a square deal! Hard work! That's all I've ever had!

CHARLES (Callously). What else were you ever good for?

ZERO. Well, that ain't the point. The point is I'm through! I had enough! Let 'em find somebody else to do the dirty work. I'm sick of bein' the goat! I quit right here and now! (He glares about defiantly. There is a thunder-clap and a bright flash of lightning.)

ZERO (Screaming). Ooh! What's that? (He clings to CHARLES.)

CHARLES. It's all right. Nobody's going to hurt you. It's just their way of telling you that they don't like you to talk that way. Pull yourself together and calm down. You can't change the rules—nobody can—they've got it all fixed. It's a rotten system—but what are you going to do about it?

ZERO. Why can't they stop pickin' on me? I'm satisfied here—doin' my day's work. I don't want to go back.

CHARLES. You've got to, I tell you. There's no way out of it.

ZERO. What chance have I got—at my age? Who'll give me a job?

CHARLES. You big boob, you don't think you're going back the way you are, do you?

ZERO. Sure, how then?

CHARLES. Why, you've got to start all over.

ZERO. All over?

CHARLES (*Nodding*). You'll be a baby again—a bald, red-faced little animal, and then you'll go through it all again. There'll be millions of others like you—all with their mouths open, squalling for food. And then when you get a little older you'll begin to learn things—and you'll learn all the wrong things and learn them all in the wrong way. You'll eat the wrong food and wear the wrong clothes and you'll live in swarming dens where there's no light and no air! You'll learn to be a liar and a bully and a braggart and a coward and a sneak. You'll learn to fear the sunlight and to hate beauty. By that time you'll be ready for school. There they'll tell you the truth about a great many things that you don't give a damn about and they'll tell you lies about all the things you ought to know—and about all the things you want to know they'll tell you nothing at all. When you get through you'll be equipped for your life-work. You'll be ready to take a job.

ZERO (*Eagerly*). What'll my job be? Another adding machine?

CHARLES. Yes. But not one of these antiquated adding machines. It will be a superb, super-hyper-adding machine, as far from this old piece of junk as you are from God. It will be something to make you sit up and take notice, that adding machine. It will be an adding machine which will be installed in a coal mine and which will record the individual output of each miner. As each miner down in the lower galleries takes up a shovelful of coal, the impact of his shovel will automatically set in motion a graphite pencil in your gallery. The pencil will make a mark in white upon a blackened, sensitized drum. Then your work comes in. With the great toe of your right foot you release a lever which focuses a violet ray on the drum. The ray playing upon and through the white mark, falls upon a selenium cell which in turn sets the keys of the adding apparatus in motion. In this way the individual output of each miner is recorded without any human effort except the slight pressure of the great toe of your right foot.

ZERO *(In breathless, round-eyed wonder)*. Say, that'll be some machine, won't it?

CHARLES. Some machine is right. It will be the culmination of human effort—the final triumph of the evolutionary process. For millions of years the nebulous gases swirled in space. For more millions of years the gases cooled and then through inconceivable ages they hardened into rocks. And then came life. Floating green things on the waters that covered the earth. More millions of years and a step upward—an animate organism in the ancient slime. And so on—step by step, down through the ages—a gain here, a gain there— the mollusc, the fish, the reptile, then mammal, man! And all so that you might sit in the gallery of a coal mine and operate the super-hyper-adding machine with the great toe of your right foot!

ZERO. Well, then—I ain't so bad, after all.

CHARLES. You're a failure, Zero, a failure. A waste product. A slave to a contraption of steel and iron. The animal's instincts, but not his strength and skill. The animal's appetites, but not his unashamed indulgence of them. True, you move and eat and digest and excrete and reproduce. But any microscopic organism can do as much. Well— time's up! Back you go—back to your sunless groove—the raw material of slums and wars—the ready prey of the first jingo or demagogue or political adventurer who takes the trouble to play upon your ignorance and credulity and provincialism. You poor, spineless, brainless boob—I'm sorry for you!

ZERO *(Falling to his knees)*. Then keep me here! Don't send me back! Let me stay!

CHARLES. Get up. Didn't I tell you I can't do anything for you? Come on, time's up!

ZERO. I can't! I can't! I'm afraid to go through it all again.

CHARLES. You've got to, I tell you. Come on, now!

ZERO. What did you tell me so much for? Couldn't you just let me go, thinkin' everythin' was goin' to be all right?

CHARLES. You wanted to know, didn't you?

ZERO. How did I know what you were goin' to tell me? Now I can't stop thinkin' about it! I can't stop thinkin'! I'll be thinkin' about it all the time.

CHARLES. All right! I'll do the best I can for you. I'll send a girl with you to keep you company.

ZERO. A girl? What for? What good will a girl do me?

CHARLES. She'll help make you forget.

ZERO *(Eagerly)*. She will? Where is she?

CHARLES. Wait a minute, I'll call her. *(He calls in a loud voice.)* Oh! Hope! Yoo-hoo! *(He turns his head aside and says in the manner of a ventriloquist imitating a distant feminine voice.)* Ye-es. *(Then in his own voice.)* Come here, will you? There's a fellow who wants you to take him back. *(Ventriloquously again.)* All right. I'll be right over, Charlie dear. *(He turns to* ZERO.) Kind of familiar, isn't she? Charlie dear!

ZERO. What did you say her name is?

CHARLES. Hope. H-o-p-e.

ZERO. Is she good-lookin'?

CHARLES. Is she good-looking! Oh, boy, wait until you see her! She's a blonde with big blue eyes and red lips and little white teeth and——

ZERO. Say, that listens good to me. Will she be long?

CHARLES. She'll be here right away. There she is now! Do you see her?

ZERO. No. Where?

CHARLES. Out in the corridor. No, not there. Over farther.

To the right. Don't you see her blue dress? And the sunlight on her hair?

ZERO. Oh, sure! Now I see her! What's the matter with me, anyhow? Say, she's some jane! Oh, you baby vamp!

CHARLES. She'll make you forget your troubles.

ZERO. What troubles are you talkin' about?

CHARLES. Nothing. Go on. Don't keep her waiting.

ZERO. You bet I won't! Oh, Hope! Wait for me! I'll be right with you! I'm on my way! *(He stumbles out eagerly.* JOE *bursts into uproarious laughter.)*

CHARLES *(Eyeing him in surprise and anger).* What in hell's the matter with you?

JOE *(Shaking with laughter).* Did you get that? He thinks he saw somebody and he's following her! *(He rocks with laughter.)*

CHARLES *(Punching him in the jaw).* Shut your face!

JOE *(Nursing his jaw).* What's the idea? Can't I even laugh when I see something funny?

CHARLES. Funny! You keep your mouth shut or I'll show you something funny. Go on, hustle out of here and get something to clean up this mess with. There's another fellow moving in. Hurry now. *(He makes a threatening gesture.* JOE *exits hastily.* CHARLES *goes to chair and seats himself. He looks weary and dispirited.)*

CHARLES *(Shaking his head).* Hell, I'll tell the world this is a lousy job! *(He takes a flask from his pocket, uncorks it, and slowly drains it.)*

CURTAIN

BEGGAR ON HORSEBACK

by George S. Kaufman
Marc Connelly

Introduction

The day after *Beggar on Horseback* opened in New York (February 12, 1924), John Corbin began his review for *The New York Times* with:

> There are no beggars in this new Kaufman-Connelly comedy and indeed no horsebacks. There is not really anything that has ever been in a play before. That was one reason why the audience rose to it at the very start. The reason why it kept on rising with ever increased delight was that it bristles with sly and caustic satire, brims with novel and richly colored theatric inventions, and overflows with inconsequent humor and the motley spirit of youth.[1]

Since its premiere in 1924 it has been anthologized at least ten times;[2] has taken its place as one of the first great satires on American big business; and has been popular with school, college, and community theatre groups for four decades.

The sophisticated reader of the 1960's, who can see almost any type of play on television with all its many resources for creating effects, atmosphere, and mood, must place himself back in 1924 to appreciate fully the extent of Kaufman's and Connelly's achievement. Although it is true that a dream sequence in a play was not new (the technique was used by Eleanor Gates in her *Poor Little Rich Girl* in about 1912), and that expressionistic plays had already begun to appear on Broadway (e.g., John Howard Lawson's *Roger Bloomer*

---

[1] Quoted by Barnard Hewitt, *Theatre U.S.A.*, p. 354.
[2] John H. Ottenmiller, *Index to Plays in Collections*, p. 113.

and Elmer Rice's *The Adding Machine*), still, *Beggar on Horseback* was breaking new ground in the American theatre by its courageous attack on the crushing effects of big-business mentality upon artistic creation.

What Kaufman and Connelly say so effectively is that one cannot buy artistic creations with money; that art cannot be produced on the assembly line; that big business, for all its much-advertised efficiency, is not so efficient after all (see, for example, the hilariously funny scenes about a lead pencil).

The early 1920's saw many novels making fun of the businessman who looks at everything from a dollars-and-cents viewpoint; perhaps Sinclair Lewis' *Babbitt* is the best exemplar. But it took some courage to write and produce on Broadway a play attacking big business. As Alexander Woollcott said in his preface to the published play:

> They (i.e., Kaufman and Connelly) offer it merely as a relieving antidote to the worship of material prosperity. It is a play written in the distaste that can be inspired by the viewpoint, the complacency and the very idiom of Rotarian America.[3]

Barrett H. Clark and George Freedley in their *History of Modern Drama* praise it as:

> the first genuinely imaginative satire of its kind that, without heat or apparent moral indignation, attempted to expose the barren machine-age efficiency that had to some extent become a religion to Homo Americanus.
> . . . Even as late as 1924 the theatre was apparently not considered a proper place to question the sacred aims and procedures of Big Business.
> But it should be noticed that the playwrights attacked their problem not as reformers but as artists—or shall we say as tolerant and intelligent gentlemen who could smile at fatuity and "kid" the theology of success.[4]

---

[3] Preface to *Beggar on Horseback*, p. 11.
[4] *A History of Modern Drama*, p. 733.

Although four decades have come and gone, and the Space Age, the Nuclear Age, and the Television Age have superseded the business boom of the early 1920's, whose excesses inspired this comedy, the basic truths expressed in the play are still very much in evidence in our own day. Art may not necessarily flourish in a freezing garret in Greenwich Village; neither will it develop in a Riviera villa furnished by all-powerful in-laws. Equally evident is the truth that millions quickly made do not guarantee to their owner artistic or any other kind of taste. Any day's newspaper can testify to the tragic failures of marriages *not* based on any mutual understanding or compatability. To have satirized some of the foibles of forty years ago and to be meaningful in our own day is no insignificant achievement—and this Kaufman and Connelly have accomplished in *Beggar on Horseback.*

George S. Kaufman (1889–1961)

George S. Kaufman was born in Pittsburgh, Pennsylvania, on November 16, 1889. After an early career as a reporter and drama critic, he began to write plays. Since 1921, when *Dulcy* appeared as his first collaboration with Marc Connelly, there was rarely a year—until his death in 1961—without a Kaufman play (usually in collaboration). His only play written alone was *The Butter-and Egg Man* (1925). Among his collaborators were Edna Ferber, Irving Pichel, Larry Evans, Marc Connelly, Katherine Dayton, Alexander Woollcott, Ring Lardner, Morrie Ryskind, and Moss Hart.

Kaufman was a master craftsman of the theatre who was frequently brought in by the producer to transform the script of a potential play into that of a successful one. He had a keen eye for comedy and never quite lost the satirical touch shown so brilliantly in *Beggar on Horseback.* He was successful in almost all varieties of theatrical art—expressionistic satire in *Beggar on Horseback;* social satire in *To the Ladies* and *Dulcy;* revues, as in *The Bandwagon;* musicals, as in the Pulitzer Prize-winning comedy *Of Thee I Sing;* and comedies, some of the greatest of the twentieth-century theatre, such as *Once in a Lifetime* and *You Can't Take It With You.*

Marc Connelly (1890–   )

Marc Connelly was born in McKeesport, Pennsylvania, was educated at Trinity School, Washington, Pennsylvania, and came to New York City in 1915, to watch a musical containing some of his lyrics. He has been a devotee of the theatre ever since, serving it as playwright, actor, director, and teacher of playwriting. His earliest plays were in collaboration with George S. Kaufman: *Dulcy* (1921), *To the Ladies* (1922), *Merton of the Movies* (1923), and *Beggar on Horseback* (1924).

His own plays have included the *Wisdom Tooth* (1927); *The Green Pastures,* fabulously successful in 1929 and frequently revived; and *Story for Strangers* (1948). In 1947 he was invited to join the Yale University faculty to teach playwriting, and he has been interested for a long time in assisting young playwrights to develop their potentialities.

As an author, Connelly has shown great skill in high comedy, a form which depends for its appeal on characterization rather than on plot. Also, in *The Green Pastures,* he demonstrated his ability to portray tenderness and pathos. In recent years he has been seen on television frequently in the role of a judge or a counselor of younger folk. He has lived to see many changes in the American theatre since the memorable opening night of *Dulcy,* with Lynn Fontanne, in 1921.

JOSEPH MERSAND

FURTHER READING

Clark, Barrett H., and Freedley, George. *A History of Modern Drama.* New York: D. Appleton-Century, 1947, p. 733.
Dickinson, Thomas H. *Playwrights of the New American Theatre.* New York: Macmillan, 1925, pp. 313-14.

Flexner, Eleanor. *American Playwrights, 1918–1938*. New York: Simon and Schuster, 1938, pp. 206-13.

Gagey, Edmond M. *Revolution in American Drama*. New York: Columbia University Press, 1947, p. 202.

Gassner, John. *Masters of the Drama* (3rd ed.). New York: Dover, 1954, p. 666.

Hewitt, Barnard. *Theatre U.S.A. 1668–1957*. New York: McGraw-Hill, 1959, pp. 353-55.

Krutch, Joseph Wood. *The American Drama Since 1918*. New York: Random House, 1939, pp. 137-38.

Lovell, John, Jr. *Digest of Great American Plays*. New York: Thomas Y. Crowell, 1961, pp. 208-10.

Mantle, Burns. *American Playwrights of Today*. New York: Dodd, Mead, 1929, p. 88.

Morehouse, Ward. *Matinee Tomorrow*. New York: Whittlesey House, 1949, p. 204.

Ottenmiller, John H. *Index to Plays in Collections* (3rd ed.). New York: The Scarecrow Press, 1957, p. 113.

Quinn, Arthur Hobson. *A History of the American Drama from the Civil War to the Present Day*. New York: F. S. Crofts, 1937, vol. 2, pp. 222-23.

Shipley, Joseph T. *Guide to Great Plays*. Washington: Public Affairs Press, 1956, pp. 373-74.

Woollcott, Alexander. Preface to *Beggar on Horseback*. New York: Horace Liveright, 1924, pp. 11-15.

BEGGAR ON HORSEBACK

Cast of Characters

DR. ALBERT RICE

CYNTHIA MASON

NEIL MC RAE

MR. CADY

MRS. CADY

GLADYS CADY

HOMER CADY

A BUTLER

JERRY

A BUSINESS MAN

MISS HEY

MISS YOU

A WAITER

A REPORTER

A JUROR

A GUIDE

A SIGHTSEER

A NOVELIST

A SONG WRITER

AN ARTIST

A POET

Part One

(The scene is NEIL MC RAE'S *apartment in a comfortable, run-down and not very expensive building. It is plainly an artist's room, and furnished with as many good-looking things as the occupant could afford—which are not many. The most luxurious piece of furniture in the room is a grand piano, which* NEIL *has probably hung on to with no little difficulty. It stands well down left. Down right is an easy chair—the only chair in the room that even suggests comfort—and against the rear wall is* NEIL'S *desk. In front of the desk is a swivel chair, and two or three other chairs, stiff-backed, stand around the room. At the left of the stage, near the piano, is a window, hung with chintz curtains that have seen better days—curtains which come to life here and there in great splotches of red. Some of the same stuff hangs in a center doorway—a doorway that leads to* NEIL'S *bedroom and thence to a "kitchenette." The door into the apartment is at the right—somewhere beyond it is the elevator, and one needs only a look at the room to know that it is an elevator that requires four minutes to ascend the three floors.*

The time is about four-thirty of a Spring afternoon. The curtain rises on the room and nothing more; then, after a second, there comes a knock on the door. The knock is repeated, then the knob is cautiously turned and the door slowly opens. DR. ALBERT RICE, *a young man of thirty or so, peers inquiringly into the room through the widening crack, sees no one, and enters.)*

ALBERT. Neil! *(There is no answer; he observes the room. Slightly to his surprise, he sees a sewing basket on the piano.)* Are you married? *(He goes up to the bedroom entrance and peers into the semi-darkness.)* Neil!

(CYNTHIA MASON, who seems to be about twenty-five, appears suddenly in the doorway at right. There is a moment of uncertainty as she and the doctor confront each other.)

CYNTHIA. Are you looking for Mr. McRae?

ALBERT. Yes. The door was open.

CYNTHIA *(Disturbed)*. Really? Was it wide open?

ALBERT. It was closed, but it wasn't locked.

CYNTHIA. Oh! *(There is a pause of uncertainty.)* Was Mr. Mc-Rae expecting you?

ALBERT. No—I just got in from Chicago. Neil and I are old friends. My name is Rice.

CYNTHIA. Oh! You're not *Doctor* Rice?

ALBERT. Yes.

CYNTHIA *(Laughing)*. I'm so relieved! My name is Cynthia Mason, Dr. Rice. I know a great deal about *you*. *(They shake hands.)*

ALBERT. Of course Neil never writes letters, so you've been concealed from me. You didn't know him a few months ago, did you, when I left New York?

CYNTHIA. No, only since he moved here. I live across the hall.

ALBERT. Oh, I see.

CYNTHIA *(Looking around)*. There's that work basket. *(She takes it from the piano, then faces the* DOCTOR *again.)* I hope you'll forgive me, when I tell you why I lingered.

ALBERT. You're forgiven.

CYNTHIA. Night before last we had burglars.

ALBERT. Really?

CYNTHIA. Not on this floor—the apartment below. The poor man lost three or four suits of clothes, so——

ALBERT *(With an understanding smile).* So Neil leaves his door
unlocked.

CYNTHIA. Probably since early this morning. Though I'm afraid
the burglar who took Neil's clothes wouldn't do very well.

ALBERT *(With a look around the room).* No, I suppose not.

CYNTHIA *(A pause; she turns, with an air of finality).* Well,
he'll be here soon.

ALBERT. You're not going?

CYNTHIA. I must. Neil has some people coming to tea.

ALBERT *(Bent on holding her).* Well—now, how do you know
I'm *not* the burglar?

CYNTHIA. Because I don't believe there are such things as
gentlemen burglars. *(She drops a half curtsy; turns again
toward the door.)*

ALBERT. Oh, wait! What did Neil tell you about me?

CYNTHIA. Let me see. He said you were extremely brilliant.
But too versatile.

ALBERT. Brilliant, yes. But versatile—on the contrary, I'm
going to become a specialist.

CYNTHIA. Sometimes I wonder what's happened to all the
young men who used to become just doctors.

ALBERT. They all died of starvation. *(There is a pause;* CYN-
THIA *looks at her watch.)*

CYNTHIA. I don't know why Neil isn't here.

ALBERT. You don't expect *him* to be prompt, do you?

CYNTHIA. But he has some people coming. You may know
them—their name is Cady.

ALBERT. Cady? Not the Cadys from Livingston?

CYNTHIA. Yes—*do* you know them?

ALBERT. I'm not sure—I think I used to. You know, I lived in
Livingston myself, a long time ago.

CYNTHIA. So Neil told me.

ALBERT *(Puzzled).* The Cadys? What are *they* coming for?

CYNTHIA. Miss Cady is Neil's pupil.

ALBERT. You mean he's giving her music lessons?

CYNTHIA. He is.

ALBERT. But he's not a teacher. *(He waits for a denial.)* Is he?

CYNTHIA. He *must* do something.

ALBERT (*With a sigh*). Things aren't any better with him, then?

CYNTHIA. Well, he isn't ready to retire.

ALBERT (*With a shake of the head*). I suppose he'll always go on this way. He's so—utterly improvident, so——

CYNTHIA (*Rallying to his defense*). Well—he's really improved in that way. He may surprise you.

ALBERT. He certainly would.

CYNTHIA. He's saving money! (*Her tone changes.*) But the trouble is—he's working so hard to get it.

ALBERT. You mean giving music lessons?

CYNTHIA. Worse. You've got to talk to him—he won't listen to me. He's been sitting up night after night——

NEIL (*Heard in the hallway*). Halloo! (*He kicks open the door and enters. He is carrying a pile of books, and on top of the pile a music portfolio. He sees* ALBERT; *dumps the books abruptly into the easy chair.*) Albert! Well, I'll be damned! (*Tosses his hat into the bedroom; seizes* ALBERT's *hand.*)

ALBERT. Mr. McRae, I believe?

NEIL. Where did you come from? Chicago?

ALBERT. This morning. Of course, you never told me you'd moved. How are you?

NEIL. Never felt better! Gosh, I'm glad you're back! You've met Cynthia?

CYNTHIA. Well, we've been talking. I thought I'd caught the burglar.

NEIL. Did you find him in here? (*To* ALBERT.) How did you get in?

ALBERT (*Elaborately*). First I turned the knob of the door——

CYNTHIA. And, as you hadn't locked it, he had no difficulty in entering. (*She turns to the books in the easy chair.*) What are these?

NEIL. Why—just some books.

CYNTHIA (*Takes one up*). "Life of Charles I." Neil!

NEIL. Well—I used to be very interested in history, and especially——

CYNTHIA (*Severely*). The truth, Neil!

NEIL. I—I bought them, that's all.

CYNTHIA. Oh, Neil. After your promise!

NEIL. Well— (*To* ALBERT.) Just take a look at this binding.

ALBERT (*Giving no encouragement*). Yes. I see it.

CYNTHIA (*Determined*). Neil, where did you get them?

NEIL (*Still to* ALBERT). There was a burglary downstairs, and this fellow lost all his clothes.

CYNTHIA (*Resigned*). And you bought these books from him.

NEIL. Well—ah——

CYNTHIA. You work at these terrible orchestrations to *make* a little money, and then—did you go to bed at all last night?

NEIL. Of course I did.

CYNTHIA. Doctor, you *will* talk to him, won't you? (*She takes up her work basket.*) I'm sure he hasn't been sleeping—he hasn't been doing *anything* he should. (*She is heading for the door.*)

NEIL. You're not going?

CYNTHIA. I am. You have people coming to tea, remember.

NEIL. Good heavens, what time is it?

CYNTHIA. Nearly five. I suppose you have everything ready?

NEIL. Why, yes—I've got—that is, I think—— (*He smiles helplessly.*) Be a darling and help me, will you?

CYNTHIA. Are you sure you have everything? (*Knowing well that he hasn't.*)

NEIL. I think so.

CYNTHIA. He thinks so. (*This to* ALBERT, *with a smile, as she goes through the bedroom doorway.*)

ALBERT. She's charming, Neil.

NEIL. Isn't she? (*He moves his portfolio from the chair to the desk.*) She's a designer in one of the big dressmaking firms. Did she tell you how we met?

ALBERT. No.

NEIL. She lives across the hall. (*He raises his voice for* CYNTHIA's *benefit.*) She thinks she can play the piano.

CYNTHIA (*In the kitchen*). I can!

NEIL. You cannot! (*To* ALBERT.) One night I knocked on her door and asked her to stop. She did. We've been great pals ever since. (*Calling to* CYNTHIA.) Can I help you, Cynthia?

CYNTHIA. No, nor anyone else. (*She returns.*) Do you remember when you last had any tea?

NEIL. The other day.

CYNTHIA. You have three leaves left. *(She exhibits them.)*

NEIL *(Inspects them)*. Four!

CYNTHIA. And did you know that your toast machine was burnt out?

NEIL. Oh, yes—I forgot. But I'm sure there's some tea—I remember—no, I used the last of it early this morning. I'll run right out—— *(He is about to start.)*

CYNTHIA *(Holding him)*. Neil!

NEIL. What?

CYNTHIA. Then you *were* up all night?

NEIL. Why—not exactly.

CYNTHIA *(To the DOCTOR)*. He's been sitting up making orchestrations for a cheap little music publisher. Neil, it's like copying bad paintings. Doctor, you must make him stop.

NEIL. Well—I'll go out and get some tea.

CYNTHIA. No! You stay and talk to the Doctor. I'll bring everything over from my place. *(Again she picks up the basket.)*

NEIL. I can't let you do that. Let me help.

CYNTHIA. I will not. *(She goes.)*

NEIL *(More to himself than to ALBERT)*. I could have sworn I had everything.

ALBERT. She'll take care of things. *(He is near the window.)* Come over here and let me see you.

NEIL. Now, you're not going to fuss over me just because I've been doing some work.

ALBERT. No. But I want to look at you. *(An orchestra, in a restaurant across the street, strikes up a jazz tune. It comes faintly through the window.)*

NEIL. Good Lord, that again!

ALBERT. What?

NEIL. That damned cabaret orchestra across the street. It begins at five every afternoon.

ALBERT. You *are* nervous, aren't you?

NEIL. Huh? No. I just don't like that music.

ALBERT. *Did* you work all night?

NEIL. Some of it.

ALBERT. It's bad business, Neil. *(He feels for his pulse.)* How many Cadys are coming to tea?

NEIL. Oh, did Cynthia tell you? You remember the Cadys?

ALBERT. Vaguely. I don't suppose they'd know me. Do they live here now?

NEIL. They moved East a few months ago. Gladys is my one and only music pupil.

ALBERT *(Watch in hand)*. Rich, I suppose?

NEIL. Lord, yes. Millions.

ALBERT. What did he make it in? *(He puts away the watch.)*

NEIL. Funny—I don't even know. Manufactures something.

ALBERT *(Trying to remember)*. Just the one daughter, isn't there?

NEIL. Yes. *(Adds, as an afterthought.)* There's a brother.

ALBERT *(Recalls him, apparently none too pleasantly)*. I remember him.

NEIL. I *had* to ask them. For heaven's sake, stay and help out.

ALBERT *(With a laugh)*. Well, I'll stay a little while. *(Feels for his pipe.)*

NEIL. Try to get away. (ALBERT *laughs, lightly.*) Well, what's the verdict on *me?*

ALBERT. You're just a little tired, that's all. Sort of nervous.

NEIL. Nonsense.

ALBERT. Got any tobacco?

NEIL. Right there on the desk.

ALBERT *(Fooling with the tobacco jar; unable to open it)*. Have you been writing *anything* of your own?

NEIL. Well, no—only snatches of things. I'm going to get back at it soon, though.

ALBERT. That's good. *(The jar in hand.)* How do you open this thing?

NEIL *(Takes up a paper knife from the piano—a knife of ivory, scimitar-shaped, and with a long black tassel hanging from it)*. I use this. Give it to me. (ALBERT *hands it over;* NEIL *opens and returns it, all without a word.*)

ALBERT *(Filling his pipe)*. How old is the daughter now?

NEIL. Gladys?

ALBERT. Yes.

NEIL. Twenty-two or three—I don't know. Why? (*He puts the knife back on the piano.*)

ALBERT. How soon will they be here?

NEIL. Any minute, I guess. Why all the questions?

ALBERT. I just wondered. (*Takes a medical case from his pocket and shakes out a pill.*) I want you to take one of these before they come, and another one later on.

NEIL. Good heavens, there's nothing the matter with me.

ALBERT. I know there isn't.

NEIL. What'll they do—make me sleep?

ALBERT. They'll quiet you.

NEIL. But I don't dare go to sleep. In the first place the Cadys are coming, and——

(CYNTHIA *re-enters. She is now hatless, and carries a folded table-cloth.*)

CYNTHIA. I hope you scolded him. (*She goes to the desk and begins to spread the cloth.*)

ALBERT. Not enough, I'm afraid. (*Pill in hand.*) Do you think you have a glass of water left?

NEIL (*Starting*). Oh, of course!

ALBERT. No, no, I can find it. (*He goes into the bedroom.*)

CYNTHIA (*With a glance at the portfolio*). You didn't let them give you more to do?

NEIL. Why, hardly any. It's all right.

CYNTHIA. It *isn't* all right. Oh, I wouldn't mind if it were something decent! But it's perfectly sickening to think of your genius being choked to death in this way!

NEIL. I'll work on the symphony soon, honestly.

CYNTHIA. And then make up for it by mere hack-work. I wish someone would subsidize you.

NEIL. That would be nice. (ALBERT *comes back with the glass of water.*)

ALBERT. Here you are! (*Gives* NEIL *pill and glass.*)

NEIL. Oh, all right. But there's nothing the matter with me. (*He takes the pill.*)

ALBERT. How was it?

NEIL. I've tasted better. *(The orchestra across the street is heard in another outburst of jazz.)* Would you believe that people actually enjoy that? Wait! I've got one here that will be next month's national anthem. *(Searches for it in portfolio.)* There aren't any words to it yet, but it's going to be called "Sweet Mamma."

CYNTHIA. Don't, Neil. Play Dr. Rice the second movement of your symphony.

NEIL. Want to hear it?

ALBERT. You bet. *(He indicates the pipe.)* Do you mind?

CYNTHIA. Not at all.

NEIL. She calls it the second movement because there isn't any first.

CYNTHIA *(Finding it).* Here! *(She spreads the manuscript on the rack.)*

NEIL. You understand this is just a movement. It's—*(He sees place that needs correction.)* Oh! *(Starts fishing for a pencil.)* Of course I never have a pencil. *(CYNTHIA gets one from his left vest pocket and hands it to him.)* Oh, thanks! *(He makes the correction.)* It's just a sketch. Not finished, you know.

CYNTHIA. But it's going to be—and soon. *(NEIL starts to play, but is not far into it when the phone rings.)*

NEIL *(Stops playing).* I'll bet that's the Cadys. *(Goes to the phone.)* Hello! *(To CYNTHIA.)* It is. Downstairs. . . . Send them right up, Jerry.

CYNTHIA. Good heavens, I'll have to bring the tea things in.

NEIL. Why not?

CYNTHIA. They don't want to meet me.

NEIL. Don't be foolish.

CYNTHIA. Well—I won't stay. *(She goes.)*

NEIL. I suppose I ought to clear things up a bit.

ALBERT *(With a glance at the books in the easy chair).* If you expect them to sit down. *(NEIL carries the books into his bedroom. He returns, counts the chairs, then tests a spindley-legged one that stands centre.)*

NEIL. I hope nobody heavy sits in this.

(Voices are heard in the hall, and MR. and MRS. CADY,

HOMER *and* GLADYS *appear at the open door.* MRS. CADY *enters first, then* GLADYS, *then* MR. CADY, *and* HOMER. *Together they make up an average Middle West family. They have no marked external characteristics except that* HOMER *is wearing a violent yellow tie.*)

MRS. CADY. Why, Neil!

NEIL. How are you, Mrs. Cady? Gladys.

MRS. CADY. After all these years!

GLADYS. Hello, Neil!

CADY. Well, well, Neil, my boy!

NEIL. Hello, Mr. Cady!

HOMER. Hello, there!

NEIL. How are you, Homer?

HOMER. Not so good.

NEIL (*Feeling keenly his position as host*). Ah—this is Dr. Rice. Mr. and Mrs. Cady, and—Miss Cady and—Cady. (*His voice trails off. There are the indistinct greetings that follow an introduction.*)

MRS. CADY. Doctor, did you say?

ALBERT. Yes, ma'am.

MRS. CADY. Homer, here's a doctor.

HOMER. Yes?

MRS. CADY. Homer's had a good deal of trouble from time to time. Sit here, Homer—in this easy chair. (HOMER *takes the only easy chair.*)

NEIL (*Delinquent*). Oh, yes—sit down, everybody. I'm sorry I —ah——

MRS. CADY. Oh, that's all right. We'll just settle ourselves. (*She sits in the swivel chair at the desk.*)

NEIL (*Stirring up conversation*). Ah—Dr. Rice comes from Livingston, too.

MRS. CADY. Really?

CADY. That so?

ALBERT. Oh, a long time ago. We moved away when I was very young.

MRS. CADY. I wonder if I—(*There is a sneeze from* HOMER)— Are you all right, Homer?

HOMER. Yes. (*Something in his tone says that he is as all right as possible, considering where he is.*)

MRS. CADY (*Blandly finishing*).——knew your people?

HOMER. I don't remember them. (*You gather that* ALBERT *just couldn't have had any people.*)

CADY (*At the telephone*). Mind if I use this?

NEIL. Oh, no, of course not.

CADY. Thanks. I left the office a little early. (*Takes the receiver off.*)

MRS. CADY (*Bent on placing the* DOCTOR). Let me see. *Old* Mrs. Rice——

CADY. Cortlandt 8262.

MRS. CADY. I guess you're not the same. (*There is a half-query in her voice.*)

ALBERT. Well, as a matter of fact, I moved away just after you came there.

MRS. CADY. Oh, I see.

GLADYS (*Producing a box of candy*). I brought you some candy for your tea, Neil.

NEIL. Oh, thanks. (*To* MRS. CADY, *who is teetering in the desk chair.*) There's another chair if——

MRS. CADY. No, I like this. Feels like my rocking chair at home. (*She sways back and forth.*)

GLADYS. Mother's favorite chair is her rocker.

MRS. CADY. There's nothing like an old-fashioned rocking chair.

CADY (*At the phone*). Let me talk to Burgess.

MRS. CADY. Mr. Cady says I'm chair-bound. Just joking, you know. (*She explains elaborately, to* ALBERT.) Mr. Cady. Says I'm chair-bound.

ALBERT (*Just the news he was waiting for*). Oh, yes.

SIMULTANEOUSLY

MRS. CADY. Let me see: there were two families of Rice out there, and I remember that one of them came here, just before we left.	CADY. Burgess? Any word from 653? . . . Hush, mother. . . . Well, I'll tell you what to do. We ought to send a tracer. . . . That's

(She finishes in a sibilant whisper, having been shushed by her husband.)

right. . . . Well, I'll tell you what to do—if you don't hear by six o'clock send a tracer. That's all. (CADY *hangs up: turns to* NEIL.)

CADY. Much obliged. When I get a foot away from a telephone I'm lost. *(He starts for the weak chair;* NEIL *makes a movement.)* What is it?

NEIL. That chair isn't very strong.

CADY. Oh, I'll be careful.

NEIL *(Not exactly at ease).* We're going to have some—tea and things—pretty soon now.

CADY *(Has taken out a cigar).* Match?

NEIL *(Starting).* How's that?

CADY. Match.

NEIL. Oh, yes! Right here. (NEIL *lights his cigar.)*

GLADYS *(Taking in the room).* See, mama, isn't it cute?

MRS. CADY. Yes, indeed.

GLADYS. There's the piano over there.

MRS. CADY. Oh, yes. *(Everybody looks at the piano.)* Neil must play something for us. *(It is Remark No. 80 and purely perfunctory.)*

CADY. It's certainly very nice. We've been hearing quite a bit about you, Neil.

NEIL. Is that so?

CADY. Hear you've become quite a musician since you went away from Livingston.

NEIL. Oh, I don't know.

CADY. Well, Gladys has been telling us so. So we thought we'd come find out for ourselves. Gave up a golf game to do it, too. Play golf?

NEIL. No, I don't.

CADY. Play golf, Doctor?

ALBERT. I'm sorry.

CADY. Well, everybody ought to. Great exercise. Keeps a man fit for business. I'd make Homer do it, if he wasn't so delicate. (HOMER *shifts in his seat.)*

MRS. CADY. Comfortable, Homer?

HOMER *(Carelessly)*. Um-hum.

(CYNTHIA comes in with the tea things.)

NEIL. Oh, here we are! I—I want you to meet Miss Mason. She's brought the things over from her place.

MRS. CADY. Oh, I see.

NEIL *(Beginning again the weary round of introductions)*. Mrs. Cady and—of course you know Gladys——

GLADYS. Yes.

CYNTHIA. How are you, Miss Cady?

NEIL. And Mr. Cady and—another Mr. Cady. *(HOMER does not rise. Mumbled greetings are exchanged.)* Miss Mason lives—just across the hall.

MRS. CADY. Yes, so Gladys has told us. Are you a musician, too, Miss Mason?

CYNTHIA. No, I'm not, Mrs. Cady.

MRS. CADY *(Turning to her husband)*. Don't she make you think of Elizabeth Merkle, Fred?

CADY. Well—I see what you mean.

HOMER *(Ever the dissenter)*. She don't me.

MRS. CADY. Of course Elizabeth's dark, but there's something about the shape of the face. *(To NEIL.)* You knew the Merkles, Neil. Mr. Merkle had the skating rink.

NEIL. Oh, yes. Elizabeth was a little girl when I knew her.

MRS. CADY. She's twenty-two or three. Twenty-three, isn't she, Fred?

CADY. Yes, I guess so.

HOMER. Lizzie Merkle's crazy. She's going to marry Lou Carmichael.

GLADYS. Oh, did grandma say when it was to be?

MRS. CADY. No, I don't think they knew themselves. You knew Lou, didn't you, Neil? *(CYNTHIA is serving tea.)*

NEIL. Did they live over on Pine Street?

MRS. CADY. I think they did.

HOMER. No, they didn't.

GLADYS. Hush up! They did. They lived next door to Dr. Endicott.

HOMER. They did not. They've always lived on Mead Avenue.

GLADYS. Well, I guess I ought to know. Didn't I go and meet his sister once? Remember that tall girl, mama?

HOMER. You're crazy.

MRS. CADY. Lou used to take Gladys to dances a lot.

GLADYS. He was a wonderful dancer! (*She giggles.*)

MRS. CADY. He was with the telephone company.

HOMER (*Scornfully*). Charlie Ferris nearly beat him up.

MRS. CADY. Remember when he and Charlie Ferris were crazy about Gladys? This girl's had more boys crazy about her, Neil. (CYNTHIA *gives tea to* CADY.)

GLADYS. Oh, I never cared for either of them.

HOMER. You never let them *think* so.

GLADYS (*Smugly*). Homer!

HOMER (*To* NEIL, *unpleasantly, as he passes tea to him*). No, thanks. Tea always sits on me.

CADY. Say, I hear your Uncle James is dead, Neil. Leave you anything?

NEIL. No—Uncle James never had anything.

CADY. Too bad. He was a fine man. Everybody was sorry when he moved to Boston.

MRS. CADY. He was nice. (*To* CYNTHIA.) We used to sing together in Sunday school when we were children.

NEIL. I remember you sang in the choir.

GLADYS. Mama still sings, when she lets herself go.

HOMER. We call her Galli-Curci.

MRS. CADY (*Genially*). They're always joking me about my voice. But I do love old hymns. Your father was a good singer too, Neil.

NEIL. I guess he was a better lawyer.

CADY. Yes, everybody had a great deal of respect for John McRae.

MRS. CADY. He was a beautiful character.

CADY. He'd give his money away to everybody. Afraid he never made very much, though. Lawyers don't, as a rule. Neil, did you know that when I was a young man I studied law—right in the same office with your father?

NEIL. No? Did you?

CADY. Yes, sir. Had it all figured out to be a judge—Judge Cady—till I found out what was the most a judge could make. (*Puts his tea down, almost untasted.*)

CYNTHIA. Too strong?

CADY. No. I'm not much of a tea drinker.

MRS. CADY. I guess Gladys and I are the tea drinkers in our family. We have it every afternoon. (NEIL *is opening the candy box.*)

GLADYS. Neil's going to come up and have some with us next week. Tuesday.

NEIL. Candy? (MRS. CADY *takes a piece; so does* MR. CADY.)

MRS. CADY. That's nice. We'll have some people in. I want you to see the new house. My, I don't know what the folks would say back in Livingston if they could see it. Remember our house in Livingston, Neil?

NEIL. Yes, indeed. (*He passes the candy box to* HOMER, *who waves it disdainfully aside.*)

MRS. CADY (*Trying to be bantering*). You ought to. You were there enough. Every afternoon, pretty near. Neil and Gladys would play together and I'd go out in the kitchen and make candy for them. (*She rocks.*)

GLADYS. Oh, yes! Wasn't it fun, Neil?

MRS. CADY. We always saved some pieces for Mr. Cady. All the Cadys are fond of candy. Aren't they, Fred? (*She taps his knee.*)

CADY (*Munching*). Guess that's right, mother.

HOMER. I'm not.

MRS. CADY. Except Homer. (*She resumes, largely to herself.*) All the Cadys eat candy.

CYNTHIA. And now—if you'll excuse me. (*Rises.*)

NEIL. Oh, you're not going? (HOMER *doesn't rise with the other men.*)

CYNTHIA. I'm afraid I must.

CADY. That's too bad.

MRS. CADY. Well, I hope we meet again.

CYNTHIA. I just ran in for a moment to be temporary hostess.

GLADYS. Goodbye, Miss Mason.

CYNTHIA (*To* ALBERT). I hope I'll see you again. (*Shakes his hand.*)

ALBERT. Oh, I'll be back in a few weeks. (*There are further goodbyes. Cynthia goes.*)

MRS. CADY (*Looking after her*). She *is* like Elizabeth.

CADY (*Noisily*). Well—how are things generally, Neil? Making a lot of money out of your music?

NEIL. No—with music you don't make a great deal of money.

CADY. I don't know about that. It's just like any other business. Maybe you're not giving them what they want.

MRS. CADY. I guess Neil's doing his best, aren't you, Neil?

CADY. We've all got to please the public. Eh, Doctor?

ALBERT. Oh, yes.

CADY. I've got to in my business. Of course I don't claim to know anything about music, but I think I represent about the average viewpoint. Now, what I like is a good lively tune—something with a little snap to it. As I understand it, though, you sort of go in for—highbrow music.

NEIL. It isn't exactly that.

CADY. Well, there's no money in it. You know what happened to your father.

MRS. CADY. Had to scrape all his life. (*Turns to* ALBERT.) Neil's father. Had to scrape all his life.

CADY. A young fellow's got to look out for his future, I claim —got to save up a little money.

NEIL (*Puzzled*). Yes, sir.

MRS. CADY (*Helping along what is clearly a prearranged conversation*). In some *business*, Mr. Cady means.

CADY. Yes. Now you take—well, my business, for example. We've always got an opening for—a bright young fellow.

NEIL. You mean—*me*—in your business?

CADY. Well, I just mentioned that for example.

NEIL. I—I'm afraid I wouldn't be much good in business, Mr. Cady.

MRS. CADY. Of course you'd be good.

NEIL. I did work once in an office, and I guess I wasn't— very——

CADY. That's all right. You'd learn. The idea is you'd be

making money. Some day you'd maybe have a nice interest in the firm. 'Tain't as though you couldn't write a little music now and then in your spare time, and we'd be sort of all together. *(The jazz orchestra is heard again—this time louder.)*

MRS. CADY. Just like one big family.

GLADYS *(Singing and swaying to the tune)*. Oh, they're playing "The Frog's Party." *(To Neil.)* Come on and dance!

NEIL. I'm sorry, but I don't dance.

GLADYS. Oh, so you don't—but I'm going to make you learn. I know a wonderful teacher. *(Turns to ALBERT.)* Dance, Doctor?

ALBERT. A little. *(GLADYS and ALBERT take a few turns about the room. MRS. CADY hums the tune, not knowing the words.)*

CADY. Great song! A man I played golf with yesterday tells me that for the first six months of the fiscal year that song'll make a hundred thousand dollars. Write something like that and you're fixed. That's music.

HOMER. We got it on the radio last night.

ALBERT *(Politely)*. You don't say?

GLADYS *(Near the piano)*. Oh, Neill *(The three remaining CADYS are grouped with ALBERT.)*

SIMULTANEOUSLY

GLADYS *(Holds up a piece of music, as NEIL crosses to her)*. What's this?

NEIL. Just something I'm working on.

GLADYS *(Sotto voce)*. I want to talk to you.

NEIL. Oh!

GLADYS. Don't you want to talk to me?

NEIL. Oh, yes.

GLADYS. Neil. *(Points to a*

CADY. Couple of hundred miles away, wasn't it?

HOMER. Three hundred.

CADY. Think of that!

ALBERT. It's wonderful.

MRS. CADY. I was going to ask you, Doctor, if you're related to those other Rices. There were two daughters, I think.

ALBERT. No, I haven't any relatives left, there.

small photograph that sits on piano.)

NEIL. Yes?

GLADYS (*Takes up the picture*). Can I have one of these?

NEIL. I'm afraid I haven't got another.

GLADYS. This was in the Musical Courier, wasn't it?

NEIL. Why, yes.

GLADYS. I saw it. You're pretty well known, Neil. I'm proud of you. I wish I could have this one. Only I wish it were of you alone, instead of you and this other girl, whoever she is. (*Puts picture back.*)

NEIL. It's just a girl I met one summer. (*A pause.*)

GLADYS. Neil?

NEIL. Well?

GLADYS. Do you like me better than you do Miss Mason?

NEIL. Well, I think she's awfully nice.

GLADYS. Don't you think I'm nice, too?

NEIL. Yes, of course.

GLADYS. Because, I think *you* are. You know that, don't you, Neil?

NEIL (*Nearly choking*). I'm—glad.

GLADYS. So, of course, I want *you* to think *I* am.

NEIL. I—do.

CADY. Live in New York, now, I suppose?

ALBERT. No, Chicago. I'm just here for a flying visit.

CADY. Chicago? Don't say? Well, that's a good town.

HOMER. Chicago a good town? Huh!

MRS. CADY. It would be nice if you could come up and see us, too, Doctor.

ALBERT. Thank you, but I'm going back soon.

MRS. CADY. Well, do come if you can. Any day after Thursday. Both our butlers are leaving, and I can't get any new ones to come until after the holiday. But we always like to have people from Livingston drop in. I always say if you don't keep in touch with your old home town, why your old home town won't keep in touch with you.

HOMER. I never want to go back there.

CADY. Well, I don't know as I do either.

MRS. CADY. Listen to that man. And to think he was president of the Board of Trade there for five mortal years.

CADY (*Thoughtfully, to* ALBERT). You know, I think I've got you placed now.

GLADYS *(Suddenly)*. Oh! That reminds me. *(Fishes in her handbag.)*

NEIL. What is it?

GLADYS *(Bringing out four or five small samples of colored cloths)*. I knew I wanted to ask you something. Which do you like best?

NEIL. Why, they're all very nice.

GLADYS. But don't you like one best?

NEIL. I don't know. They're all sort of—ah—why—

GLADYS. Because I'd like to get the one you'd like. *(NEIL is puzzled. She spreads the samples on his arm.)* They're samples, silly! I'm going from here to the dressmaker's to pick one out.

NEIL. Oh, I see. *(He removes the samples.)*

GLADYS *(Pouting)*. Of course if you don't care what I wear, why, all right.

NEIL *(Not enthusiastic)*. I do care.

GLADYS *(Eager again)*. Well, which one would you rather see me in? The blue?

NEIL. Yes, that would be nice.

GLADYS. I like the pink one myself.

Was your father E. J. Rice in the lumber business?

ALBERT. No, he was an architect.

MRS. CADY. An architect—you don't say? Put up buildings, did he?

ALBERT. Yes, a few.

MRS. CADY. Put up any buildings in Livingston?

ALBERT. Why, yes.

CADY. Not the First National?

ALBERT. No, he designed the Mechanics' Building, right next door.

CADY. You don't say?

MRS. CADY. Well, that's a nice building, too.

HOMER. I remember it.

MRS. CADY. Mr. Cady had his offices in the First National Building.

ALBERT. Is that so?

CADY. I guess there's been quite a building boom since you were there. That whole block is pretty solid now.

ALBERT. Really?

MRS. CADY. My, yes. You wouldn't know the place.

CADY. Yes, sir! I guess there's been a good many million dollars invested there in the last five years.

ALBERT. You don't say?

MRS. CADY. Mr. Cady put up a building himself.

ALBERT. That so?

CADY. Just a warehouse. Of course we still have a plant there——

HOMER (*Heard by himself*). It's half past, pop. (*Rises.*)

CADY. Yes, I guess we'll have to be going. (*Rises.*)

MRS. CADY. Ready, Gladys? (*Rises.*)

GLADYS. Yes, mama. (*Starts, then turns back to* NEIL.)

SIMULTANEOUSLY

GLADYS (*Suddenly, to* NEIL). Oh, Neil!

NEIL. Yes?

GLADYS. I won't go home for dinner—if you don't want me to.

NEIL. Well, I did sort of think I'd do some work—

GLADYS. I'll go with *you* to a new restaurant I just heard about! I'll tell you what! I'll only be at the dressmaker's a few minutes. Then you can meet me.

NEIL. Well, I don't know exactly how I'll be fixed.

GLADYS. I'll telephone you the minute I'm finished.

NEIL. But, Gladys, I'm going to be tied up, I'm afraid, and——

GLADYS. Well, anyway, I'll phone.

MRS. CADY. Well, now, don't forget, Doctor! Come and see us, if you can.

ALBERT. Thank you.

CADY. Or have a round of golf with me some time. Play golf?

ALBERT. I'm sorry, I don't.

CADY. I remember—I asked you before.

HOMER (*Impatient*). Oh, come on!

MRS. CADY. Just a second, Homer. Gladys is talking.

HOMER. She's always talking.

MRS. CADY (*To* ALBERT, *with a laugh*). Just like a brother, isn't he?

CADY. Well, goodbye, Doctor.

ALBERT. Goodbye, Mr. Cady.

CADY. Come on, Gladys.

GLADYS. All right. (*To* NEIL.) I'll telephone you from the dressmaker's when I'm through.

MRS. CADY. And, Neil—you're coming Tuesday, remember.

NEIL. Oh, thanks. I'm sorry I couldn't have had a nicer party for you.

MRS. CADY. It was elegant. Only next time we come, you must play something for us.

NEIL. I'll ring for the elevator.

MRS. CADY. Oh, that's nice. Come on, Homer. (NEIL, MR. CADY *and* MRS. CADY *pass into the hall.*)

GLADYS. Goodbye, Doctor.

ALBERT. Goodbye, Miss Cady. (GLADYS *follows them out;* HOMER *lingers with the Doctor.*)

HOMER. What about him? Do you know him well? (*He takes out a box of powders.*)

ALBERT. Who? Neil?

HOMER. Yeh. Is he all right?

ALBERT. Why?

HOMER. Well, I just like to know things about a possible brother-in-law.

ALBERT. I see.

HOMER. Gladys is nutty about him. Thinks he's artistic, my God! And did you hear the old man? Just because his father was John McRae! (*Puts the powder on his tongue—takes a glass of water.*)

MRS. CADY (*In the hall*). Hurry, Homer!

HOMER (*Calling*). All right! (*He swallows the words, drinking at the same time.*) So long. Well, I hope it don't happen. (*He strolls out.*)

ALBERT. So long. (*The voices of the departing guests are heard in the hall.* NEIL *returns; looks back into the hall.*)

NEIL. What was all that about?

ALBERT. Oh, nothing in particular.

NEIL. How did you like the Cadys?

ALBERT. They seem to be all right. They must be richer than mud. Did you hear Mrs. Cady on her "butlers"?

NEIL. No.

ALBERT. I never heard of anybody having more than one butler before, but the Cadys seem to have 'em in pairs.

NEIL (*Laughing*). I haven't been to their house yet. I'm going next week, though. (*His glance going to the door.*) Say! Homer's a dirty dog, isn't he?

ALBERT (*Thoughtfully*). Neil, I want to talk to you.

NEIL. Good Lord, again?

ALBERT. In the first place, I want you to go to bed.

NEIL. At half past five o'clock?

ALBERT. You haven't slept for days.

NEIL. But I can't go to bed now. I've got work to do. (*A second's pause.*) You don't mean I'm sick?

ALBERT. No, but you need rest. I want you to put on your dressing gown and lie down for a while. And then take another one of these. (*Produces the pills.*)

NEIL. But I can't afford to go to sleep. I told you that. I've got work to do.

ALBERT. You can't work tonight.

NEIL. I must.

ALBERT. On those orchestrations?

NEIL. Yes. (*A pause.*)

ALBERT. Neil.

NEIL. What?

ALBERT. I want to talk to you about something else.

NEIL. Good heavens!

ALBERT. All right, but—somebody has to. (*Neil looks up, sensing something important.*) What are you going to do about your work?

NEIL. Huh?

ALBERT. Your *real* work, I mean. How much have you done since I went away?

NEIL. Well, what you heard. And Miss Mason and I are working out a little pantomime together. It's going to be a lot of fun——

ALBERT. How much of it is written?

NEIL. A lot. About half, I guess.

ALBERT. About half a movement of a symphony and about half a pantomime.

NEIL. I still have to eat.

ALBERT. But Neil, don't you see—you're wasting your genius!

NEIL. Genius, my hat!

ALBERT. You're wasting the best years you'll ever have doing odd jobs just to keep alive. You've got to be free to write.

NEIL. Well, maybe some day I'll write a popular song and make a million.

ALBERT. If you ever did you'd either burn it or sell it for ten dollars. You'll never make any money, Neil. You know that as well as I do.

NEIL. Then what's the answer? Are you going to subsidize me?

ALBERT. I wish to God I could! But there's no reason why you shouldn't subsidize yourself.

NEIL. What do you mean?

ALBERT. I mean the Cadys.

NEIL. What are you talking—Oh, don't be foolish!

ALBERT. Why is it foolish?

NEIL. Gladys would never—why, you're crazy!

ALBERT. Am I? Think back. How did she behave this afternoon? And Papa Cady? "Nice little share in the business?" And—well, I know what I'm talking about.

NEIL. You mean you're seriously advising me to ask Gladys Cady to marry me?

ALBERT. That's exactly what I'm doing. She's a nice girl, and pretty. You'd have comfort and money and time——

NEIL (*Interrupting, with growing excitement*). Well, what about *me*? Do you think money and music and time would make up for everything else? No, sir! I'd rather keep on living right here—just as I am now—all my life long.

ALBERT. Now, now! Don't get temperamental! If you'll just ——(CYNTHIA *opens the door.*)

CYNTHIA. May a poor girl call for her dishes?

NEIL. I'm sorry—I should have brought them over.

CYNTHIA (*Detecting a note in his voice*). Neil, there's nothing the matter?

ALBERT. I've been trying to persuade him to rest. (*To* NEIL.) Won't you go in and—get ready?

NEIL. I—I can't now.

CYNTHIA. Neil, please. (*A pause.*)

NEIL. All right. But don't go away. I want to talk to you. (*He goes into the bedroom.*)

CYNTHIA. He *is* difficult.

ALBERT. Yes, he is.

CYNTHIA. I'm glad you've taken charge of him. *(She is collecting the tea dishes.)*

ALBERT. He'll be all right. Just needs sleep, that's all. I'm not worrying about him physically so much as—well, spiritually.

CYNTHIA. I know. I've been worrying about it for weeks.

ALBERT. You do see his genius, don't you?

CYNTHIA. Oh, yes! He has it, if anyone ever had.

ALBERT. And this hack-work—it must be killing his spirit.

CYNTHIA. When I think of his keeping on, year after year! And he's such a babe-in-arms about practical things. He *does* so need——*(She hesitates.)* We must do something, mustn't we?

ALBERT. Yes, we must. *(A pause.)* There *is* a possible way out, you know. *(A pause.)*

CYNTHIA *(Slowly).* Yes, I know. *(A longer pause.)*

ALBERT. It's the only way, I'm afraid.

CYNTHIA. Oh, I've been thinking about it ever since she began coming here! You really *do* think it's the right thing for him? The wisest?

ALBERT. I'm sure of it.

CYNTHIA. But could he be happy?

ALBERT. That's the only way he *can* be happy, permanently— if he's free to write his music. That's the most important thing in the end.

CYNTHIA. It seems—and yet I'm afraid you're right.

ALBERT. We only hurt people by being sentimental about them. That's one of the first things a doctor learns. Let's put this through. Will you?

CYNTHIA. Oh, I couldn't!

ALBERT. You can do more than I can. You'll be here, and I've got to go away. And anyway, a woman can always do more than a man about this sort of thing. *(Holds out his hand to her.)* For Neil's sake. *(He takes a step away from her as he hears* NEIL *returning.* NEIL *comes back, wearing a dressing gown.)* That's right! Now!

NEIL. Of all the rot! Putting a grown man to bed at half past five!

ALBERT. Who ever accused you of being a grown man? Here! *(Produces a pill.)* Be brave. One swallow and it's over.

NEIL. Oh, all right—give it to me.

ALBERT. Here! *(NEIL takes it.)* And another before you go to bed. I'll put them here. *(He takes up his hat.)*

NEIL. You're going?

ALBERT. Got to—dining uptown. *(Taps NEIL lightly with his gloves as he passes.)* I'll look in in the morning. You'll be all right then. Good night, Miss Mason.

CYNTHIA. Goodbye, Doctor. *(ALBERT goes.)*

NEIL *(To CYNTHIA, who is gathering the last of her dishes).* He's been talking to you about me, hasn't he?

CYNTHIA. Why—you and other things. *(Not looking up.)*

NEIL. What did he say?

CYNTHIA. Don't you wish you knew—curiosity!

NEIL. I *do* know. I know exactly. He said the same thing to me. He said I was a failure—practically. That I'd have to depend on other people all my life.

CYNTHIA. Neil, you're just exciting yourself. You're tired, and you know he wants you to——

NEIL. No, wait! We've got to talk about this, you and I. He said more than that. He said that I ought to ask Gladys Cady to marry me. *(A pause.)* Well! You don't seem—surprised.

CYNTHIA. No, I'm not.

NEIL. Don't you even think it's—funny, a little bit?

CYNTHIA. No.

NEIL. Cynthia! *(Looks at her for a moment and then with a cry.)* Oh, Cynthia—dear! *(Takes her hand.)*

CYNTHIA. Don't, Neil!—*Please* don't!

NEIL. But Cynthia, don't you know—without my telling you —that I love only you and no one else?

CYNTHIA. Oh, Neil, please! *(Then, with an attempt at lightness.)* This is so sudden!

NEIL *(Hurt).* Oh, Cynthia, please don't!

CYNTHIA. Oh, please don't *you!*

NEIL. You know I love you, Cynthia! Of course you know; you couldn't help knowing! I thought maybe you—don't you, at all, Cynthia?

CYNTHIA (*Regaining control of herself*). Neil, let me tell you something. I *have* seen that you were growing to care for me, and I've—I've tried to think what I ought to do about it.

NEIL. Do about it! What can you do about it if——

CYNTHIA. You can do lots of things—if you're practical and sensible.

NEIL. Oh, my dear!

CYNTHIA. I said to myself, I think he's beginning to care about me more than he ought to, considering how we're both situated, and that nothing could come of it. And if I stay here I mightn't be sensible either. So, I'm going away.

NEIL. What!

CYNTHIA. I'm going to move uptown and live with Helen Noland. I'm going tomorrow.

NEIL. Cynthia—do you mean that you don't care about me at all?

CYNTHIA. Oh, yes, I do, Neil. I care about you very much. I think you're a great artist.

NEIL. Artist! (*He turns away from her.*)

CYNTHIA. And I think it would be the greatest possible misfortune for your music for you to go on this way, living from hand to mouth. So—when Dr. Rice suggested that you marry Miss Cady, it seemed to me a very sensible thing to do.

NEIL (*Faces her again*). Cynthia—do you know what you're talking about?

CYNTHIA. Perfectly.

NEIL. You can't mean that music or no music I ought to marry Gladys.

CYNTHIA. I think you ought to do just that for the sake of your music.

NEIL (*Hurt*). Oh! You're like Albert! You think my music is the only thing about me that's worth while! (*He again turns away.*)

CYNTHIA. Oh, Neil!

NEIL *(Continuing)*. It never *was* me that you cared about—only the music.

CYNTHIA. I want you to be happy, Neil.

NEIL *(Laughs mirthlessly)*. I certainly got it all wrong, didn't I? *(A pause.)* Well, goodbye, Cynthia.

CYNTHIA. Oh, Neil! Don't say goodbye like that.

NEIL. What other way is there? You're all being so sensible and practical. I might as well be practical and sensible too. *(CYNTHIA starts to speak, chokes up, goes out—stifling her tears. After a moment NEIL turns and sees that she is gone.)* My music! *(Then, less viciously.)* My music! *(The phone bell rings. NEIL looks toward it—plainly, GLADYS has finished at the dressmaker's. For a second he hesitates; then he makes up his mind and strides to the phone. There is grim determination in his voice, from the opening greeting.)* Hello, Gladys!

GLADYS *(Over the phone)*. Hello, Neil!

NEIL. Well, is the fitting over? *(He stifles a yawn; the pills are beginning to work.)*

GLADYS. Yes, but it wasn't a fitting.

NEIL. Well, whatever it was.

GLADYS. I took the pink one.

NEIL. The pink one. That's fine.

GLADYS. Oh, you don't care which at all!

NEIL. Of course I care which.

GLADYS. Can you meet me?

NEIL. Well, I don't think I can do that.

GLADYS. What?

NEIL. I say I can't go out. The doctor says I must stay in for a while.

GLADYS. Oh, my goodness! Are you sick?

NEIL. Oh, no. Just tired. Really, that's all. I have to—sleep for about an hour. *(He is growing momentarily more listless.)*

GLADYS. Oh dear!

NEIL. Well, why don't you come up here instead?

GLADYS. Shall I?

NEIL. Of course.

GLADYS. Why?

NEIL. Well, there's something I want to say to you, to ask you —something we all want to—I mean something I want to ask you——

GLADYS. I wish I knew!

NEIL. Maybe you do know. We thought—that is, I thought— how would you like to marry a great composer? *(The receiver nearly falls from his grip.)*

GLADYS. Oh, darling! Do you mean it?

NEIL. Sure I mean it.

GLADYS. Of course I'll marry you!

NEIL. Would you, honestly?

GLADYS. Yes, indeed!

NEIL. Well, that's fine. We'll show them, won't we?

GLADYS. Who?

NEIL. Oh, everybody.

GLADYS. Can I tell them?

NEIL. Yes, tell them all. Homer and——

GLADYS. Oh, darling, I'm so happy!

NEIL *(His tone dull)*. Well, I'm happy, too.

GLADYS. Let me hear you say "Sweetheart."

NEIL. Do I have to say it?

GLADYS. Of course.

NEIL *(Barely audible)*. Sweetheart.

GLADYS. Go ahead.

NEIL. Didn't you hear it?

GLADYS. No.

NEIL *(Viciously)*. Sweetheart!

GLADYS. Do you love me?

NEIL. Of course I do.

GLADYS. Well, I'll come over in about an hour.

NEIL. All right. *(A sleepy pause.)* In about an hour. You come, and—I'll sleep for an hour. I'll—sleep. *(He tries to replace the receiver, but is too sleepy. It dangles from its cord. NEIL rouses himself from the chair with difficulty.)* And that's that! *(Across the street the jazz orchestra begins again to play "The Frog's Party." It seems louder than before—al-*

ready NEIL's *imagination is causing it to swell. He wheels toward the window.)* Now go ahead and play! *(He staggers to the easy chair and drops into it.)* Play the wedding march, damn you! Play the wedding march! *(The tune resolves itself into a jazzy version of Lohengrin's "Wedding March." At the same time* NEIL *finally collapses into the chair, and the lights of the room begin to go down. As it grows dark the music swells. Then, after a moment, it begins to grow light again—but it is no longer* NEIL's *room. It is a railway station, with the arch of Track 37 prominently visible, and other arches flanking it at the side. A muddled train schedule is printed on the station walls, with strange towns that never existed.* NEIL's *piano, however, has remained where it was, and so has his easy chair. Then, down the aisles of the lighted theatre, there comes suddenly a double wedding procession. One section is headed by* MR. CADY *and* GLADYS —MR. CADY *in golf knickers and socks, knitted vest, and frock coat, with a silk hat prominently on his arm.* GLADYS *is the gorgeously attired bride, bearing proudly a bouquet that consists entirely of banknotes. Behind them stream four* USHERS—*spats, frock coats, and high hats, to say nothing of huge bridal veils, draped over their heads. If you could peer beneath their veils, however, you would find that all four of them look just alike. The procession that comes down the other aisle is headed by* MRS. CADY *and* HOMER. MRS. CADY *wears a grotesque exaggeration of the dress that* NEIL *has seen her in, and* HOMER's *yellow tie has assumed tremendous proportions. Behind* MRS. CADY *and* HOMER *are four* BANDSMEN. *Like the* USHERS, *they all look alike, all wearing bridal veils, through which they play their instruments.)*

(At the foot of the stage the processions halt; the music stops. ALBERT *appears from nowhere in particular; he has turned into a minister.)*

GLADYS. Oh, Neil!

NEIL *(In his sleep).* Huh? *(*ALBERT *gently rouses him.)*

ALBERT. Neil! Did you forget that you were being married today?

NEIL. Oh! Why—I'm afraid I did. (*He looks wonderingly at the railway station, then turns and sees* GLADYS.) Oh, hello, Gladys! I'm sorry. (*The two processions stream up onto the stage. The* USHERS *and the* BANDSMEN *line up behind the* CADY *family.*)

GLADYS. Neil, I want you to meet my ushers. They're all boys I used to know pretty well. (*As* GLADYS *begins the introductions the entire thing turns into a rhythmic chant, to an orchestral accompaniment.*) This is Alf and this is Georgie.

NEIL. Glad to meet you!

ALF. Glad to meet you!

GLADYS. This is Steve.

NEIL. I'm glad to meet you!

GLADYS. This is Fatty.

NEIL. How d'you do?

GLADYS. This is Lou.

LOU. I'm glad to meet you!

NEIL. Glad to meet you!

LOU. Glad to meet you!

GLADYS. And this last is Cousin Harry.

HARRY. Glad to meet you!

NEIL. How d'you do?

CADY. Hurry up, now! Let's get at it!

ALBERT. Take this man to be your husband? (*A* TRAINMAN, *in uniform, enters through the gates of the railway station.*)

TRAINMAN. Wolverine, for Monte Carlo!

ALBERT. Have and hold him . . .

GLADYS. Yes, I do!

(*They all begin to rise and fall on their toes, to the beat of the music.*)

ALBERT. All your worldly goods and chattels . . .

(*A* TRAINBOY, *carrying the usual magazines, chocolates, etc., comes through the gates.*)

TRAINBOY. Latest magazines and papers!
MRS. CADY. Going off to leave her mama!
HOMER. Say, it's cold here! Ah, ker-choo!

(The USHERS *begin to march around* GLADYS *and* NEIL, *faster and faster.)*

CADY. Train pulls out in just a minute!
ALBERT. Both for richer and for richer . . .
TRAINMAN. Pasadena, Paris, London!
ALBERT. Better, worser . . .
GLADYS. Sure I will!
CADY. Special car Apollinaris!

*(*GLADYS *is kissing the* USHERS *as they march.)*

TRAINBOY. Nothing sold after the train leaves!
MRS. CADY. Don't know *what* I'll do without her!
TRAINMAN. Show your tickets!
HOMER. Ma, keep still!
CADY. Get aboard! I'll tip the preacher!
TRAINMAN. Right this way, please! Right this way, please!
TRAINBOY. Huyler's chocolates and bonbons!
MRS. CADY. Oh, my baby!
HOMER. Oh, good Lord!
TRAINMAN. Lenox, Palm Beach, Narragansett!
ALBERT. I pronounce you—got the ring, Neil?
ALL THE USHERS. Bet he's lost it! Bet he's lost it!
GLADYS. Here's another!
TRAINMAN. All aboard!

*(The procession starts through the gates—*ALBERT *and* CADY *first, then the rest of the* CADYS, *then the* USHERS *and the* BANDSMEN. *As they all file through the* USHERS *continue the chant, calling out in unison.)*

Well, goodbye! Congratulations!
Goodbye, Gladys! Goodbye, Gladys!

Send us back a picture postal!
Hope you're happy!
Well, goodbye!

(GLADYS *tosses her bouquet back to them; the* USHERS *scramble for the banknotes. As the last of the procession disappears through the doors the lights die down. A moment later they come up again, revealing a row of white marble columns, with crimson curtains hung between them.* NEIL'S *piano, however, is still incongruously in the left corner, and his easy chair stands at the right. Immediately* NEIL *and* GLADYS *enter through side curtains.* NEIL *is still wearing his bathrobe—a somewhat sad spectacle amid all this grandeur.* GLADYS *is no longer in bridal costume, but wears a pleated dress—an exaggeration of the dress that she has worn in real life, with great pleats several inches thick.*)

GLADYS. We're married, Neil!

NEIL. Yes.

GLADYS. I'm your little bride.

NEIL. My little bride.

GLADYS (*Giggles*). Isn't it all just too wonderful? (*Runs into his arms.*) This is our beautiful home—see! (*The curtains behind the front columns part, revealing a magnificent interior consisting entirely of more marble columns and velvet curtains.*) You're going to have everything you've always needed! Mama and papa both say so!

NEIL. Oh! Do they?

GLADYS. Yes, indeed! You just wait—they'll be here any minute!

NEIL. They're coming here?

GLADYS. Of course they are! There're a lot of people coming— all coming to see our beautiful new home! Wait a minute —I'll show you! (*Calls.*) Butlers! (*Two* BUTLERS *appear. They are exactly alike.*) Announce somebody!

THE TWO BUTLERS. Mrs. Cady and her chair and knitting! (MRS. CADY *enters with a rocking chair attached to her. She begins knitting immediately. The two* BUTLERS *depart.*)

MRS. CADY. Two little lovebirds! Gladys and Neil! Gladys and Neil! Are they happy? Oh, my dear, you never *saw* anyone so happy! I was saying to Mr. Cady, "Well, Mr. Cady, what do you think of your little daughter now? *(She sits.)* How's this for a happy family?" And Mr. Cady says to me, "Well, I never would have believed it." And I says to Mr. Cady, and Mr. Cady says to me, and I says to Mr. Cady, and Mr. Cady says to me, and I says——

NEIL. Stop! *(MRS. CADY stops.)* So—so you're my wife's mother?

GLADYS. Why, of course she is! I think she's a pretty nice mother-in-law, don't you? Most people don't like their mothers-in-law, but I think *she's* pretty nice.

NEIL. But is *she* going to be—always——

GLADYS. Yes, indeed! Won't it be lovely? And that isn't all! *(Calls.)* Butlers! *(Four BUTLERS enter.)*

THE FOUR BUTLERS. Mr. Cady, her father! *(MR. CADY enters. He is in complete golf attire, and there is a telephone attached to his chest. As he enters the BUTLERS depart.)*

CADY *(Into the telephone).* Yep! Yep! Hullo! Well, I'll tell you what to do! Sell eighteen holes and buy all the water hazards. Yep! Yep! Hullo! Well, I'll tell you what to do! I expect caddies will go up any time now. How's the eighth hole this morning? Uh-huh. Well, sell it in three. Yes, sir. That's fine. Yep! Yep! Hullo! Well, I'll tell you what to do! Buy——

NEIL. No, no! *(CADY stops; looks at NEIL.)* You must stop—both of you! Do you know me?

CADY. My son! My new son! Well, Neil, how's the nice music and everything? Making a lot of money?

NEIL. Are we all going to live together?

GLADYS. Yes, indeed, darling.

CADY. Yes, indeed.

MRS. CADY. Yes, indeed.

GLADYS. And that isn't all. *(Six BUTLERS enter. Of course they are all alike.)* I've *another* surprise for you!

THE SIX BUTLERS. Her brother, Homer. He makes me sick.

FIRST BUTLER. I don't think *he's* sick at all. *(The BUTLERS go. HOMER enters—the yellow tie is bigger than ever.)*

HOMER. Oh, there you are, you dirty dog! I'm on to you! You married her just because Dad's got a lot of money, and you think you're going to have a cinch. But if you think you're going to get all of Dad's money, you're mistaken, because I'm going to get my share and don't you forget it. (*He makes straight for the easy chair, sits in it, and sneezes.*)

MRS. CADY. Now, Homer! Homer's sick.

CADY. Yes, he's sick.

GLADYS. It's all right, dearest.

NEIL. It isn't all right. I don't want the money. All I want to do is write my music. That's what I want to do—work. Do you think I'll be able to?

GLADYS. Why, of course you will, dear. We've just had this whole room done over for you to work in.

MRS. CADY. It's awfully pretty, Neil.

CADY. Cost a lot of money, too. (*His phone rings.*) Hello! . . . No—wrong number! (*He hangs up.*)

GLADYS. Don't you just love it, Neil, keeping house together? Say "Sweetheart!"

NEIL (*Automatically*). Sweetheart.

GLADYS. And next week we're going to have everything done over in some *other* color. Here are the samples—the samples. (*She produces another set of samples, larger than those used in real life.*) Now which color would you like? It's going to be whichever color you like.

NEIL. Why, any one. (*He removes the samples from his arm.*)

HOMER. Make him pick one! Make him pick it!

GLADYS. Here, I'll tell you! You stop in and get them matched! Get some of this one, and some of that one, and maybe some of the other one—on your way home from business tomorrow. It'll give you something to do.

NEIL. Am I going to business tomorrow?

CADY. Yes, sir! Start right in at the bottom and work up. Learn all the ins and outs. Lots of people think the ins and outs don't amount to anything; but you can't get anywhere in business without them.

NEIL. But if I have to go to business tomorrow I'd like to work on my symphony now—if you'll only go.

HOMER. Huh! The symphony!

GLADYS. That old thing!

CADY. That's no good!

MRS. CADY. I wouldn't have it in the house!

NEIL. But it is good—and I've got to finish it.

CADY. Highbrow music—that's what it is.

NEIL. Well, then, I'll work on the pantomime—that's not so
highbrow. *(He goes to the piano.)*

MRS. CADY. For my part I like hymns. There's nothing like
the old familiar hymns. *(She sings—"Oh, Blessed Be the
Tie That Binds.")*

GLADYS. Anyhow, you can't work now. It's tea time!

MRS. CADY *(To the tune of the hymn).* Yes, tea time! It's tea
time! It's tea time!

CADY. So it is. *(Into his phone.)* Hello! . . . Don't disturb me
now—I'm busy. . . . Tea!

CADY. Quite a crowd coming this afternoon.

MRS. CADY. Yes, coming to meet Neil! Yes, Gladys and Neil!
Gladys and Neil!

GLADYS. Now, Neil, you be nice to everybody. I want you to
make a nice impression. *(Eight BUTLERS enter.)*

THE EIGHT BUTLERS. A friend of her family's. *(The BUTLERS
go. No one enters, but apparently the CADYS see someone.
They greet the invisible guest.)*

GLADYS. How do you do?

CADY. How do you do? *(They bring her down to MRS. CADY.)*

MRS. CADY. How do you do? Oh, what a nice new ear trumpet!

GLADYS. I'm so glad you were able to come! *(NEIL peers, trying
his best to see what it is all about.)*

MRS. CADY. Well, it's wonderful to see you again!

GLADYS. Doesn't she look well, mama?

MRS. CADY. You're the picture of health! No one would ever
say *you* had an operation. I say—no one would ever say
you had an operation. Yes, it always does it if you were
heavy before. Oh, was it a year ago? Well, tempus does
fugit, as Homer says. You remember Homer?

HOMER. I said hello.

MRS. CADY. Homer's sick.

GLADYS. Oh, Neil! I want you to meet an old friend of mama's. She's deaf. You'll have to talk loud. (*Ten* BUTLERS *enter.*)

THE TEN BUTLERS. Another friend of the family's! (*The* BUTLERS *go.*)

GLADYS (*Greeting the newcomer*). How do you do?

CADY. How do you do?

GLADYS. So glad to see you again. And little Hattie! Oh, look, mama! (CADY *and* GLADYS *bend over, as though greeting a child.*)

MRS. CADY. Why, if it isn't little Hattie! Look, Gladys! Isn't she cunning?

GLADYS. Isn't she? Those cute little curls! Do you want to meet your great big cousin Neilie? Neil, darling, this is your little cousin Hattie. Isn't she a big girl? Say something cute to her. (GLADYS *turns away from* NEIL *and he passes his foot over the spot where the child is supposed to be. Twelve* BUTLERS *enter.*)

THE TWELVE BUTLERS. A great many other friends of the family.

FIRST BUTLER. And all pretty terrible, if you ask me. (*They go.*)

CADY. Hello, Alf! You remember Mrs. Cady?

HOMER. Hello, Fatty.

MRS. CADY. How do you do?

CADY. Say, I called you up a couple times but couldn't get any answer.

GLADYS. Why, how do you do, Alf? I'm awfully glad you were able to come. Oh, Neil! I want you to meet an old friend of papa's. He's known me ever since I was—how high? Yes, but you couldn't lift me now. (*The invisible guest tries to lift her and fails. She giggles.* BUTLERS *enter with imaginary trays.*)

MRS. CADY. And now we'll have some nice tea to drink.

HOMER (*Probably to* FATTY). He married Gladys for her money.

MRS. CADY. And then Neil will play for us.

GLADYS. Oh, hello! Haven't seen you in a long time! No, I guess I wasn't engaged then.

(It is a Babel. The CADYS *are all speaking together, moving around and greeting guests.* NEIL *moves through it all, walking through guests, passing his hands through the butlers' trays—bewildered.)*

CADY. Oh, hello, Ralph. I want you to meet my new son-in-law. Neil, this is Mr. Umn.

GLADYS. Oh, have you been out to California? Did it rain much?

CADY. Yes, he's going to be very valuable to me in business, too.

HOMER. I'll bet he's rotten.

CADY. But after all there's nothing like business. It'll all be his when I retire—his and Homer's, his and Homer's. *(Slaps* NEIL *on back.)*

(The following four speeches are spoken simultaneously.)

MRS. CADY. Well, Miss Mmmm, you know Mmm, don't you? He's a cousin of John's who knew Francis very well. She's Ted's aunt. Yes. It's such a long time since you've been to see us. Gladys is always saying: "Mama, why is it Mrs. Mmm doesn't come and visit us, or why don't we go out and see her?" and all like that. You know Mrs. Mmm, don't you? You've become very plump, or you've become very thin. You don't mind my not getting up, do you? Mr. Cady always says I'm chair-bound. But that's his way of making a joke. He's always making a joke. You know Neil, of course. Would you like to have Neil play for us? Neil, play for us.

HOMER. Look at him, the dirty dog! He married her for her money all right, but if he thinks he's going to get it he's got another think coming. Pop's going to put him in the business! Huh! He thinks he's going to get the business, too. Well, I'll show him—the dirty dog! He isn't going to get the business away from me—not while I'm alive and kicking. All because he's a musician. Yes, he thinks he plays the piano. Well—let him play it and see if I care. I dare him to play it. Go on and play for us.

MR. CADY. Well, well, well! You know Judge Mmm of course. Old man, I want you to meet the Judge. Yes, they've got a very beautiful home here. Would you like a cocktail, eh? Yes, sir! Well, Judge, how's everything been going? Say, you know Mr. Mmm, don't you? How are you? How have you been all these years? Have a cocktail—that's the boy. Yes, she's a big girl now. Grown up—married. That's her husband there. That's the one I bought for her. Very talented. I'll get him to play. Neil, we'd like to hear you play. Come on, Neil, play something on the piano.

GLADYS. Oh, how do you do, Aunt Gertrude? You know Willie, of course. Willie, you remember Aunt Gertrude. Aunt Gertrude, you remember Willie. Yes, this is our beautiful home. My husband's very talented. No, you didn't interrupt him a bit. He's awfully glad you came. He wasn't going to do anything this afternoon. Anway, we always have tea. And if it isn't tea, it's something else. We're always having such a good time, Neil and I. Yes, that's my husband there. He plays the piano beautifully. Shall I get him to play? I think he would if I ask him. Oh, Neil, darling, play something. Please, Neil! Neil, for my sake, you'll play, won't you?

(MR. and MRS. CADY, GLADYS and HOMER reach the "Come on and play" lines simultaneously.)

THE CADYS. Play something for us! Play something for us! Play something for us!

NEIL *(In quiet desperation)*. All right. *(Crosses to piano, seats himself and turns on them.)* I'll play, but I'll play what I want to—and I don't think you'll like it. *(He plays— music that is soft and flowing, and reminiscent of* CYNTHIA. *The lights fade on the* CADYS *and their reception; the curtains fall. Through the window by the piano comes* CYNTHIA.)

NEIL (*As he continues playing*). Cynthia! I thought that would bring you—I hoped so.

CYNTHIA. Of course, Neil, dear.

NEIL. Cynthia, it was a mistake! I'm terribly unhappy!

CYNTHIA. I'm so sorry, Neil. Because I want you to be happy, always.

NEIL. But I can't be happy with these people. I should have married you, Cynthia. I wanted to, you remember? But you wouldn't. And now it's too late.

CYNTHIA. Yes, it's too late. And I'm sorry, too.

NEIL. I don't want you to be sorry, Cynthia. I don't want you to regret anything. It was all my own fault. (NEIL's *music turns to jazz as he plays.*)

CYNTHIA. Oh, Neil, don't let your music do that! (*She begins to draw back into the window.*)

NEIL (*Desperately, as the music becomes more and more jazzy*). I can't help it! It's these people. I'm trying—but I can't help it. (CYNTHIA's *image begins to fade.*) No—no! Don't leave me, Cynthia! I need you! Don't leave me with these people! They don't understand! They never can understand! (*But* CYNTHIA *is gone now.* NEIL *ends the jazz music with a treble crash, and buries his head on the keyboard. Immediately* MR. CADY *enters—his hat on and a morning newspaper in his hand.*)

CADY (*As he passes*). Hurry up, Neil! Mustn't be late for business. (*An* ELEVATOR MAN, *the same who was the trainman during the wedding scene, enters from the other side and meets* MR. CADY *at centre.*) Good morning, Jerry.

ELEVATOR MAN. Good morning, Mr. Cady. Express elevator going up! Watch your step!

(NEIL *looks up. There is no elevator, but this time even* NEIL *is persuaded, and he believes that he sees it. Four* BUSINESS MEN, *all with hats and newspapers, and all looking just alike, enter one at a time and step into the imaginary elevator.*)

CADY (*To the first of them*). Good morning! Made it in twenty-eight minutes this morning!

FIRST BUSINESS MAN. Good morning! I got the eight-six this morning!

SECOND BUSINESS MAN. Good morning! I missed the seven-forty-three.

THIRD BUSINESS MAN. Good morning! I always take the nine-two.

FOURTH BUSINESS MAN. Good morning! I thought you were on the eight-sixteen. (NEIL *gets into the car; the men huddle together*.)

STARTER (*Clicking his signal*). All right! Twentieth floor first stop!

CADY. No, sir, I wouldn't sell under a million five! No, sir, a million five! Oh, good morning, Neil!

NEIL. Well, I'm starting.

CADY. Good boy, Neil! I want you to meet some of my associates. This is my son-in-law, gentlemen. Just bought him for my daughter. Mr. Canoo, statistical department.

FIRST BUSINESS MAN. Four out! (*As* MR. CADY *thus introduces him the* FIRST BUSINESS MAN *walks out of the elevator, and goes off, paying no attention to* NEIL, *who nods at his retreating back*.)

CADY. Mr. Deloo, traffic department.

SECOND BUSINESS MAN. Five out! (*He goes*.)

CADY. Mr. Meloo, tax department!

THIRD BUSINESS MAN. Six out! (*He goes*.)

CADY. Mr. Beloo, general department.

FOURTH BUSINESS MAN. Eight out. (*He goes*.)

CADY. Well, well, Neil, starting in to work? You'll like it. You'll learn the ins and outs in no time. Hey! Wait a minute. I said nine out! (*He goes*.)

NEIL. Excuse me, Jerry! Can you tell me where I can learn the Ins and Outs?

STARTER. Ins and Outs Department! Room three hundred and thirty-three and one-third. Try and find it. (*He goes*.)

NEIL. Thank you.

(*The curtains between the marble columns at right part.*

A small office is disclosed. MISS HEY, *a stenographer, is typing at a small desk behind a railing.)*

NEIL. I beg your pardon?

MISS HEY. Well?

NEIL. I want a pencil.

MISS HEY *(Still typing).* What is it?

NEIL. I want a pencil.

MISS HEY. Who sent you?

NEIL. I don't know. But I have to have a pencil. I worked in a place like this once before. I had a great deal of difficulty getting a pencil then, I remember.

MISS HEY. It's just as hard to get one here.

NEIL. I thought it would be. I suppose there's a lot of red tape to go through.

MISS HEY *(Turning toward him).* Yes. Now as I understand it, you want a pencil.

NEIL. That's right.

MISS HEY. Of course you've filled out a requisition.

NEIL. No, I haven't. A piece of paper, isn't it? *(She hands him a tremendous sheet of paper. It is about twenty by thirty inches. He studies it.)* What I want is a pencil. There's a place for that to be put in, I suppose?

MISS HEY *(Wearily).* Yes—where it says: "The undersigned wishes a pencil to do some work with." How old are you?

NEIL. Thirty-two.

MISS HEY *(Taking the paper away).* That's the wrong form. *(She gives him another—a blue one this time.)* Parents living?

NEIL. No.

MISS HEY. What did you do with your last pencil?

NEIL. I didn't have any.

MISS HEY. Did you have any before that?

NEIL. I don't think I ever had any. *(He indicates the form.)* Is that all right?

MISS HEY. It isn't as regular as we like, but I guess it'll do.

NEIL. What do I do now? Go to someone else, don't I?

MISS HEY. Oh, yes. Sometimes you travel for days.

NEIL. Are we all crazy?

MISS HEY. Yes. *(She resumes typing.)* You might try Room E —right down the corridor.

(The curtains close over her, and the curtains at the left simultaneously open, revealing another office, just like the first. Another stenographer, MISS YOU, is at work on a type-writer. NEIL approaches her, requisition in hand.)

NEIL. Is this Room E?

MISS YOU *(Mechanically).* Did you have an appointment?

NEIL. No—you don't understand. I'm trying to get a pencil.

MISS YOU. Well, what do you want to see him about?

NEIL *(Handing over the requisition).* It's this. Somebody has to sign it.

MISS YOU *(Takes requisition).* Oh! *(Looks at it.)* Mr. Bippy! The man is here to see about getting a pencil or something.

NEIL. It *is* a pencil.

MISS YOU. Did you see Mr. Schlink?

NEIL. Yes.

MISS YOU. Mr. Woodge?

NEIL. Yes.

MISS YOU. Mr. Meglup?

NEIL. Yes.

MISS YOU. What did *they* say?

NEIL. Why, they seemed to think it would be all right.

MISS YOU *(Calls again).* Oh, Mr. Bippy! *(To NEIL.)* Belong to the Employes' Mutual Mutual?

NEIL. Oh, yes.

MISS YOU. Cady Golf and Building Fund?

NEIL. Yes.

MISS YOU. Well—all right. *(She stamps the requisition with an elaborate machine, which rings a bell as it works. She hands the paper back to NEIL.)*

NEIL. Oh, thanks. Do I get a pencil now?

MISS YOU. Oh, no! It has to be O.K.'d by the President. All requisitions have to be O.K.'d by the President.

NEIL. Is he around here some place?

MISS YOU. Oh, no! He's in a big office. Just keep going until you find a great big office.

NEIL. Where?

MISS YOU. Oh, somewhere in the new building. Mr. Bippy!

(NEIL turns away. The curtains close.)

NEIL. The new building. A big office.

(The centre curtains open, revealing a larger office. MR. CADY, seated at a long table, is dictating, in alternate sentences, to MISS YOU, MISS HEY, and to a dictaphone which stands before him. NEIL tries to attract MISS HEY's attention.)

SIMULTANEOUSLY

NEIL *(To MISS YOU)*. I beg your pardon. . . . *(To MISS HEY.)* I beg your pardon . . . would you mind if I—is this the President's office? Excuse me. . . . Excuse me.

MISS HEY *(To NEIL)*. Well, what is it?

NEIL. I want to see the President.

MISS HEY. What do you want to see him about?

CADY *(Dictating)*. And so beg to state—yours of the 19th instant—hoping to receive your valued order—yours received and would say—our Mr. Mmm will call on you—in re our No. 2160 —yours sincerely—annual sales convention—beg to state—beg to state—beg to state—pursuant to your instructions of the 13th ultimo—F.O.B. our factory—beg to state—beg to state—beg to state—as per your terms and specifications—would say—would say——*(By this time, hearing NEIL's voice, CADY turns.)*

CADY. Why, Neil!

NEIL. Here I am—at work!

CADY. Yes, sir! Business! Big business!

NEIL. Yes. Big business. What business are we in?

CADY. Widgets. We're in the widget business.

NEIL. The widget business?

CADY. Yes, sir! I suppose I'm the biggest manufacturer in the world of overhead and underground A-erial widgets. Miss You!

MISS YOU. Yes, sir.

CADY. Let's hear what our business was during the first six months of the fiscal year. (*To* NEIL.) The annual report.

MISS YOU (*Reading*). "The turnover in the widget industry last year was greater than ever. If placed alongside the Woolworth Building it would stretch to the moon. The operating expenses alone would furnish every man, woman and child in the United States, China and similar places with enough to last for eighteen and one-half years, if laid end to end."

CADY. How's that?

NEIL. It's wonderful!

CADY. And wait for September 17th!

NEIL. Why?

CADY. That's to be National Widget Week! The whole country!

NEIL. That's fine, but what I came up about——

CADY. Never mind that now—we've got more important things. Conferences, mostly. (*To* MISS HEY *and* MISS YOU.) Any good conferences on for today?

MISS HEY AND MISS YOU (*Together*). One at 3:19 this afternoon. (*They go.*)

CADY. That's fine! Ever been to a conference, Neil?

NEIL. No, but I've heard a lot about them.

CADY. They're great! You make speeches and decide things, and nobody can get in while they're going on. (MISS YOU *and* MISS HEY *re-enter excitedly.*)

MISS YOU AND MISS HEY. All ready! They're going to start the conference, the conference, the conference! (*They rush out.*)

CADY. Fine! Come right in, gentlemen!

(Half a dozen BUSINESS MEN *enter. They wear clothes that suggest fatness and prosperity. They walk in stiffly, in a line, repeating the phrases "Overhead," "Turnover," "Annual Report," "Overhead," "Turnover," "Annual Report." They sit, in stiff poses.)*

We are going to have a conference! *(Calls off.)* Bolt the doors, out there! Gentlemen—this is our annual quarterly meeting. *(He drops a gold piece in front of each man.)* I want to introduce a young man who has been showing great promise in our factory. I don't know what he will have to say to you——

NEIL. I know what to say! *(Rises.)* I remember now—I know exactly what to say!

CADY. Gentlemen, Mr. Neil McRae!

(As NEIL *rises to speak the* MEN *all fall into mechanical positions, reminiscent of the board of directors pictures in the advertisements.* NEIL *pounds the table occasionally during his speech, but there is no sound.)*

NEIL. I know you must be surprised to see so young a man stand up before you, but I have *trained* myself to occupy the position I am now in. I have learned my facts. That is how I happen to own my own home. It simply took up my spare time in the evenings. Then, one day, the head of the factory came through the room where I happened to be working on a very difficult piece of machinery. "Who is that?" he asked the foreman. "He seems to be brighter than the others." "Not at all," answered the foreman. "He has simply applied himself and I think we must raise his pay, if we want to hold him." A few weeks later I was able to solve in five minutes a problem that had puzzled the best brains in our organization. I am now the head of my department, and my old foreman is working under me. *(*NEIL *sits; there is applause; the* MEN *lean over and shake his hand, congratulating him.)*

BUSINESS MEN. Wonderful! Wonderful!

CADY. I knew he could do it! Gentlemen, he has saved us millions!

FIRST BUSINESS MAN. Why, he is going to be the biggest man in the organization.

OTHERS. Yes! The very biggest!

FIRST BUSINESS MAN. What do you say to signing up with us for ten years at half a million dollars a year?

SECOND BUSINESS MAN. And becoming sales manager?

CADY. How about a bonus?

FIRST BUSINESS MAN. Yes, a bonus!

SECOND BUSINESS MAN. Here's my check for one hundred thousand dollars!

CADY. And here's mine! Two hundred thousand dollars.

FIRST BUSINESS MAN. And mine for one hundred thousand!

OTHER BUSINESS MEN. And mine—one hundred and fifty thousand dollars!

NEIL. Oh, thank you, thank you! (*He looks at the checks; they are of various-colored paper—pink, blue, yellow.*) It's an awful lot of money, isn't it?

CADY. A million dollars!

NEIL. A million dollars!

CADY. Well, gentlemen, that was a dandy conference!

FIRST BUSINESS MAN. One of the best!

CADY. Let's have another!

SECOND BUSINESS MAN. Yes, another.

(CADY *hands out gold pieces again as the curtains close in.* NEIL, *however, has stepped out of the scene and stands facing the audience. Curtains fall behind him.*)

NEIL. Just think, a million dollars. (*He looks at the checks in his hand, but they have turned into samples of colored cloth.*) Blue and pink and yellow. Blue and yellow and pink. I was to match them. *I* know! I was to match them for——

GLADYS (*Heard in the distance*). Oh, Neil!

NEIL. For Gladys! (*Then, mechanically.*) Sweetheart! (GLADYS, *resplendent in evening dress and wrap, joins him.*)

GLADYS. Did you have a hard day at the office, Neil?

NEIL. Here they are. It's a million dollars—I think.

GLADYS. Oh, good. I always knew you'd be a big success, Neil.

NEIL *(Dully)*. But I'm not doing what I want to do. My music —I want to write my music.

GLADYS. Oh, not now! It's time to go somewhere! We're going to dance!

NEIL. No, no! I've got to write my music. I want to go home now!

GLADYS. Oh, nobody ever goes home. We're going to go and dance!

NEIL. But we've got to eat dinner first!

GLADYS. Of course! We're going to eat right here!

NEIL. In this restaurant again? But we were here last night, and the night before. You don't want to come here every night, do you?

GLADYS. Why, of course I do! Suppose it *is* expensive, you can afford it now! And nobody comes here but the best people! We'll come here every night from now on! They have the nicest little lamps on the tables!

(A CHECK-ROOM BOY *enters from one side and a* HEADWAITER *from the other. A second glance reveals the fact that the* HEADWAITER *is* ALBERT. *The* CHECK BOY *takes* GLADYS's *wrap and* NEIL's *bathrobe.)*

ALBERT. *Bon soir. (Holds up two fingers.)* How many, please?

NEIL. Two.

ALBERT. Two?

NEIL *(Counts them)*. Two.

ALBERT. Two?

NEIL. Why, hello, Albert!

ALBERT. Hello, Neil!

NEIL. Oh, yes! You were a waiter at college, weren't you? You know Gladys?

GLADYS. Of course. *(*ALBERT *and* GLADYS *shake hands. Then* ALBERT *immediately becomes again the formal waiter.)*

ALBERT. How many, please?

NEIL. Two.

ALBERT. Two?

NEIL. (*Looks around to see if a third has mysteriously appeared*). Yes—two.

ALBERT. I will see if I can find you a table. (*He consults his chart.*) All our reserved tables are reserved.

(*The centre curtains part, revealing a gaudy cabaret interior. In the centre, at the rear, is a window, set in a frame of wrought iron. There is a single table, set with much fancy glassware and two table lamps of the sort so dear to* GLADYS's *heart. As this scene is revealed an unseen orchestra strikes up the jazz tune, "The Frog's Party."*)

ALBERT. Ah! Right this way, please! Here is a nice one— right by the window! (*He seats them with an elaborate flourish, simultaneously uttering the meaningless ritual of headwaiters everywhere.*) Yes, Madame! Yes, sir! (*A* CIGA-RETTE GIRL, *Spanish in attire, enters and circles around the table.*)

GIRL. Cigars and cigarettes! Cigars and cigarettes! (ALBERT *presents the menu, a huge affair, to* NEIL.)

GLADYS. See, Neil? Isn't it wonderful? (*She sways to the music.*) Order! He's waiting! Hurry up—you've got to order!

NEIL (*Scanning the card*). I—I can't decide right away.

GLADYS. Oh, that music! I can't stand it any longer! (*She rises and seizes* ALBERT.) Dance? (*She whirls around the table with him, to the accompaniment of the jazz tune and the* CIGARETTE GIRL's *chorus of "cigars, cigarettes."*)

ALBERT (*When the dance is over*). Perhaps Madame would care for some Bordelaise à la Bordelaise, or some Bordelaise à la Bordelaise, or some Bordelaise à la Bordelaise.

GLADYS. Why, yes—I'd like that!

ALBERT. And what will Monsieur have?

NEIL (*Studying card*). What *is* Bordelaise à la Bordelaise?

ALBERT. Very nice, sir.

NEIL. Yes, I know, but what is it?

ALBERT. It's served in a little round dish—very nice.

NEIL. Can't I find out what it is?

ALBERT. I'll see if anybody knows, sir. (*He turns his back.*)

GLADYS. Neil!

NEIL. Well?

GLADYS. People don't do that— making a scene in a restaurant!

NEIL. I only want to know what it is.

GLADYS. But you must pretend that you *do* know! *That's* the thing! (ALBERT *turns back to* NEIL.)

ALBERT. I'm sorry, sir—nobody knows.

NEIL. It doesn't matter. I'll take it.

ALBERT. Yes, sir. Thank you, sir. (*Four* WAITERS *enter, with dishes.*)

GLADYS. Oh, here's dinner! (*The* WAITERS *circle the table, clanking the lids of their dishes as they exhibit the food. They go slowly at first, then faster and faster, in time to the constantly accelerating music.*)

NEIL (*Springing up*). Stop! I can't stand it! (*The waiters halt in their tracks; the music stops.*) Is it going to be like this always?

GLADYS. What?

NEIL. Our life! (ALBERT *dismisses the waiters.*)

GLADYS. Why, I think it's wonderful! You're going ahead being a big success in papa's office, and every night we'll go out and dance! You'll have to learn!

NEIL. I won't dance! I don't want to dance! I wouldn't ever have had to dance if I hadn't married you! (*It gives him a thought.*) If I hadn't married you——

GLADYS. Well, I don't care whether you dance or not. *I'm* going to! Albert—— (*She rises and seizes* ALBERT; *they dance off.*) If you hadn't married me you'd have starved to death—starved to death—starved to death——

(*Her voice dies down in the distance as she and* ALBERT *dance off to the accompaniment of the jazz tune. As* NEIL *starts the next speech the jazz tune slowly changes into the* CYNTHIAN *theme, and at the same time the gaudy cabaret changes into a sunny cottage.*)

NEIL. I don't think so. I might have been poor, but we'd both have work to do. It's a small house, I know, but the sun finds it the first thing every morning. And flowers live longer in our windows than anywhere else, because she cares for them so.

(The wrought-iron window has turned into a simple thing of chintzes; chintz curtains appear in the doorways, and a box of jonquils takes its place at the foot of the window. The table no longer contains restaurant silver and electric lamps, but is simply furnished with a few breakfast things, with a vase of jonquils to keep them company. The place is flooded with sunlight.)

NEIL *(Calling)*. Cynthia!

CYNTHIA. I'm coming!

NEIL. *Are* you coming, or must I use force?

CYNTHIA. It's the toast machine. You sit down and begin.

NEIL. As though I ever begin without you! Besides, I have something beautiful for you. (CYNTHIA *enters, bringing a tray laden with breakfast.*) See what I've done!

CYNTHIA. What?

NEIL. Nothing at all! Merely created an utterly beautiful morning!

CYNTHIA. *You* did? I started it an hour ago.

NEIL. Perhaps; but see those little powder-puff clouds? *They* weren't there ten minutes ago.

CYNTHIA. They *are* nice, darling. I didn't think you were so clever.

NEIL. And wait till you see the sunset I'm planning.

CYNTHIA. You can't beat last night's. What a scarlet!

NEIL. It blushed because we flattered it so. *(A pause.)*

CYNTHIA. Darling.

NEIL. What?

CYNTHIA. A letter. *(They stare at the envelope corner.)*

NEIL. Didn't you dare open it?

CYNTHIA. No. But let's be brave. *(They hold hands and take a long breath.)* Now—one, two, three! *(They tear the letter open; read it in silence.)* Do you believe it? *(The voice is ecstatic.)*

NEIL. No! Do you?

CYNTHIA. Darling!

NEIL. Darling!

CYNTHIA. But it *must* be real—it's typewritten.

CYNTHIA AND NEIL *(Reading in unison).* "Your symphony will be played by our orchestra on December the tenth."

NEIL. Darling!

CYNTHIA. Darling! They'll applaud and applaud! You'll have to come out and bow!

NEIL. I won't!

CYNTHIA. You'll have to have a new dress suit!

NEIL. And you'll have to have a new evening dress—yellow chiffon, too. I can do their damned orchestrations now. I can do a hundred of them between now and October.

CYNTHIA. No, you won't!

NEIL. But, my youngest child, we must continue to eat.

CYNTHIA. But, my dear, we're extremely wealthy. Have you seen my new housekeeping book?

NEIL. No.

CYNTHIA. Look! I ruled every one of those columns myself.

NEIL *(Rises).* Oh! Sit down!

CYNTHIA. That's why my middle finger is all red. *(NEIL kisses her finger.)* This is serious. This is finance. Listen! *(Reading from book.)* "To Mrs. Neil McRae—debtor. Ninety-seven dozen eggs from the little red hen at seventy-nine a dozen —ninety-seven, seventy-nine. Four hundred and forty-six quarts of milk from the little dun cow at sixty-four—four hundred and sixty-four. Thirty-six pots of jonquils sold Mr. Frost, the florist, at thirty-six sixty-six—six sixty-six, sixty-six." And there's the total!

NEIL. But, Cynthia, that can't be right; it's impossible!

CYNTHIA. Add it up for yourself.

NEIL. Sixty-three and eight are forty-two——

CYNTHIA. Neil, you may be one of the minor gods, but you can't add. *(Takes pencil.)* There! Look!

NEIL. But that means——

CYNTHIA. It means we're billionaires, that's all.

NEIL. We have a hundred and seventy-seven dollars and—seventy-seven cents?

CYNTHIA *(Nods)*. And we can keep on just as we have been doing.

NEIL. Cynthia, do you suppose *any* two people *ever?* *(He kisses her.)*

CYNTHIA. No, I don't believe *any* two people *ever.* *(The voice of* GLADYS *comes out of the distance, faintly.)*

GLADYS. Oh, Ne-il!

CYNTHIA. What is it, dear?

NEIL. I thought I heard someone calling.

CYNTHIA. You did that last night at tea time. I'm frightened.

NEIL. You mustn't be—there are no fears in this house.

GLADYS *(Louder this time—the same old call)*. Oh, Ne-il!

NEIL. Cynthia, it's calling me!

CYNTHIA. What?

NEIL. I don't know. I must go to it. *(He steps out of the cottage.)*

CYNTHIA. I'll go along! *(The voice grows weaker as* GLADYS'S *gets stronger.)*

NEIL. You can't, my dear! It's too absurd. *(The curtains close on the cottage; the jazz begins again.)*

GLADYS. Oh, Ne-il!

CYNTHIA *(Faintly)*. O-o-o-h!

NEIL. Yes, what is it?

GLADYS. Oh, Neil! *(*GLADYS *enters—so do the* CHECK BOY, *the* CIGARETTE GIRL, ALBERT, *and the four* WAITERS. *They stand in a line with outstretched palms.)*

NEIL. Yes, what is it? *(*GLADYS, *as she speaks, dances with each* WAITER *in turn.)*

GLADYS. Come on, sweetheart! We're going home now! Tip the waiters! Tip the waiters!

NEIL. For heaven's sake, stop that dancing!

GLADYS. I should say not! Tip the waiters! Tip them big! Tip them big! *(She dances off with the last of the waiters.* NEIL *hands out large bundles of money to the* WAITERS, *then as he proceeds along the line, he comes suddenly to* ALBERT.)*

NEIL. Albert! *(The music stops.)* You got me into this! You've got to tell me how I'm going to get out of it!

ALBERT. What's the matter?

NEIL. I can't stand it! I can't live with Gladys any longer. What am I going to do about her?

ALBERT. Why, that's easy.

NEIL. What do you mean?

ALBERT. Just kill her—that's all.

NEIL. Kill her?

ALBERT. Of course. It's simple and practical.

NEIL. Do you know I never thought of that? I'm not very practical, am I?

ALBERT. No, you're not.

NEIL. Of course, I wouldn't like to do it unless it were absolutely necessary.

ALBERT. Still, it's worth thinking about. *(He leaves him with this thought.)*

NEIL. Yes, it is. *(The music starts;* GLADYS *and the* WAITER *dance on again.)*

GLADYS. We're going home now! Tip the waiters! Did you tip them all? We're going home! Mama and papa will be there, and Homer!

(The WAITERS *are now gone, and the curtains reopen on the* CADY *home of pillars.* HOMER *is working a radio set;* MR. CADY *is playing golf with an imaginary ball;* MRS. CADY *rocks, knits and sings. All is pandemonium.)*

CADY. Fore! Everybody, fore!

HOMER. I've got the radio fixed! Listen!

RADIO. Stock market reports! Stock market reports! *(Ad infinitum.)*

GLADYS. Oh, Neil! Isn't it nice to be in our own home again? *(She leaps into his lap.)*

MRS. CADY *(Singing).* "Bringing in the sheaves! Bringing in the sheaves!"

CADY. Give me the niblick! Give me the niblick!

NEIL. I wish you'd all keep still.

GLADYS. What, darling? Wait! Wait! *(Everyone subsides.)* I hear them! The dancing teachers! The dancing teachers! *Now* you'll learn to dance.

NEIL. I won't, I tell you!

GLADYS. Oh, yes, you will! Here they are! The dancing teachers! Come in, dancing teachers! Now you'll learn to dance! *(Six* DANCING TEACHERS *enter—exquisite gentlemen, one like another.)*

NEIL. Gladys, I won't!

GLADYS. You've got to! Look! Aren't they wonderful? Here he is—my husband! You're to teach him to dance!

LEADER OF THE DANCING TEACHERS. Ah! *(He circles around* NEIL, *about to pounce.)*

NEIL. Gladys, I warn you! If you go ahead with this, you'll be sorry!

GLADYS. Teach him to dance! Teach him to dance!

LEADER *(Advancing upon* NEIL*).* You've got to dance! We teach the world to dance! We make it dance. *(He seizes him.)* We've got him.

GLADYS. *Now* you'll learn to dance!

LEADER. Now watch me! One foot out and one foot in! One foot out and one foot in!

GLADYS. He's learning to dance! He's learning to dance!

ALL THE DANCING TEACHERS *(Forcing* NEIL's *arms, shoulders and feet).* One foot out and one foot in! One foot out and one foot in! Now your shoulder, now your elbow! Now your shoulder, now your elbow! One foot out and one foot in! One foot out and one foot in. Now your shoulder—

NEIL *(Tears himself loose).* No! No! I tell you! Get out! All of you! *(They fall back.)* Get out, every one of you! I won't learn to dance! *(They have disappeared.)*

GLADYS. Neil!

NEIL *(The* CADYS *meantime unconcernedly continue their customary occupations, but in subdued tones).* Thank God! Now I'm going to write!

GLADYS. Neil, do you realize how you're behaving?

NEIL. I do! I won't go on with this any longer! If this is to be

our life together then I can't stand it! I won't! That's all
—I won't!

GLADYS. Neil! After all I've done for you! After all papa's done
for you!

NEIL. Done for me? You've ruined me, that's all! You've given
me a lot of money that I didn't want, and you won't let me
do the one thing I want to do! Well, now I'm going to write
my music! I'm going to finish my symphony!

GLADYS. Oh, no, you're not! (*Crosses quickly to the piano and
tears up the manuscript.*) There's your old symphony! Now,
what have you got to say?

NEIL. You tore it up! It was the only reason I married you, and
you tore it up! All right—there's only one thing to do! (*He
takes up the paper knife from the piano—it is about twice
the size that it was when the audience last saw it.*)

GLADYS. Neil, Neil! What are you going to do?

NEIL. I'm going to kill you! (*She stands looking at him, transfixed. He stabs her, and she falls dead.*)

MRS. CADY (Quietly). Now you've done it!

NEIL. It was her fault! She killed my work!

MRS. CADY. She was a sweet girl. The police will get you. (*She
sings "Bringing in the Sheaves."*)

NEIL. Stop that singing!

MRS. CADY. I won't!

NEIL. And stop that damned knitting!

MRS. CADY. I won't! "Rock of Ages, cleft for me." (NEIL *stabs
her. She dies, falling over backward, chair and all.*)

CADY (*Blandly continuing his golf game*). This is outrageous!
The idea of killing a man's daughter and wife! I'm ashamed
of you!

NEIL. You're to blame, too! Just as much as the others! Look!

CADY. What is it?

NEIL. *You're* dead, too.

CADY. Oh! (MR. CADY *dies.*)

NEIL. Thank God, they're out of the way! Peace! I can work
at last!

THE RADIO. Stock market reports! Stock market reports!

HOMER *(Coming from behind the radio machine).* Is that so?
I guess you forgot all about *me*, didn't you?

NEIL. Forget you? Indeed I didn't! Homer, my boy! *(He stabs
him;* HOMER *crumples up on the floor.)* I guess that ends
that! Free! Free!

HOMER *(Sitting up).* Free nothing! We'll sue you for this, you
dirty dog! *(He falls dead again.)*

NEIL. It won't do you any good! Not when they know why I
did it! Not when I show them what you killed! Not when
I play them my music! *(Half a dozen* NEWSPAPER REPORTERS
*enter. They are dressed alike and look alike; each has a
pencil expectantly poised over a piece of paper.)*

THE REPORTERS *(Speaking one at a time, as they surround*
NEIL). The Times! The World! The Post! The Globe! The
Sun! The News! The Times! The World! The Post! The
Globe! The Sun! The News!

NEIL *(Indulging in a gesture with the paper knife).* Gentlemen,
this is purely a family affair. I don't think I should say anything at this time, but do come to my trial.

THE REPORTERS *(Again speaking one at a time).* A statement!
A statement! A statement! A statement! A statement! A
statement!

NEIL. Well, gentlemen, it's a long story.

(Instantly a dozen NEWSBOYS *rush down the aisles of the
theatre, crying "Extra! Extra! All about the murders!" The
din is terrific. Simultaneously the theatre lights up; the
audience turns for a second to look at the newsboys, and
in that second the curtain falls. The* NEWSBOYS *pass out
copies of The Morning-Evening, containing a full account
of the quadruple murder.)*

Part Two

(The scene is now a courtroom. Against curtains of black stand three major objects of red—the same red that appeared fitfully in NEIL's chintz curtains, and again as draperies for the pillars in the Cady home. Squarely in the centre is a block of twelve seats mounted on a platform. They are designed, obviously, for the jury, but instead of being the customary jurors' chairs they are of the kind found in theatres. NEIL's piano and easy chair, of course, remain in their accustomed places. At the right, also vividly red, is the judge's bench, and against it leans a frame of photographs, of the sort that you see in theatre lobbies. The pictures show MR. CADY in various costumes and poses. The witness's box is at the left, and beside it a ticket taker's box, presided over by the ubiquitous JERRY. Near him is a HAT-CHECK BOY recognizable as the same youth who took NEIL's robe in the restaurant, and who also sold chocolates during the wedding ceremony. A couple of USHERS, GIRLS, stand chatting beside the jury box. NEIL, of course, is also present, walking up and down somewhat nervously, and consulting his watch. The JURORS are beginning to arrive as the curtain ascends—three or four are streaming in. To NEIL's surprise they all turn out to be dancing teachers.)

TICKET TAKER *(As the curtain ascends).* Oyez! Oyez! Oyez! *(He takes the tickets of the JURORS, returns the stubs, and drops the remainder into his box.)*

CHECK BOY. Check your coat! Check your coat!

1ST JUROR. I guess we're early.

NEIL. Excuse me, but are you some of the jurors?

2ND JUROR. We certainly are.

153

NEIL. But—but you're dancing teachers, aren't you?

1ST JUROR. Best in the world.

NEIL. Are you going to try me? My music?

1ST JUROR. That's what.

NEIL. But it doesn't seem fair. I'm afraid you'll be prejudiced against something really good.

(The SECOND *and* THIRD JURORS *meet and automatically shake hands.)*

2ND JUROR. Hello, Ed!

3RD JUROR. Hello, Ed!

2ND JUROR. Well, you old son-of-a-gun!

3RD JUROR. Well, you old son-of-a-gun!

2ND JUROR. Glad to see you!

3RD JUROR. Glad to see you. *(They put their hands in their pockets simultaneously.)*

2ND JUROR. Fine! How's every little thing?

3RD JUROR. Fine! How's every little thing?

2ND JUROR. Well, glad I saw you!

3RD JUROR. Well, glad I saw you!

2ND JUROR. Goodbye, Ed!

3RD JUROR. Goodbye, Ed!

1ST JUROR *(At the frame of photographs).* Say, who's this?

NEIL. That's the judge. It's the opening night of my trial, you know. That's the way he appeared in several famous cases.

2ND JUROR *(Joining them and pointing to a picture).* Oh, yes! That's the way he looked in the Watkins trial. He was terrible good. Did you see it? *(A fourth JUROR is shown to a first row seat by an USHER.)*

1ST JUROR. No, I was out of town. *(Points to another picture.)* There he is in the Ferguson case! Gosh, he was good in that!

NEIL. Yes, I heard he was.

2ND JUROR. Was he funny?

1ST JUROR. Funny? He had that courtroom roaring half the time.

2ND JUROR. I don't know another judge in the country who

can deliver a charge to a jury like he can. Pathos, comedy, everything.

1ST JUROR. They say this will be the best trial he's ever done. I hear they were sold out last Monday. (*More* JURORS *are entering.*)

TICKET TAKER. Tickets, please!

HAT-CHECK BOY. Coats checked! Check your coat! (*The* THIRD JUROR *presents his ticket stub to an* USHER.)

USHER. Other aisle, please! (*He crosses to the other side of the jury box and presents the stub to the other* USHER.)

USHER. Other aisle, please! (*He returns to the* FIRST USHER.)

USHER. Right this way! (*She indicates a seat in the middle of the box.*)

3RD JUROR (*Looking at the stub*). Ain't this an aisle seat?

1ST USHER. No, sir. Fourth seat in.

3RD JUROR. After paying all that money to a speculator! (*He takes his seat in the middle of the back row.*)

4TH JUROR. There ought to be a law against them. (*Other* JURORS *are being seated.*)

(NEIL, *at the footlights, catches the attention of the* ORCHESTRA LEADER.)

Now, the overture to the trial, please.

(*The orchestra plays the overture—a few bars of cheap musical comedy strains, the modulation from one tune to another being most elaborate. As the orchestra plays, more* JURORS *are seated, leaving empty only the seat next the Judge's bench for the* FOREMAN, *and another in the middle of the first row. The* JURORS *look at their programs, talk, adjust opera glasses, etc. As the overture ends,* ALBERT *enters, a camera slung over his shoulder.*)

NEIL. Why, hello, Albert!

ALBERT. Hello, Neil!

NEIL. What are you doing here?

ALBERT. I'm covering the trial.

NEIL. "Covering" it? For a newspaper?

ALBERT (*Nods*). I'm a reporter on the Illustrated.

NEIL. Oh, yes! You used to write, didn't you?

ALBERT. I understand they're going to try some of your music?

NEIL. Yes. You'll give it a fair criticism, won't you—in the paper?

ALBERT. In what paper?

NEIL. Why, your paper.

ALBERT. The Illustrated? We don't use any writing. It's an *illustrated* paper. Didn't you ever see it—in the subway?

NEIL. Of course! I remember—just pictures. But how do people know what they are?

ALBERT. Oh, we always have a few simple words, saying what the picture is about. A good many of our subscribers can read, and they tell the others. (*A* CANDY SELLER *appears.*
He has the usual tray of chocolates and peppermints seen in the theatres.)

CANDY SELLER. Chocolates and bonbons! Fresh chocolates and bonbons! Assorted chocolates!

1ST JUROR (*Leaning out of the jury box*). Here you are. (*Buys a box of candy.*)

(*The* CANDY SELLER *goes out again. There is a sudden burst of activity in the jury box.*)

NEIL. What's all that?

ALBERT. They are getting ready to elect a foreman for the jury.

(*There is something like a cheer from the jury box. At one end a sign appears reading: JONES FOR FOREMAN. At the other side: SMITH FOR FOREMAN. The* FIRST JUROR *rises to speak. He receives hearty applause.*)

1ST JUROR. Mr. Chairman and ladies and gentlemen of the Fifth Jury District: I don't think anybody here has to be told at this late date that Harry J. Smith, retired, is the logical man for foreman of this grand jury. I guess everybody here knows Mr. Smith's record. You have all known him since childhood. He is an old Eighth Ward boy and will give a jury a business administration.

OTHER JURORS. Hooray! *(The FIRST JUROR sits. The SECOND JUROR immediately demands attention.)*

2ND JUROR. Mr. Chairman and ladies and gentlemen of the Fifth Jury District: I don't think anybody here has to be told at this late date that Thomas A. Jones, retired, is the logical man for foreman of this grand jury. I guess everybody here knows Mr. Jones's record. You have all known him since childhood. He is an old Eighth Ward boy and will give the jury a business administration.

VOICE. What about Ireland? *(There are cries of "Throw him out!" NEIL holds up a hand for silence.)*

NEIL. Wait! *(He goes into the witness box.)* Ladies and gentlemen of the Fifth Jury District: I know it is late to be putting forward a new candidate for foreman of this grand jury, but this is my trial, and it is my music that you're going to hear. Both of the candidates who are now up before you are good dancers, but it is only fair that there should be someone on the jury who knows good music.

JURORS. Hooray!

NEIL. Therefore, when the light on the Times Building swings on tonight, I want it to be a steady red light, which will show that we have elected the Hon. Albert Rice, of Chicago, a man of the people, for the people, and by the people, and the stars and stripes forever in the good old U.S.A.!

JURORS. Hooray!

(Almost immediately a red light shines across the group, and the orchestra strikes up Sousa's march, "Stars and Stripes." The JURORS, cheering, march around the jury box, carrying American flags, banners, noise-makers, etc. There are cries of "Rice Wins! Hoorah for Rice!" ALBERT, still mindful of the fact that he has been sent to get the news, makes ready his camera and calls on the crowd to halt.)

ALBERT. Hold it, please! *(They stop—there is a scurrying to get into the photograph. ALBERT snaps them.)*

NEIL. Hold it! *(He takes the camera and ALBERT automatically prepares to have his own picture taken. One of the ushers tries to slip into the picture, but* NEIL *waves her aside. He snaps* ALBERT.) Will they be out soon?

ALBERT. Soon? They are out! (*He pulls a copy of the Illustrated from his pocket—a newspaper covered with a front page crowded with photographs, but entirely blank elsewhere.*) I brought one with me.

NEIL. They're on the front page.

ALBERT. Sure! We put everything on the front page. (*He points.*) There's a picture of the judge delivering his charge.

NEIL. But he hasn't delivered it yet.

ALBERT. Well, we have to get things quick. Our readers expect it. (ALBERT *takes his place in the jury box. The other* JURORS *lean over and shake his hand.*)

NEIL. The Hon. Albert Rice assumes office as thousands cheer. (*He waits for the cheer—it does not come. He motions to the jury. They clap their hands perfunctorily.*)

ALBERT. Thank you, gentlemen.

TICKET TAKER (*Announcing*). His Honor, the Judge!

(*Everyone rises. The orchestra begins the "Soldiers' Chorus" from* Faust. *The* JUDGE *enters. He is* MR. CADY, *his golf suit handsomely covered by an enormous red robe. He also wears an enormous Judge's wig. He throws away all dignity, however, by lifting the skirts of his gown and skipping into view. The music ends on a long note in the brasses, such as attends the finish of an acrobat's trick.* CADY *curtsies toward the jury box in response to unanimous applause, and blows a kiss.* He goes up to his chair and holds the picture of a satisfied actor as he waits for another burst of applause to subside.*)

CADY (*At last—to* NEIL). Got a match?

NEIL. What?

CADY. Got a match?

NEIL. Oh, yes! (*He strikes a match. Although several feet away from the cigar, the cigar lights.* MR. CADY *and jury are about to sit when* NEIL *hisses.*) Look out!

CADY. What is it?

NEIL. That chair. It isn't very strong, you know.

CADY. Oh, I'll be careful. (*He sits. The* JURORS *sit.*)

TICKET TAKER. Oyez! Oyez! Oyez! (*The final* JUROR *enters and presents his ticket.*)

CADY. Ladies and gentlemen, I——

NEIL (*Noticing the tardy* JUROR). Just a minute! He's late. (*To the* JUROR.) Can't you people ever be on time? (*The tardy* JUROR *gives his seat check to an* USHER, *who starts to lead him to his place, in the middle of the second row, but finds somebody already in it.*)

CADY (*Blandly*). Ladies and gentlemen, I declare the Court— (*The confusion makes him break off again.*)

USHER. (*Leaning far over*). May I see your check, please?

CADY. I declare the Court——

USHER. May I see your check?

JUROR (*Searching his pockets*). I had it here some place. Ah! (*Gives stub to the* USHER. *The* USHER *examines the ticket stub.*)

USHER. Oh, you belong in the row ahead. This gentleman has a ticket for this seat. (*People in both rows have to stand up while the exchange is made. It is a good deal of trouble, to put it mildly.*)

NEIL (*To* CADY). All right now. I'm sorry.

CADY. I declare the court to be in session. (*There is a round of applause.* CADY *bows.*) The business of the day is the trial of Neil Wadsworth McRae for murder. (*There is more applause.* NEIL *is finally compelled to bow.* CADY *again addresses* NEIL *confidentially.*) Am I right?

NEIL. Yes. And don't forget, I'm going to play my symphony. That was the reason I did it, you know.

CADY. Yes, I remember. (*He is quite conversational.*) Now, the first thing to be done, I should say, is to have the prosecuting attorney make a sort of general charge. (*To* NEIL.) What do you think?

NEIL. I guess that's right. How about it, Albert?

ALBERT (*Looking up from his program*). Yes, that's right. (NEIL *nods to the* TICKET TAKER.)

TICKET TAKER (*Announcing*). The prosecuting attorney!

(HOMER *enters to the tune of "Tammany." He wears a long black robe. He receives a hearty round of applause, with a few hisses.*)

NEIL. Oh, it's you!

HOMER (*Quietly*). I'll get you now, you dirty dog!

NEIL. I think not.

CADY. Come, come, we can't be all day at this. I've got to get back to the office. Now, just what were these murders all about?

HOMER (*Reads from document. As* HOMER *begins to read* USHER *and* CHECK BOY *begin a whispered conversation that soon dominates the scene*).

SIMULTANEOUSLY

HOMER. "On such and such a blank date, the defendant, Neil Wadsworth McRae, did brutally murder, maim, assault, detroy, stab, injure, kill and cause the death of Gladys Virginia Cady, his wife; Mr. Cady, her father; Mrs. Cady, her mother, and Homer Cady, her brother, destroying one and all of the aforesaid Gladys Virginia Cady, his wife; Mr. Cady, her father; Mrs. Cady, her mother, and Homer Cady, her brother —by the use of a large paper knife, of bone manufacture and curious design, a picture of which appeared in the newspapers at the time." (*Hands the newspaper containing the picture to* CADY.)

USHER. Did you sell much candy?

CHECK BOY. Sure—enough to buy a couple seats for the movies.

USHER. Oh, let's see the one up the street!

CHECK BOY. Oh, that's punk! You always want to see the sad ones.

USHER. I hate comedies.

CHECK BOY. Well, I hate sad ones.

NEIL. Quiet, please; some of us would like to hear the show! (*They grudgingly leave the room.*)

CADY. Yes, I saw it. A great, big, long one. Exhibit A. *(He hands it to the* FOREMAN.*)*

ALBERT. Exhibit A! *(Passes it to the other* JURORS.*)* *(The other* JURORS *repeat "Exhibit A," passing the newspaper from one to another.)*

HOMER. Having caused the death of the aforesaid and aforementioned people, I therefore call upon the Court to punish said Neil Wadsworth McRae in one of two ways prescribed by law—death or hard labor for life, whichever they do in this state.

CADY *(Realizing that maybe it's serious after all).* Oh, no! Is that so?

NEIL *(Lightly).* Just wait!

CADY *(To* HOMER*).* Yes. Just wait, please.

1ST JUROR *(Leans toward his neighbor, with open program, and reads from it, as though confiding a bit of real news).* Say, this courtroom, with every seat occupied, can be emptied in less than three minutes.

CADY. Silence in the court! *(A pause.)*

HOMER. The State rests. *(He sits in the easy chair and is immediately seized with a fit of coughing.* MRS. CADY *instantly appears behind* HOMER; *she has her knitting, but no chair.)*

MRS. CADY. Are you all right, Homer?

HOMER. I guess so.

MRS. CADY *(To the jury).* Homer's sick. He was always delicate. But he was a good boy though. When Homer wanted to be he was as good a boy as you'd find in a month of Sundays. There was no reason on earth why Neil shouldn't have allowed him to live, just like a lot of other people are allowed to live. *(The* JURORS *applaud her.)*

CADY. You are his mother?

MRS. CADY. Yes, sir. *(*CADY *shakes her hand, sympathetically.)*

CADY. You were also a victim, I believe?

MRS. CADY. That's right. *(*CADY *shakes her hand again.)* You heard how he did it? With a paper knife.

CADY. Oh, yes! You see, we're trying him today.

MRS. CADY. For the murders?

CADY. Yes.

MRS. CADY. Oh, I beg your pardon! *(Begins to back away in confusion.)* I wouldn't have intruded, if I'd known.

NEIL. Wait a minute! I'd like to have Mrs. Cady take the stand, please.

MRS. CADY *(Flustered)*. Who? Me?

NEIL. If you don't mind.

HOMER. What! Going to make her take the stand? A mother? *(There are hisses from the jury.)*

NEIL. Over here, please! *(Leads her to the witness box.)* Do you swear to tell the truth—the truth—and—the truth?

MRS. CADY. Yes.

NEIL. You can't tell the truth unless you raise your hand, you know.

MRS. CADY. No?

NEIL. No. *(She puts up her hand.)* You're Mrs. Cady, aren't you?

MRS. CADY. Yes. *(To MR. CADY.)* Is that right, Fred?

CADY. Yes—that's all right.

NEIL *(Suddenly wheeling on MRS. CADY)*. Now then. *(MRS. CADY jumps.)* Where were you on Friday, June third?

MRS. CADY. Knitting. *(She suits the action to the word.)*

NEIL. But you used to sing in the choir, didn't you?

MRS. CADY. Oh, yes. *(Sings.)* "Just as I am, without one plea." *(The JURORS stand and join in. CADY stops smoking for a moment and also sings a bar or two.)*

CADY *(Suddenly rapping for order)*. Silence in the court!

NEIL *(Waves a warning finger at MRS. CADY, as though to intimate that another question is about to come)*. Prove an alibi!

HOMER. I object, Your Honor!

CADY. Objection sustained and overruled! *(To MRS. CADY.)* Answer the question! *(NEIL smiles mockingly at HOMER.)*

MRS. CADY. What was it?

NEIL. Prove an alibi!

MRS. CADY. What kind?

NEIL *(To CADY)*. I didn't know there were different kinds.

CADY. Oh, yes—there are several kinds of alibis.

NEIL. Then prove any kind.

HOMER. Your Honor, I object!

CADY. You object?

HOMER. Yes! *(He goes to NEIL and looks sinisterly at him.)* I object to his looks!

NEIL. Why, what's the matter with them?

CADY *(It is apparently a point of great import).* An objection has been raised to the prisoner's looks. *(Looks at NEIL carefully.)* Hm! Have you anything to say?

NEIL. Sir?

CADY *(Quite casual).* Have you anything to say about your looks?

NEIL. Why—I think they're all right. *(There is a weighty pause.)*

CADY. This is a serious question. *(He removes his wig. The jury breaks out in chatter; CADY raps.)* Order, please! Now, the prisoner thinks that his looks are all right.

HOMER. But he can't prove it!

CADY *(To NEIL).* Can you prove it?

NEIL. Why— *(Here's an awful situation!)*

CADY. You see, this is a court of law. Everything has to be proved.

NEIL. Well, well—can't the jury tell by looking? *(NEIL looks toward the jury, which peers at him closely, but is puzzled. The JURORS shake their heads, uncertain.)*

CADY. You see, it's illegal for a jury to know anything until it's been instructed. Now, as I understand it, the point is that you think your looks are all right?

NEIL. Yes.

CADY. But you can't prove it?

NEIL *(If he can only have a moment's peace in which to think it over!).* Oh, Lord! *(One of the jurors is noisily unwrapping a candy box.)* Quiet! Good heavens—how can I think if they're going to— Your Honor, they *must* be quiet!

CADY. Quiet!

THE JUROR. But it's candy! *(It is a big box full and it is passed up to the JUDGE.)*

CADY. Oh, really? *(GLADYS enters in a brilliant dinner gown and an ornate cloak.)*

GLADYS. Oh, candy! *(She crosses to the Judge's stand and be-gins rifling the box.)* Hello, Neil! I didn't mean to interrupt! I just ran in to get the boys! We're going dancing! *(Some of the* JURORS *rise; one or two even begin climbing over the railing to join her.)* There's a big new place opening tonight and they're going to take me there! Got some money, papa?

CADY. Ten thousand enough? *(He gives her a handful of bills.)*

GLADYS. Oh, thanks. Come on, boys! *(The* JURORS *make further gestures toward going.)*

NEIL. No, wait! *(All movement is suspended.)* You mean you want to take—*them*—away with you?

GLADYS. Of course!

NEIL. But—but I'm being tried for the murders. And if you take the jury away——

GLADYS. I'm sorry, Neil, but I couldn't miss the opening, could I? Are you ready? *(The* JURORS *step toward her.)*

NEIL. No, no! *(Again the* JURORS *halt.* NEIL *appeals to* CADY.*)* She can't do that, can she?

CADY *(Who has been eating so much candy he has had little time for the trial's new aspect).* What?

NEIL. Take the jury away, right in the middle of things?

CADY *(Licking his fingers).* She can if it's habeas corpus.

NEIL *(Not at all sure).* Well—is it?

CADY *(He licks his fingers).* It's beginning to look that way.

NEIL. But it isn't fair! They've got to hear my music. I know what I'll do! *(He faces* CADY.*)* I'll take it to a higher court!

CADY *(Just a bit hurt).* Oh, don't you like this court?

NEIL. It isn't that. It's a good court, I guess, and the people are lovely, but——

CADY. About how high a one would you want?

NEIL. I'd want the highest I could get.

CADY. All right. *(*JUDGE CADY *slowly goes up in the air, as his stand grows two or three feet higher.)* Is this high enough for you?

NEIL. I guess so. Is this the superior court?

CADY. Oh, yes. Much superior. And more up-to-date. We send out all our verdicts by radio.

NEIL. She can't take them away with her now, can she—in this court?

CADY. Oh, no! You see, in a higher court the lower court is reversed.

NEIL. Good! *(The* JURORS *resume their old positions.)*

GLADYS. Oh, the devil! Well, then I'll take Albert. He's only the foreman. *She grabs* ALBERT *by the hand and leads him out of the courtroom.)*

CADY *(Sucks a sticky thumb).* Well, are the rest of you ready to bring in a verdict? All in favor will say——

NEIL. No, wait! I'm not through—you haven't heard the music yet.

CADY. Oh, that's right! You're going to play for us.

NEIL. Of course. That's why I killed them, you know—on account of the music. I want to prove that I was justified. Listen! *(He goes to the piano.)* You won't blame me when you've heard the music. *(He strikes a chord.)* This is a symphony in C Minor. *(He starts to play. The result is disconnected, meaningless. There is a budding hissing from the* JURORS. NEIL, *with a cry, jumps to his feet, holding up the torn sheet of music. He finds it almost impossible to speak.)* She destroyed it! She tore it up, and now I can't play it! Cynthia! Cynthia! *(CYNTHIA appears at the piano. She is calm and sympathetic, as always.)*

CYNTHIA. Yes, dear?

NEIL. Cynthia, she tore up the symphony! I can't remember it, and they're waiting for me to play!

CYNTHIA. You still have the pantomime, haven't you?

NEIL. Yes.

CYNTHIA. Then play that for them instead. *(She finds the pantomime music.)* They'll think it's better, anyhow. *(Puts the music before him.)*

NEIL. But it isn't finished.

CYNTHIA. Well, now you *can* finish it.

NEIL. Can I?

CYNTHIA. Of course. It'll be all right, dear—you'll see.

NEIL. You—you think we ought to do it?

CYNTHIA. Of course.

NEIL. All right. (*He faces his inquisitors.*) Ladies and gentlemen, instead of the symphony, we're going to play a little
pantomime, called "A Kiss in Xanadu"—written by Cynthia
Mason and Neil McRae. We'll need quite a lot of room, so
if you don't mind clearing the court— (*The Judge's dais and
the witness box disappear. The jury box, too, moves into
blackness.*) The scene is the royal palace in Xanadu. It's
a night in June—one of those spring nights that you find
only in Xanadu. Now, if you're all ready—music! (*The
music of the pantomime begins.*) Cynthia, we ought to have
a window to show what kind of night it is. (*In the distance
a great open window appears. Beyond a moonlit balustrade
are flowers and trees and stars.*)

CYNTHIA. It's coming!

NEIL. Thanks! The scene is the bedchamber of the Prince
and Princess. On the right is the bed of the Princess and on
the left the bed of the Prince. (*Two fairy-tale beds appear
from the darkness. They are canopied in pink. Above them
are flower-draped testers that rise to golden points.* NEIL
and CYNTHIA *seat themselves at the piano and the pantomime begins.*)

A LORD OF THE BEDCHAMBER *and a* LADY OF THE BEDCHAM-
BER *enter and bow to each other ostentatiously. They are
followed into the room by two small black* PAGES, *carrying
tiny bed tables. The one for the Princess' bed bears a small
lamp with a dainty shade. The Prince's has a candle and
shade, and a small phonograph. As the* LORD *and* LADY *examine the room the* PAGES *go out and return with a pillow,
which is placed at the foot of the Princess' bed, and a
costumer, which is for the convenience of the Prince. The
attendants convince themselves there are no intruders under
the beds and depart. A clock strikes nine.*

The PRINCESS *enters. She is very beautiful, but very
bored. The lovely night lures her to the window. She goes
out on the little balcony and sighs. She is a married Princess.
She returns to the bedchamber and snappishly commands*

the LADY *to undress her. Nothing to do but go to bed! The* LADY *draws the curtains and leaves.*

The PRINCE *enters with his* LORD. *He would like to be a Gay Dog Prince and he twirls his mustache bravely. He, too, would like to find romance again, but here he is—a married Prince! A* PAGE *puts his royal dressing gown and crown on the costumer. The* LORD *attaches curlers to the royal mustache and leaves the* PRINCE. *The* PRINCE *turns on the phonograph and tries to do his Nightly Dozen. But the night outside distracts him. He goes to the window. It is too much for him. A second attempt to exercise is abandoned. He will go out to Adventure. If he turns the royal dressing gown inside out it should make a rather good disguise. He does so. The lining of the crown makes a serviceable cap. He tiptoes to the other bed. The* PRINCESS *is asleep. He draws the canopy across his own bed and steals out the window.*

CYNTHIA. But the Princess wants to go adventuring, too. I know! Let's have the moon wake her!

NEIL. Yes! Come on, moon! *(The moon obligingly sends its beams across the bed of the Princess.)* Thank you!

The pantomime proceeds. The PRINCESS' *head pops through the draperies. It is such a beautiful night! She observes the closed canopy of her lord's bed. He is asleep—the dull, conventional husband. She goes to the window. What a night! Romance lies out there. She hesitates. She decides. Frightened, but determined, she takes a cover from her bed. An excellent shawl it makes! But something is wrong. She stands undecided, her hands touching her lovely hair. The music stops.*

NEIL. We skipped a place here. We've got to disguise the Princess. She mustn't be recognized, either, you know.

CYNTHIA. Of course not. I have it! Let her put on her lamp-shade for a bonnet!

NEIL. And she can use the Prince's candle-shade for a mask!

The music starts again and the PRINCESS *dons the lamp-shade and puts two finger holes through the candle-shade. She is very happy and goes out to the trees and stars. There is darkness—and here we are in a public park in Xanadu. There are a good many flowery bushes to be seen, but they are not noticed by the* PRINCE, *who sits, depressed, on a park bench, under a street lamp. A* POLICEMAN, *a* LAMP-LIGHTER *and two small* ATTENDANTS *enter on patrol, and sedately go about their business. The* PRINCESS *comes into the park. A* MAN, *a romantic-looking man, even if he is masked by that upturned coat collar! A girl, a charming girl, even if she is holding a small mask before her eyes! She skips away, but returns. She drops her handkerchief. She quietly and politely sneezes. He springs to her aid with her handkerchief. She sits beside him on the bench. He plucks a rose from the bush behind them and offers it timidly. She tosses it away. The light in the lamp is much too bright. A mighty puff from the* PRINCE *and it goes out. But the* WATCH *returns. The lamp is relighted. The* PRINCE *and the* PRINCESS *sit a little closer. He offers another rose. This time she accepts it. But that lamp! He has a permanent solution. He breaks the lamp in two. Masks are not needed in the darkness, but the moon comes up. He waves it away. She kisses him. A clock strikes five. The sun rises. The adventure is over. She runs away. He calls, but she does not answer. He picks up the rose she spurned. His grief is covered by considerate darkness.*

Once more it is the Royal bedchamber. The PRINCESS *creeps into the room and into bed. The* PRINCE *steals in a moment later. He goes to the* PRINCESS' *bed. Still asleep! He goes to his bed. The clock strikes eight. The* LORD *and* LADY *arrive. The* PAGES *fetch a breakfast table. The royal pair are awakened. They sit down to eat. She starts to pour her husband's coffee. Oh, yes, she had forgotten! She rises and offers a cheek to be kissed. He mechanically obliges. They sit down again. But they cannot eat. The music of the night is still with them. They steal wistful looks at the window.*

The PRINCESS *looks at the rose he gave her. The* PRINCE *looks at the one she first refused. The flowers are stealthily put away. The* PRINCE *and the* PRINCESS *unfold their napkins. It is the humdrum life once more.*

(The curtain falls, slowly. Then, slowly, the footlights go down, plunging the auditorium into complete darkness. Immediately we hear the verdict from the vastly Superior Court—sent out, as JUDGE CADY *had said, by radio. It comes, through magnifiers, from the rear of the auditorium, and takes the form of loud and derisive laughter, punctuated by cries of "Rotten!" "No good!" "Highbrow!" "Terrible!" In the darkness the curtain again rises. Seated cross-legged on* NEIL'S *piano, still in the red wig and with a red light playing on him, is* JUDGE CADY. *As always, he is smoking a cigar.* NEIL *sits facing him on the piano stool.)*

CADY *(To the invisible voices).* Silence! *(The voices stop.)* Now, was that what you wanted to show us?

NEIL. Yes, sir.

CADY. Well, of course we don't want to hurt your feelings, Neil, but I'm afraid it's a little bit highbrow. Don't you think so?

NEIL. No, sir. Not very.

CADY. Well, I don't think it's what they want. *(To the unseen* JURORS.*)* How about it? *(A single voice comes over the radio. It says "Rotten!")*

CADY. Are you ready to bring in a verdict?

FIRST JUROR'S VOICE. Yes, I move we bring in a verdict!

SECOND JUROR'S VOICE. I second the motion!

FIRST JUROR'S VOICE. It is moved and seconded that we bring in a verdict. Remarks? *(A pause.)* All those in favor say "Aye."

CHORUS OF VOICES. Aye!

FIRST JUROR'S VOICE. Opposed—"No?" *(Pause.)* The motion is carried.

CADY. Well, what sort of a verdict do you want to bring in? There are several kinds of verdicts.

FIRST JUROR'S VOICE. I move we bring in a verdict of guilty!

SECOND JUROR'S VOICE. I second that motion!

FIRST JUROR'S VOICE. It is moved and seconded that we bring in a verdict of guilty. Remarks? All those in favor say "Aye."

CHORUS OF VOICES. Aye!

FIRST JUROR'S VOICE. Opposed—"No?" *(Pause.)* Well, I guess the motion's carried.

CADY. See, Neil? I told you so.

NEIL. Well—well, what are you going to do with me?

CADY. This thing of using the imagination has got to stop. We're going to make you work in the right way. You see, your talents belong to us now, and we're going to use every bit of them. We're going to make you the most wonderful song writer that ever lived.

NEIL. But I can't write that kind of music! You know I can't!

CADY. You can do it by our system. You are sentenced to be at the Cady Consolidated Art Factory at eight o'clock tomorrow morning!

NEIL. Art factory?

CADY. At eight o'clock tomorrow morning!

(The lights slowly dim and fade out, and instantly there is a burst of noise. Pianos are playing discordantly; there is the sound of machinery in the distance, a voice is singing a jazz tune, and other voices are heard in loud declamation. The lights go up again on a tier of four cells. In the first a MAN is dictating to a STENOGRAPHER; in the second NEIL is working away at a piano, while a YOUTH in a belted coat and a straw hat, atilt on his head, sings to the accompaniment of NEIL's music; in the third cell an ARTIST works before an easel, and in the fourth a YOUNG MAN is loudly reciting poetry, apparently moved to do so by the posturings of two other YOUTHS who are in the cell with him. After a moment of this pandemonium a GUIDE enters, followed by three VISITORS. All four are dancing teachers, so far as outward appearances go, but they are marked apart by the fact that the GUIDE wears an official-looking cap, and the VISITORS carry umbrellas and open Baedekers. The GUIDE raises his voice for silence; a gong sounds somewhere,

*and all activity ceases. The figures in the cages come down
to the bars and stand waiting.)*

GUIDE. Now this, gentlemen, is the manufacturing department.
In this studio—*(he indicates the first)*—we have Walter
Carp Smith, the world's greatest novelist——

NOVELIST *(More or less routine)*. How are you?

GUIDE *(Passing to the second cage)*. In this studio, Neil McRae,
the world's greatest composer!

NEIL *(Listlessly)*. How are you?

GUIDE *(At the third cage)*. In this one, Finley Jamison, the
world's greatest magazine artist!

ARTIST. How are you?

GUIDE *(At the fourth cage)*. And in this, James Lee Wrex, the
world's greatest poet!

POET. How are you?

GUIDE *(Indicating the unseen cages beyond)*. The studios beyond are devoted to science and religion. Mr. Cady was
the first person in the world to put religion up in ten-cent
packages, selling direct to the consumer.

FIRST VISITOR. You don't say so!

GUIDE. He also prides himself on having the largest output of
literature and music in the world. He's going to open two
more plants the first of the month. Now, would you like
to see how these men work?

FIRST VISITOR. Yes, indeed! *(Goes toward the first cage.)* Did
you say this was the novelist?

GUIDE. The world's greatest. Author of more than two thousand published works.

FIRST VISITOR. What an imagination!

GUIDE. Yes, sir, none at all. Now if you're ready, I'll show you
how he works. Go!

NOVELIST *(Begins at once to dictate from a book in his hand)*.
"Something closely resembling a tear fell from the old pa-
trician's cheek. 'Margaret,' he cried, 'the people of the West
have learned to love you, too.' 'Jackie boy,' she whispered.
'They have made you governor after all.' Far off on the—
the—"*(he hesitates; the* STENOGRAPHER *takes up the story.)*

STENOGRAPHER. "—desert, the caravan faded away. Night took them in its arms and a great hush fell on the forest. The two lovers——"

GUIDE. Stop! (*He turns to the* VISITORS.) There you are!

FIRST VISITOR. Was *she* writing it?

GUIDE. Oh, no! Sometimes she gets a little ahead of him, that's all.

FIRST VISITOR. Isn't he wonderful!

GUIDE. Forty-five minutes after he finishes a novel we have it printed and assembled and on its way to the movie men.

FIRST VISITOR. May we talk to him?

GUIDE. Certainly.

FIRST VISITOR (*To the* NOVELIST). I've enjoyed your novels very much.

NOVELIST. Thank you.

FIRST VISITOR. I see you're writing a new one.

NOVELIST. Of course. I'm under contract.

FIRST VISITOR. What's that? (*Indicating the book in the* NOVELIST'S *hand.*)

NOVELIST. It's my last one.

FIRST VISITOR. But weren't you just dictating from it, for your new one?

NOVELIST. Yes. They like it that way.

GUIDE. Under the old system they wrote it all new each time. Here—let the gentleman have it as a souvenir.

FIRST VISITOR (*Reading the title*). "Eternal Love." What's your new one called?

NOVELIST. "Love Eternal."

GUIDE. Don't forget—you're lecturing at three o'clock at Wanamaker's.

SECOND VISITOR. Say, will you show us how the artist works?

GUIDE. Certainly. What will you have—a cover or an advertisement?

SECOND VISITOR. What's the difference?

GUIDE. There isn't any.

SECOND VISITOR. Well, then, I'll take an advertisement.

GUIDE. All right. Go! (*The* ARTIST *draws without looking at the*

canvas. He hands it to the GUIDE, *who hands it to the* VISI-
TOR. *The canvas is blank.*) There you are!

SECOND VISITOR. What beautiful eyes!

THIRD VISITOR. Wonderful!

GUIDE. Do you want to talk to him?

SECOND VISITOR. Oh, thanks. I suppose it'll be used on a magazine?

ARTIST. Oh, yes—thousands.

SECOND VISITOR. Must be worth five or six hundred dollars.

ARTIST *(Bored to death).* Thirty-five hundred.

FIRST VISITOR. You don't say so!

GUIDE. And here, gentlemen, is our poet. His "Jolly Jingles" are
printed in three million newspapers a day.

FIRST VISITOR *(Pointing to the* MEN *in back).* Who are those
men?

GUIDE. Those are his models. He is the only poet in the world
who works from living models. That's why all his poetry
is so true, so human. He'll show you. Go!

POET. I will now write a friendship poem. *(Motions to his*
MODELS.) Friendliness No. 3, please. "Friendship." *(The*
MODELS *strike a pose, hands clasped. The* POET *recites.*)
"Goodbye, old pal; hello, old pal; the greatest pal I ever
knew. A dog's your finest friend, my lad, when all the world
is blue."

SECOND VISITOR. Ain't it human?

GUIDE. And here, gentlemen, is Mr. Neil McRae, America's
foremost composer.

FIRST VISITOR. Who's that in back?

GUIDE. That's his lyric writer. You will now see how they work.
What kind of a song will it be, McRae?

NEIL. A pathetic. *(Sits at the piano.)*

GUIDE. A pathetic. Go! *(*NEIL *plays.)*

SINGER *(In a horrible voice).* "You've broken my heart like you
broke my heart, So why should you break it again?" *(*NEIL
comes to the bars again.)

GUIDE. That will sell one and one-half million.

SECOND VISITOR. I suppose you write other kinds of songs, too?

NEIL. Oh, yes—mammies, sweeties and fruit songs. The ideas

are brought from the inspiration department every hour on the hour. After I turn them into music they are taken to the purifying department, and then to the testing and finishing rooms. They are then packed for shipment.

FIRST VISITOR. A wonderful system!

THIRD VISITOR. I should say so!

SECOND VISITOR. Do you work all the time?

NEIL. No, the night shift comes on at eight.

FIRST VISITOR. How long have you been here?

NEIL. For years and years.

SECOND VISITOR. Say, will you write another song for us—just as a souvenir?

NEIL *(Desperately)*. Oh, why don't you all go away?

GUIDE. What's that? What was that? You get busy there and write another song!

NEIL. No! I've been writing forever—I'm tired of it.

GUIDE. Do you want me to call Mr. Cady?

NEIL. I don't care! I don't care what you do!

GUIDE. I'll give you one more chance.

NEIL. No! I won't!

GUIDE. All right, then! Mr. Cady! Mr. Cady!

(The GUIDE *rushes out. The* VISITORS *slink away. A gong sounds. Those in the cages huddle in fear.* MR. CADY *appears behind the cages. He carries a large snake whip.)*

CADY. What's the matter here?

GUIDE. McRae says he won't go on!

CADY. He won't, eh? Well, we'll see about that!

NEIL. I can't go on! I'm tired!

CADY. What's that got to do with it? You've got to go on!

NEIL. I *can't*, I tell you. I *can't* keep on at this sort of thing.

CADY. You know your sentence, don't you? You've got to work our way until you die.

NEIL *(Dully)*. Yes, I know.

CADY. We own you now. The family. The family owns you. *(He falls into rhythmic measure.)*

You take our money and you live our life,
　We own you, we own you.
You take our money and you live our life,
　We own you, we own you.
You take our money and you live our way,
　We pay the piper and we tell him what to play.
You sold your soul and you can't get away,
　We own you, we own you.

(The CADY *family and others enter at back, and weave back and forth joining in the chant, reaching through the bars at* NEIL.)

NEIL. Until I die! I can be free from you if I die! I *can* die! You can't keep me from it! That's how I can get away from you! Open the door! Open the door! *(He shakes the door on the audience's side of the cage. It opens.)* It was never locked! *(He steps out and closes the door.* CYNTHIA *enters.)* Cynthia, Cynthia, I'm free! I can die! *(Those in the background disappear.)* Cynthia, how are we going to do it?

CYNTHIA. We'll go to an executioner. I know a good one. You mustn't be afraid. It won't hurt. *(An* EXECUTIONER *appears masked, with a black robe and a huge paper knife.)* See— it's Jerry!

JERRY. Hello, Mr. McRae. *(Takes off his mask and cap.)*

NEIL. Oh, hello, Jerry! You're going to do it, are you?

JERRY. Sure. *(Feels the edge of his knife.)*

NEIL. Oh, that's good.

CYNTHIA. Do we have to wait long?

JERRY. No—you're next.

NEIL. Oughtn't we to have a block?

CYNTHIA *(Moving the armchair).* We'll use this. It'll be more comfortable.

NEIL. Oh! And you'll stay with me?

CYNTHIA. Always. *(She stands beside him.)* But it won't hurt. *(*ALBERT *enters, wearing a short medical apron and jacket.)* Albert will give you a pill.

NEIL. Oh, yes! Hello, Albert!

ALBERT. Hello, Neil! Got a glass of water?

CYNTHIA *(Glass of water in hand)*. We're ready, Doctor. *(ALBERT goes to the chair; tests its strength.)*

ALBERT *(To the* EXECUTIONER*)*. Is the light all right? *(The cabaret orchestra is heard in the distance.)*

JERRY. I think so.

NEIL. There's that music again.

ALBERT. You're nervous, that's all. Here! *(*NEIL *swallows a pill.)*

CYNTHIA. Now it can't possibly hurt you.

ALBERT *(Motions* NEIL *to the chair)*. Here we are! *(*NEIL *sits.)* That's it—way back. *(To* JERRY.*)* Right?

NEIL. Shall I take off my collar?

ALBERT. Oh, no. There's room, I think.

NEIL. Just a once-through, please.

ALBERT. Of course. It'll be all over in a minute.

NEIL. Cynthia!

CYNTHIA. Yes.

NEIL. I was afraid you'd gone.

CYNTHIA. No, dear. *(*JERRY *taps his knife on the floor.)* Are you ready, Neil?

NEIL. Yes, except for that music. Charles the First didn't have any music. *(The lights begin to fade.)*

CYNTHIA. He's ready, Doctor.

NEIL. Don't go away, Cynthia!

ALBERT. All ready. *(*JERRY *taps the knife again on the floor.)*

NEIL. Goodbye! I'll see you soon.

CYNTHIA. Are you comfortable?

NEIL. Yes. You'll be with me always, won't you, Cynthia? *(There is darkness, save for a cloudy moving light on* NEIL.*)*

CYNTHIA. Always.

ALBERT. All right.

NEIL. Cynthia, are you there?

CYNTHIA. Yes, darling.

(There is a hum of voices. Presently one can discern several chanting, "You take our money and you lead our life." MRS. CADY is heard saying, "Homer's sick." MR. CADY is apparently telephoning somewhere. He is shouting, "Well, I'll

tell you what to do!" HOMER's *voice repeats, "You dirty dog!"* GLADYS *shrilly calls out, "He's learning to dance!" The voices become a chant, finally unintelligible. The lights slowly go up again. We are back in* NEIL's *apartment. He is asleep in his chair. It is sunset. There is a knock, a real knock, on the door.)*

NEIL *(Half asleep).* Yes? *(*CYNTHIA *enters.)*

CYNTHIA. Is anything the matter, Neil? I thought I heard you talking.

NEIL. It didn't hurt. Was it a success?

CYNTHIA. Neil, are you all right?

NEIL *(Takes her hand).* I need you, Cynthia!

CYNTHIA. Oh, Neil, do you? Are you sure you do? I—I couldn't stay away, Neil. I tried to, but I couldn't. Because I need you, too. I just couldn't give you up to anyone else on earth.

NEIL. Cynthia, dear.

CYNTHIA. It wouldn't have worked, Neil—with those people. Don't you know it wouldn't?

NEIL. I think I do.

CYNTHIA. I've been sitting out on a bench in the square, trying to think out what it would mean—what it would do to you.

NEIL. I know. Widgets.

CYNTHIA. That would be worse for you than any amount of poverty.

NEIL. Poverty in our cottage.

CYNTHIA. Did you think of a cottage, too?

NEIL. Of course—I lived there.

CYNTHIA. We could manage. I know quite a lot about raising chickens.

NEIL *(Reminiscently).* A little red hen and a little dun cow.

CYNTHIA. Yes, we might have a cow. Have you been thinking about it, too? *(Rises.)*

NEIL. Well—let's say dreaming. *(He rises and goes to the desk.)* It was terrible, Cynthia—do you know, I dreamed I was married to *her?*

CYNTHIA. To Gladys?

NEIL. When I thought you didn't care, I was hurt and angry. And I dreamed she telephoned—— (*Sees the receiver off the hook.*) My God! Did she telephone! Oh, Cynthia, it's real! I *did* do it! I did!

CYNTHIA. Did what?

NEIL. I did ask her to marry me!

CYNTHIA. Neil! You didn't! And she—accepted you?

NEIL. Yes.

CYNTHIA. Oh, Neil. (*A knock at the door.* JERRY *puts his head in. He wears a uniform somewhat like the one that accompanied him through the dream.*)

JERRY. It's me, Jerry. I've been ringing your phone for the last five minutes. Yeh, I thought so—you left it off the hook again. (NEIL *replaces the receiver.*) The young lady that came before was waiting, so I brought her right up.

GLADYS (*In the doorway*). It's me, Neil—may I come in? (*Enters.*) Oh, hello again, Miss Mason!

CYNTHIA. I—I forgot my tea things. (*Half choking, she takes up her tray of tea things.*)

GLADYS. Well, here we are. Isn't it exciting! We're engaged.

NEIL. Yes.

GLADYS. Did you have a good nap?

NEIL. Yes, thank you.

GLADYS (*Obviously something on her mind*). Do you love me a lot, Neil? Enough to do me a great big favor?

NEIL. What?

GLADYS. It's a big one, and maybe you won't want to do it.

NEIL. What is it?

GLADYS. Well, it's this way. Coming back from the dressmaker's I met Walter Craig. I told you about him, didn't I? He's a boy that sort of used to like me.

NEIL. Oh, yes.

GLADYS. Now, mind you, Neil, you can say "No" to this if you want to, but—he said, "What are you doing tonight?" Now, you won't be angry, Neil?

NEIL. No, no.

GLADYS. Well, then he said he didn't know any other girl in

New York, and would I sort of play around with him this week. So all I wondered was—well—you know how a fellow is—if he thinks a girl's engaged, why, he won't come near her at all. Now mind, you don't have to do it—and I won't be a bit hurt if you don't, but what I thought was—if we could start being engaged, say, a week from today—you wouldn't mind, would you, Neil? Of course, next week, after we *are* engaged, we'll just go everywhere together.

NEIL. I see.

GLADYS. I know a dozen people, pretty near, that'll give big parties for us. It's an awful lot of fun, being engaged.

NEIL. Is it? I'm afraid I wouldn't fit in with that sort of thing.

GLADYS. Why, half the fun of being engaged is—well——

NEIL. Gladys, just what is your idea of being engaged?

GLADYS. Why—I've just been telling you. (NEIL *smiles.*) What's the matter?

NEIL. Well, it's just that your idea of an engagement is different from mine.

GLADYS. What is yours?

NEIL. I think I'd want to be somewhere alone, just the two of us, where we could talk.

GLADYS. Talk about what?

NEIL (*With a meaning look*). I don't know.

GLADYS. You don't mean you'd *always* be like that, do you? I mean, when you're married?

NEIL. I might.

GLADYS. Well, where would I come in? Do you mean you'd expect *me* to sit around *every* evening and—just talk? I did think you'd be willing to—play around the way other people do.

NEIL. I see.

GLADYS. But, of course, if you wouldn't—well—why—there doesn't seem to be much sense in our being engaged, does there?

NEIL. It's to be just as you say, Gladys.

GLADYS. Well, I don't think we're exactly suited to each other —if you think it over. Honestly, I don't. Do you?

NEIL. No, Gladys.

GLADYS. I noticed the difference the minute I saw Walter again! I can kind of let myself go with Walter. You're sure you don't think I'm a quitter?

NEIL. I think you're all right.

GLADYS. And we'll still be friends, won't we? I've always thought you were nice, Neil. *(She gives a sigh.)* It's a sort of a relief, isn't it?

NEIL. Yes, it is—rather.

GLADYS. Well, goodbye. I've got to go because I left Walter downstairs. *(She departs.)*

NEIL. Oh! *(Laughs. Starts to call out.)* Cyn—*(Looks across the hall, crosses to the piano and begins to play the music of the pantomime. After a moment* CYNTHIA *comes slowly into the room.)*

CYNTHIA *(Hesitatingly)*. Want me, Neil?

NEIL. Do I want you? *(He continues playing as he hears her approaching.)*

CURTAIN

ALL MY SONS

by Arthur Miller

For Elia Kazan

Introduction

In appreciating Arthur Miller's *All My Sons*, which was first presented in New York on January 29, 1947, we are fortunate in having his own description of his intentions, his long period of thought about the play, and the rationale of his dramaturgy. All this and much more to enhance one's understanding of Arthur Miller can be found in his introduction to the edition of the *Collected Plays* published in 1957.[1] The introduction reminds one at times of Shaw's prefaces in its clarity, sincerity, and revelation of the mind of the creative artist. It should be read in its entirety by all students of Arthur Miller.

When *All My Sons* opened in 1947 it was widely hailed by most of the dramatic critics, with some exceptions, notably George Jean Nathan, John Chapman of the *Daily News,* and Robert Coleman of the *Daily Mirror*. Most of the critics were impressed by Miller's strong sense of dramatic situations, his feeling for and ability to create living characters, and his talent for trenchant dialogue.[2] Louis Kronenberger, writing in *PM*, also praised him for his human and moral sense. The New York Critics' Circle Award was given to Miller that year.

The playwright had come a long way in his struggle for expression and recognition since he wrote his first play as a student at the University of Michigan in the spring term of his freshman year. *All My Sons* was not in any sense his first play, although it was his first success. In 1944 his *Man Who*

---

[1] *Arthur Miller's Collected Plays,* Introduction, pp. 12-23.
[2] See Ward Morehouse, *Matinee Tomorrow,* p. 292. Compare with the following critics, included in the *New York Theatre Critics' Reviews* for February 3, 1947: Brooks Atkinson, p. 475; Robert Garland, p. 476; William Hawkins, p. 475; Louis Kronenberger, p. 477; Ward Morehouse, p. 477; and Richard Watts, Jr., p. 476.

Had All the Luck was produced on Broadway, but closed after a few performances. Prior to that time there were eight or nine plays which he had written but which had never been produced.[3] We have, then, in *All My Sons,* a successful play by a young playwright (he was thirty-two), but by no means an inexperienced one; Miller already knew enough about his craft to discard and keep in his desk drawer most of his dramatic *juvenilia.*

What so impressed and edified both the critics and the audiences on that opening night in 1947 still shines through the pages as one reads the play today, more than fifteen years later. The moral judgment that the play expresses about the businessman who places his personal aggrandizement above his responsibility to the rest of mankind is as cogent in 1964 as it was in 1947; and as it has been throughout human history. No man is an island, to use a noble utterance which has become almost an empty cliché; when Joe Keller, having realized that he too is part of the human mainland, refuses to participate in its preservation, he does the only thing possible by removing himself physically, as he has already done morally and spiritually.

Critics have made much of the Ibsenesque qualities in this play.[4] Miller, in his introduction, already mentioned, expresses his admiration of Ibsen's craftsmanship and his moral integrity.[5] The exposition of the past to explain the present and motivate the future which is so characteristic of the Norwegian giant is well demonstrated in *All My Sons.* Likewise, Miller does not hesitate to admit that his plays do more than entertain, that they reveal the mainsprings of human nature and hence reveal ourselves. Such revelation, he hopes, will cause our horizons to widen, our moral sense to grow, and our responsibilities to the world of humanity to take on new dimensions. If this means teaching through drama, Miller is proud to be another representative of a long line of dramatists

---

[3] Introduction to *Arthur Miller's Collected Plays,* p. 13.
[4] See especially George Jean Nathan, *The Theatre Book of the Year, 1946–1947,* p. 292; and John Mason Brown, *Still Seeing Things,* p. 197.
[5] Miller, *op. cit.,* p. 12.

—teachers of mankind—which runs all the way through history from Aeschylus to Bernard Shaw.

Much praise has been heaped upon Miller for his craftsmanship, for his dialogue, and for the effective realization of his characters. All of these qualities are apparent in the reading of his play. The magic of Elia Kazan's direction; the artistry of the acting, by Ed Begley as Joe Keller, Arthur Kennedy as Chris Keller, Beth Merrill as Kate, Karl Malden as George, and Lois Wheeler as Ann—these of course cannot be recaptured. But for one playgoer, at least, who was present on that memorable occasion on January 29, 1947, the rereading for purposes of this Preface brought back the excitement and the profound effect of that performance.

The Playwright Arthur Miller (1915–   )

Arthur Miller, whose *Death of a Salesman* won the Pulitzer Prize in 1949, and whose *All My Sons* was awarded the New York Critics' Circle Award in 1947, was born in New York City on October 17, 1915, in the Harlem section of Manhattan. After an uneventful career in the public schools of New York City he managed to enter the University of Michigan, and was graduated in 1938.

Although his first Broadway success did not come until he was thirty-two, with *All My Sons,* he had been writing plays in college at the rate of two a year and had won several money prizes. Professor Kenneth T. Rowe of the University of Michigan was his instructor in playwriting, and Miller acknowledges his indebtedness to him for giving him confidence and helping him emotionally.

Before Miller succeeded as a playwright he had written a book of reportage of World War II, *Situation Normal* (1944), and a novel, *Focus* (1945), about the dangers of racial prejudice. He returned to the subject of mob prejudice in his adaptation of Ibsen's *An Enemy of the People* (1951) and in *The Crucible* (1953), which dealt with the Salem witchcraft trials of 1692. Miller—in all his work, whether it be drama or fiction—is serious about man's responsibility to the community of mankind and to the dislocations, personal and moral, which result when that responsibility is ignored. To Miller, the consequences of an action are as real as the action itself. An Arthur Miller play is not an evening of light entertainment but an experience that moves, emotionally cleanses, and stimulates one to a re-examination of one's moral concepts.

JOSEPH MERSAND

FURTHER READING

Brown, John Mason. *Still Seeing Things*. New York: McGraw-Hill, 1950, pp. 197-98.

Hewitt, Barnard. *Theatre U.S.A., 1668–1957*. New York: McGraw-Hill, 1959, p. 444.

Kunitz, Stanley J. *Twentieth Century Authors: First Supplement*. New York: H. W. Wilson, 1955, pp. 669-70.

Miller, Arthur. Introduction to *Arthur Miller's Collected Plays*. New York: Viking, 1957, pp. 12-23.

Morehouse, Ward. *Matinee Tomorrow*. New York: Whittlesey House, 1949, pp. 291-92.

Nathan, George Jean. *The Theatre Book of the Year, 1946–1947*. New York: Alfred A. Knopf, 1947, pp. 290-93.

New York Theatre Critics' Reviews. New York: Critics' Theatre Reviews, Inc., 1947, pp. 475-78.

ALL MY SONS

Cast of Characters

JOE KELLER, *a factory owner*
KATE KELLER, *his wife*
CHRIS KELLER, *their son*
ANN DEEVER, *their house-guest*
GEORGE DEEVER, *her brother*
DR. JIM BAYLISS, *friend of the Kellers*
SUE BAYLISS, *his wife*
FRANK LUBEY } *the Kellers' next-door neighbors*
LYDIA LUBEY
BERT, *a neighborhood eight-year-old*

Synopsis of Scenes

ACT I: The back yard of the Keller home in the outskirts of an American town. August of our era.
ACT II: Scene, as before. The same evening, as twilight falls.
ACT III: Scene, as before. Two o'clock the following morning.

Act One

(The back yard of the KELLER *home in the outskirts of an American town. August of our era.*

The stage is hedged on right and left by tall, closely planted poplars which lend the yard a secluded atmosphere. Upstage is filled with the back of the house and its open, unroofed porch which extends into the yard some six feet. The house is two stories high and has seven rooms. It would have cost perhaps fifteen thousand in the early twenties when it was built. Now it is nicely painted, looks tight and comfortable, and the yard is green with sod, here and there plants whose season is gone. At the right, beside the house, the entrance of the driveway can be seen, but the poplars cut off view of its continuation downstage. In the left corner, downstage, stands the four-foot high stump of a slender apple tree whose upper trunk and branches lie toppled beside it, fruit still clinging to its branches.

Downstage right is a small, trellised arbor, shaped like a sea-shell, with a decorative bulb hanging from its forward-curving roof. Garden chairs and a table are scattered about. A garbage pail on the ground next to the porch steps, a wire leaf-burner near it.

On the rise: It is early Sunday morning. JOE KELLER *is sitting in the sun reading the want ads of the Sunday paper, the other sections of which lie neatly on the ground beside him. Behind his back, inside the arbor,* DOCTOR JIM BAYLISS *is reading part of the paper at the table.*

KELLER *is nearing sixty. A heavy man of stolid mind and build, a business man these many years, but with the imprint of the machine-shop worker and boss still upon him. When he reads, when he speaks, when he listens, it is with the terrible concentration of the uneducated man for whom there is still wonder in many commonly known things, a man whose judgments must be dredged out of experience and a peasant-like common sense. A man among men.*

DOCTOR BAYLISS *is nearing forty. A wry self-controlled man, an easy talker, but with a wisp of sadness that clings even to his self-effacing humor.*

At curtain, JIM *is standing at left, staring at the broken tree. He taps a pipe on it, blows through the pipe, feels in his pockets for tobacco, then speaks.)*

JIM. Where's your tobacco?

KELLER. I think I left it on the table. (JIM *goes slowly to table on the arbor at right, finds a pouch, and sits there on the bench, filling his pipe.)* Gonna rain tonight.

JIM. Paper says so?

KELLER. Yeah, right here.

JIM. Then it can't rain.

*(*FRANK LUBEY *enters, from right, through a small space between the poplars.* FRANK *is thirty-two but balding. A pleasant, opinionated man, uncertain of himself, with a tendency toward peevishness when crossed, but always wanting it pleasant and neighborly. He rather saunters in, leisurely, nothing to do. He does not notice* JIM *in the arbor. On his greeting,* JIM *does not bother looking up.)*

FRANK. Hya.

KELLER. Hello, Frank. What's doin'?

FRANK. Nothin'. Walking off my breakfast. (*Looks up at the sky.)* That beautiful? Not a cloud.

KELLER (*Looks up*). Yeah, nice.

FRANK. Every Sunday ought to be like this.

KELLER (*Indicating the sections beside him*). Want the paper?

FRANK. What's the difference, it's all bad news. What's today's calamity?

KELLER. I don't know, I don't read the news part any more. It's more interesting in the want ads.

FRANK. Why, you trying to buy something?

KELLER. No, I'm just interested. To see what people want, y'know? For instance, here's a guy is lookin' for two Newfoundland dogs. Now what's he want with two Newfoundland dogs?

FRANK. That is funny.

KELLER. Here's another one. Wanted—Old Dictionaries. High prices paid. Now what's a man going to do with an old dictionary?

FRANK. Why not? Probably a book collector.

KELLER. You mean he'll make a living out of that?

FRANK. Sure, there's a lot of them.

KELLER (*Shakes his head*). All the kind of business goin' on. In my day, either you were a lawyer, or a doctor, or you worked in a shop. Now . . .

FRANK. Well, I was going to be a forester once.

KELLER. Well, that shows you; in my day, there was no such thing. (*Scanning the page, sweeping it with his hand.*) You look at a page like this you realize how ignorant you are. (*Softly, with wonder, as he scans page.*) Psss!

FRANK (*Noticing tree*). Hey, what happened to your tree?

KELLER. Ain't that awful? The wind must've got it last night. You heard the wind, didn't you?

FRANK. Yeah, I got a mess in my yard, too. (*Goes to tree.*) What a pity. (*Turns to* KELLER.) What'd Kate say?

KELLER. They're all asleep yet. I'm just waiting for her to see it.

FRANK (*Struck*). You know?—It's funny.

KELLER. What?

FRANK. Larry was born in August. He'd been twenty-seven this month. And his tree blows down.

KELLER *(Touched).* I'm surprised you remember his birthday, Frank. That's nice.

FRANK. Well, I'm working on his horoscope.

KELLER. How can you make him a horoscope? That's for the future, ain't it?

FRANK. Well, what I'm doing is this, see. Larry was reported missing on November 25th, right?

KELLER. Yeah?

FRANK. Well, then, we assume that if he was killed it was on November 25th. Now, what Kate wants . . .

KELLER. Oh, Kate asked you to make a horoscope?

FRANK. Yeah, what she wants to find out is whether November 25th was a favorable day for Larry.

KELLER. What is that, favorable day?

FRANK. Well, a favorable day for a person is a fortunate day, according to his stars. In other words it would be practically impossible for him to have died on his favorable day.

KELLER. Well, was that his favorable day?—November 25th?

FRANK. That's what I'm working on to find out. It takes time! See, the point is, if November 25th was his favorable day, then it's completely possible he's alive somewhere, because . . . I mean it's possible. *(He notices* JIM *now.* JIM *is looking at him as though at an idiot. To* JIM—*with an uncertain laugh.)* I didn't even see you.

KELLER *(To* JIM*).* Is he talkin' sense?

JIM. Him? He's all right. He's just completely out of his mind, that's all.

FRANK *(Peeved).* The trouble with you is, you don't *believe* in anything.

JIM. And your trouble is that you believe in *anything.* You didn't see my kid this morning, did you?

FRANK. No.

KELLER. Imagine? He walked off with his thermometer. Right out of his bag.

JIM *(Gets up).* What a problem. One look at a girl and he takes her temperature. *(Goes to driveway, looks upstage toward street.)*

FRANK. That boy's going to be a real doctor; he's smart.

JIM. Over my dead body he'll be a doctor. A good beginning, too.

FRANK. Why? It's an honorable profession.

JIM *(Looks at him tiredly)*. Frank, will you stop talking like a civics book? (KELLER *laughs.*)

FRANK. Why, I saw a movie a couple of weeks ago, reminded me of you. There was a doctor in that picture . . .

KELLER. Don Ameche!

FRANK. I think it was, yeah. And he worked in his basement discovering things. That's what you ought to do; you could help humanity, instead of . . .

JIM. I would love to help humanity on a Warner Brothers salary.

KELLER *(Points at him, laughing)*. That's very good, Jim.

JIM *(Looks toward house)*. Well, where's the beautiful girl was supposed to be here?

FRANK *(Excited)*. Annie came?

KELLER. Sure, sleepin' upstairs. We picked her up on the one o'clock train last night. Wonderful thing. Girl leaves here, a scrawny kid. Couple of years go by, she's a regular woman. Hardly recognized her, and she was running in and out of this yard all her life. That was a very happy family used to live in your house, Jim.

JIM. Like to meet her. The block can use a pretty girl. In the whole neighborhood there's not a damned thing to look at. *(Enter* SUE, JIM'S *wife, from left. She is rounding forty, an overweight woman who fears it. On seeing her* JIM *wryly adds.)* . . . Except my wife, of course.

SUE *(In same spirit)*. Mrs. Adams is on the phone, you dog.

JIM *(To* KELLER*)*. Such is the condition which prevails, *(Going to his wife.)* my love, my light. . . .

SUE. Don't sniff around me. *(Points to their house, left.)* And give her a nasty answer. I can smell her perfume over the phone.

JIM. What's the matter with her now?

SUE. I don't know, dear. She sounds like she's in terrible pain— unless her mouth is full of candy.

JIM. Why don't you just tell her to lay down?

SUE. She enjoys it more when you tell her to lay down. And when are you going to see Mr. Hubbard?

JIM. My dear; Mr. Hubbard is not sick, and I have better things to do than to sit there and hold his hand.

SUE. It seems to me that for ten dollars you could hold his hand.

JIM (*To* KELLER). If your son wants to play golf tell him I'm ready. (*Going left.*) Or if he'd like to take a trip around the world for about thirty years. (*He exits left.*)

KELLER. Why do you needle him? He's a doctor, women are supposed to call him up.

SUE. All I said was Mrs. Adams is on the phone. Can I have some of your parsley?

KELLER. Yeah, sure. (*She goes left to parsley box and pulls some parsley.*) You were a nurse too long, Susie. You're too . . . too . . . realistic.

SUE (*Laughing, points at him*). Now you said it! (*Enter* LYDIA LUBEY *from right. She is a robust, laughing girl of twenty-seven.*)

LYDIA. Frank, the toaster . . . (*Sees the others.*) Hya.

KELLER. Hello!

LYDIA (*To* FRANK). The toaster is off again.

FRANK. Well, plug it in, I just fixed it.

LYDIA (*Kindly, but insistently*). Please, dear, fix it back like it was before.

FRANK. I don't know why you can't learn to turn on a simple thing like a toaster! (FRANK *exits right.*)

SUE (*Laughs*). Thomas Edison.

LYDIA (*Apologetically*). He's really very handy. (*She sees broken tree.*) Oh, did the wind get your tree?

KELLER. Yeah, last night.

LYDIA. Oh, what a pity. Annie get in?

KELLER. She'll be down soon. Wait'll you meet her, Sue, she's a knockout.

SUE. I should've been a man. People are always introducing me to beautiful women. (*To* JOE.) Tell her to come over later; I imagine she'd like to see what we did with her house. And thanks. (SUE *exits left.*)

LYDIA. Is she still unhappy, Joe?

KELLER. Annie? I don't suppose she goes around dancing on her toes, but she seems to be over it.

LYDIA. She going to get married? Is there anybody . . . ?

KELLER. I suppose . . . say, it's a couple years already. She can't mourn a boy forever.

LYDIA. It's so strange . . . Annie's here and not even married. And I've got three babies. I always thought it'd be the other way around.

KELLER. Well, that's what a war does. I had two sons, now I got one. It changed all the tallies. In my day when you had sons it was an honor. Today a doctor could make a million dollars if he could figure out a way to bring a boy into the world without a trigger finger.

LYDIA. You know, I was just reading . . . *(Enter* CHRIS KELLER *from house, stands in doorway.)*

LYDIA. Hya, Chris . . . *(*FRANK *shouts from off right.)*

FRANK. Lydia, come in here! If you want the toaster to work don't plug in the malted mixer.

LYDIA *(Embarrassed, laughs).* Did I . . . ?

FRANK. And the next time I fix something don't tell me I'm crazy! Now come in here!

LYDIA *(To* KELLER*).* I'll never hear the end of this one.

KELLER *(Calling to* FRANK*).* So what's the difference? Instead of toast have a malted!

LYDIA. Sh! sh! *(She exits right laughing.)*

*(*CHRIS *watches her off. He is thirty-two; like his father, solidly built, a listener. A man capable of immense affection and loyalty. He has a cup of coffee in one hand, part of a doughnut in other.)*

KELLER. You want the paper?

CHRIS. That's all right, just the book section. *(He bends down and pulls out part of paper on porch floor.)*

KELLER. You're always reading the book section and you never buy a book.

CHRIS (*Coming down to settee*). I like to keep abreast of my ignorance. (*He sits on settee.*)

KELLER. What is that, every week a new book comes out?

CHRIS. Lot of new books.

KELLER. All different.

CHRIS. All different.

KELLER (*Shakes his head, puts knife down on bench, takes oil-stone up to the cabinet*). Psss! Annie up yet?

CHRIS. Mother's giving her breakfast in the dining-room.

KELLER (*Crosses, downstage of stool, looking at broken tree*). See what happened to the tree?

CHRIS (*Without looking up*). Yeah.

KELLER. What's Mother going to say? (BERT *runs on from driveway. He is about eight. He jumps on stool, then on* KELLER's *back.*)

BERT. You're finally up.

KELLER (*Swinging him around and putting him down*). Ha! Bert's here! Where's Tommy? He's got his father's thermometer again.

BERT. He's taking a reading.

CHRIS. What!

BERT. But it's only oral.

KELLER. Oh, well, there's no harm in oral. So what's new this morning, Bert?

BERT. Nothin'. (*He goes to broken tree, walks around it.*)

KELLER. Then you couldn't've made a complete inspection of the block. In the beginning, when I first made you a police-man you used to come in every morning with something new. Now, nothin's ever new.

BERT. Except some kids from Thirtieth Street. They started kicking a can down the block, and I made them go away because you were sleeping.

KELLER. Now you're talkin', Bert. Now you're on the ball. First thing you know I'm liable to make you a detective.

BERT (*Pulls him down by the lapel and whispers in his ear*). Can I see the jail now?

KELLER. Seein' the jail ain't allowed, Bert. You know that.

BERT. Aw, I betcha there isn't even a jail. I don't see any bars on the cellar windows.

KELLER. Bert, on my word of honor, there's a jail in the basement. I showed you my gun, didn't I?

BERT. But that's a hunting gun.

KELLER. That's an arresting gun!

BERT. Then why don't you ever arrest anybody? Tommy said another dirty word to Doris yesterday, and you didn't even demote him.

KELLER (*He chuckles and winks at* CHRIS, *who is enjoying all this*). Yeah, that's a dangerous character, that Tommy. (*Beckons him closer.*) What word does he say?

BERT (*Backing away quickly in great embarrassment*). Oh, I can't say that.

KELLER (*Grabs him by the shirt and pulls him back*). Well, gimme an idea.

BERT. I can't. It's not a nice word.

KELLER. Just whisper it in my ear. I'll close my eyes. Maybe I won't even hear it.

BERT (*On tiptoe, puts his lips to* KELLER's *ear, then in unbearable embarrassment steps back*). I can't Mr. Keller.

CHRIS (*Laughing*). Don't make him do that.

KELLER. Okay, Bert. I take your word. Now go out, and keep both eyes peeled.

BERT (*Interested*). For what?

KELLER. For what! Bert, the whole neighborhood is depending on you. A policeman don't ask questions. Now peel them eyes!

BERT (*Mystified, but willing*). Okay. (*He runs off right back of arbor*).

KELLER (*Calling after him*). And mum's the word Bert.

BERT (*Stops and sticks his head thru the arbor*). About what?

KELLER. Just in general. Be v-e-r-y careful.

BERT (*Nods in bewilderment*). Okay. (BERT *exits downstage right.*)

KELLER (*Laughs*). I got all the kids crazy!

CHRIS. One of these days, they'll all come in here and beat your brains out.

KELLER. What's she going to say? Maybe we ought to tell her before she sees it.

CHRIS. She saw it.

KELLER. How could she see it? I was the first one up. She was still in bed.

CHRIS. She was out here when it broke.

KELLER. When?

CHRIS. About four this morning. *(Indicating window above them.)* I heard it cracking and I woke up and looked out. She was standing right here when it cracked.

KELLER. What was she doing out here four in the morning?

CHRIS. I don't know. When it cracked she ran back into the house and cried in the kitchen.

KELLER. Did you talk to her?

CHRIS. No, I . . . I figured the best thing was to leave her alone.

(Pause.)

KELLER *(Deeply touched)*. She cried hard?

CHRIS. I could hear her right through the floor of my room.

KELLER *(Slight pause)*. What was she doing out here at that hour? *(CHRIS silent. An undertone of anger showing.)* She's dreaming about him again. She's walking around at night.

CHRIS. I guess she is.

KELLER. She's getting just like after he died. *(Slight pause.)* What's the meaning of that?

CHRIS. I don't know the meaning of it. *(Slight pause.)* But I know one thing, Dad. We've made a terrible mistake with Mother.

KELLER. What?

CHRIS. Being dishonest with her. That kind of thing always pays off, and now it's paying off.

KELLER. What do you mean, dishonest?

CHRIS. You know Larry's not coming back and I know it. Why do we allow her to go on thinking that we believe with her?

KELLER. What do you want to do, argue with her?

CHRIS. I don't want to argue with her, but it's time she realized that nobody believes Larry is alive any more. *(KELLER simply moves away, thinking, looking at the ground.*) Why shouldn't she dream of him, walk the nights waiting for him? Do we contradict her? Do we say straight out that we have no hope any more? That we haven't had any hope for years now?

KELLER (*Frightened at the thought*). You can't say that to her.

CHRIS. We've got to say it to her.

KELLER. How're you going to prove it? Can you prove it?

CHRIS. For God's sake, three years! Nobody comes back after three years. It's insane.

KELLER. To you it is, and to me. But not to her. You can talk yourself blue in the face, but there's no body and there's no grave, so where are you?

CHRIS. Sit down, Dad. I want to talk to you.

KELLER (*Looks at him searchingly a moment, and sitting . . .*). The trouble is the Goddam newspapers. Every month some boy turns up from nowhere, so the next one is going to be Larry, so . . .

CHRIS. All right, all right, listen to me. (*Slight pause.* KELLER *sits on settee.*) You know why I asked Annie here, don't you?

KELLER (*He knows, but . . .*). Why?

CHRIS. You know.

KELLER. Well, I got an idea, but . . . What's the story?

CHRIS. I'm going to ask her to marry me. (*Slight pause.*)

KELLER (*Nods*). Well, that's only your business, Chris.

CHRIS. You know it's not only my business.

KELLER. What do you want me to do? You're old enough to know your own mind.

CHRIS (*Asking, annoyed*). Then it's all right, I'll go ahead with it?

KELLER. Well, you want to be sure Mother isn't going to . . .

CHRIS. Then it isn't just my business.

KELLER. I'm just sayin'. . . .

CHRIS. Sometimes you infuriate me, you know that? Isn't it your business, too, if I tell this to Mother and she throws a fit about it? You have such a talent for ignoring things.

KELLER. I ignore what I gotta ignore. The girl is Larry's girl . . .

CHRIS. She's not Larry's girl.

KELLER. From Mother's point of view he is not dead and you have no right to take his girl. *(Slight pause.)* Now you can go on from there if you know where to go, but I'm tellin' you I don't know where to go. See? I don't know. Now what can I do for you?

CHRIS. I don't know why it is, but every time I reach out for something I want, I have to pull back because other people will suffer. My whole bloody life, time after time after time.

KELLER. You're a considerate fella, there's nothing wrong in that.

CHRIS. To hell with that.

KELLER. Did you ask Annie yet?

CHRIS. I wanted to get this settled first.

KELLER. How do you know she'll marry you? Maybe she feels the same way Mother does?

CHRIS. Well, if she does, then that's the end of it. From her letters I think she's forgotten him. I'll find out. And then we'll thrash it out with Mother? Right? Dad, don't avoid me.

KELLER. The trouble is, you don't see enough women. You never did.

CHRIS. So what? I'm not fast with women.

KELLER. I don't see why it has to be Annie. . . .

CHRIS. Because it is.

KELLER. That's a good answer, but it don't answer anything. You haven't seen her since you went to war. It's five years.

CHRIS. I can't help it. I know her best. I was brought up next door to her. These years when I think of someone for my wife, I think of Annie. What do you want, a diagram?

KELLER. I don't want a diagram . . . I . . . I'm . . . She thinks he's coming back, Chris. You marry that girl and you're pronouncing him dead. Now what's going to happen to Mother? Do you know? I don't! *(Pause.)*

CHRIS. All right, then, Dad.

KELLER (*Thinking Chris has retreated*). Give it some more thought.

CHRIS. I've given it three years of thought. I'd hoped that if I waited, Mother would forget Larry and then we'd have a regular wedding and everything happy. But if that can't happen here, then I'll have to get out.

KELLER. What the hell is *this?*

CHRIS. I'll get out. I'll get married and live some place else. Maybe in New York.

KELLER. Are you crazy?

CHRIS. I've been a good son too long, a good sucker. I'm through with it.

KELLER. You've got a business here, what the hell is this?

CHRIS. The business! The business doesn't inspire me.

KELLER. Must you be inspired?

CHRIS. Yes. I like it an hour a day. If I have to grub for money all day long at least at evening I want it beautiful. I want a family, I want some kids, I want to build something I can give myself to. Annie is in the middle of that. Now . . . where do I find it?

KELLER. You mean . . . (*Goes to him.*) Tell me something, you mean you'd leave the business?

CHRIS. Yes. On this I would.

KELLER (*Pause*). Well . . . you don't want to think like that.

CHRIS. Then help me stay here.

KELLER. All right, but . . . but don't think like that. Because what the hell did I work for? That's only for you, Chris, the whole shootin'-match is for you!

CHRIS. I know that, Dad. Just you help me stay here.

KELLER (*Puts a fist up to* CHRIS' *jaw*). But don't think that way, you hear me?

CHRIS. I am thinking that way.

KELLER (*Lowering his hand*). I don't understand you, do I?

CHRIS. No, you don't. I'm a pretty tough guy.

KELLER. Yeah. I can see that. (MOTHER *appears on porch. She is in her early fifties, a woman of uncontrolled inspirations, and an overwhelming capacity for love.*)

MOTHER. Joe?

CHRIS (*Going toward porch*). Hello, Mom.

MOTHER (*Indicating house behind her. To* KELLER). Did you take a bag from under the sink?

KELLER. Yeah. I put it in the pail.

MOTHER. Well, get it out of the pail. That's my potatoes. (CHRIS *bursts out laughing—goes up into alley.*)

KELLER (*Laughing*). I thought it was garbage.

MOTHER. Will you do me a favor, Joe? Don't be helpful.

KELLER. I can afford another bag of potatoes.

MOTHER. Minnie scoured that pail in boiling water last night. It's cleaner than your teeth.

KELLER. And I don't understand why, after I worked forty years and I got a maid, why I have to take out the garbage.

MOTHER. If you would make up your mind that every bag in the kitchen isn't full of garbage you wouldn't be throwing out my vegetables. Last time it was the onions. (CHRIS *comes on, hands her bag.*)

KELLER. I don't like garbage in the house.

MOTHER. Then don't eat. (*She goes into the kitchen with bag.*)

CHRIS. That settles you for today.

KELLER. Yeah, I'm in last place again. I don't know, once upon a time I used to think that when I got money again I would have a maid and my wife would take it easy. Now I got money, and I got a maid, and my wife is workin' for the maid. (*He sits in one of the chairs.* MOTHER *comes out on last line. She carries a pot of stringbeans.*)

MOTHER. It's her day off, what are you crabbing about?

CHRIS (*To* MOTHER). Isn't Annie finished eating?

MOTHER (*Looking around preoccupiedly at yard*). She'll be right out. (*Moves.*) That wind did some job on this place. (*Of the tree.*) So much for that, thank God.

KELLER (*Indicating chair beside him*). Sit down, take it easy.

MOTHER (*She presses her hand to top of her head*). I've got such a funny pain on the top of my head.

CHRIS. Can I get you an aspirin?

MOTHER (*Picks a few petals off ground, stands there smelling them in her hand, then sprinkles them over plants*). No more roses. It's so funny . . . everything decides to happen at the

same time. This month is his birthday; his tree blows down,
Annie comes. Everything that happened seems to be coming back. I was just down the cellar, and what do I stumble
over? His baseball glove. I haven't seen it in a century.

CHRIS. Don't you think Annie looks well?

MOTHER. Fine. There's no question about it. She's a beauty
. . . I still don't know what brought her here. Not that I'm
not glad to see her, but . . .

CHRIS. I just thought we'd all like to see each other again.
(MOTHER *just looks at him, nodding ever so slightly—almost
as though admitting something.*) And I wanted to see her
myself.

MOTHER (*Her nods halt. To* KELLER). The only thing is I think
her nose got longer. But I'll always love that girl. She's one
that didn't jump into bed with somebody else as soon as it
happened with her fella.

KELLER (*As though that were impossible for Annie*). Oh,
what're you . . . ?

MOTHER. Never mind. Most of them didn't wait till the tele-
grams were opened. I'm just glad she came, so you can see
I'm not *completely* out of my mind. (*Sits, and rapidly breaks
stringbeans in the pot.*)

CHRIS. Just because she isn't married doesn't mean she's been
mourning Larry.

MOTHER (*With an undercurrent of observation*). Why then
isn't she?

CHRIS (*A little flustered*). Well . . . it could've been any number
of things.

MOTHER (*Directly at him*). Like what, for instance?

CHRIS (*Embarrassed, but standing his ground*). I don't know.
Whatever it is. Can I get you an aspirin? (MOTHER *puts her
hand to her head.*)

MOTHER (*She gets up and goes aimlessly toward the trees on
rising*). It's not like a headache.

KELLER. You don't sleep, that's why. She's wearing out more
bedroom slippers than shoes.

MOTHER. I had a terrible night. (*She stops moving.*) I never
had a night like that.

CHRIS *(Looks at* KELLER*).* What was it, Mom? Did you dream?

MOTHER. More, more than a dream.

CHRIS *(Hesitantly).* About Larry?

MOTHER. I was fast asleep, and . . . *(Raising her arm over the audience.)* Remember the way he used to fly low past the house when he was in training? When we used to see his face in the cockpit going by? That's the way I saw him. Only high up. Way, way up, where the clouds are. He was so real I could reach out and touch him. And suddenly he started to fall. And crying, crying to me . . . Mom, Mom! I could hear him like he was in the room. Mom! . . . it was his voice! If I could touch him I knew I could stop him, if I could only . . . *(Breaks off, allowing her outstretched hand to fall.)* I woke up and it was so funny . . . The wind . . . it was like the roaring of his engine. I came out here . . . I must've still been half asleep. I could hear that roaring like he was going by. The tree snapped right in front of me . . . and I like . . . came awake. *(She is looking at tree. She suddenly realizes something, turns with a reprimanding finger shaking slightly at* KELLER*.)* See? We should never have planted that tree. I said so in the first place; it was too soon to plant a tree for him.

CHRIS *(Alarmed).* Too soon!

MOTHER *(Angering).* We rushed into it. Everybody was in such a hurry to bury him. I *said* not to plant it yet. *(To* KELLER*.)* I *told* you to . . . !

CHRIS. Mother, Mother! *(She looks into his face.)* The wind blew it down. What significance has that got? What are you talking about? Mother, please . . . Don't go through it all again, will you? It's no good, it doesn't accomplish anything. I've been thinking y'know?—maybe we ought to put our minds to forgetting him?

MOTHER. That's the third time you've said that this week.

CHRIS. Because it's not right; we never took up our lives again. We're like at a railroad station waiting for a train that never comes in.

MOTHER *(Presses top of her head).* Get me an aspirin, heh?

CHRIS. Sure, and let's break out of this, heh, Mom? I thought the four of us might go out to dinner a couple of nights, maybe go dancing out at the shore.

MOTHER. Fine. (*To* KELLER.) We can do it tonight.

KELLER. Swell with me!

CHRIS. Sure, let's have some fun. (*To* MOTHER.) You'll start with this aspirin. (*He goes up and into house with new spirit. Her smile vanishes.*)

MOTHER (*With an accusing undertone*). Why did he invite her here?

KELLER. Why does that bother you?

MOTHER. She's been in New York three and a half years, why all of a sudden . . . ?

KELLER. Well, maybe . . . maybe he just wanted to see her . . .

MOTHER. Nobody comes seven hundred miles "just to see."

KELLER. What do you mean? He lived next door to the girl all his life, why shouldn't he want to see her again? (MOTHER *looks at him critically.*) Don't look at me like that, he didn't tell me any more than he told you.

MOTHER (*A warning and a question*). He's not going to marry her.

KELLER. How do you know he's even thinking of it?

MOTHER. It's got that about it.

KELLER (*Sharply watching her reaction*). Well? So what?

MOTHER (*Alarmed*). What's going on here, Joe?

KELLER. Now listen, kid . . .

MOTHER (*Avoiding contact with him*). She's not his girl, Joe; she knows she's not.

KELLER. You can't read her mind.

MOTHER. Then why is she still single? New York is full of men, why isn't she married? (*Pause.*) Probably a hundred people told her she's foolish, but she's waited.

KELLER. How do you know why she waited?

MOTHER. She knows what I know, that's why. She's faithful as a rock. In my worst moments, I think of her waiting, and I know again that I'm right.

KELLER. Look, it's a nice day. What are we arguing for?

MOTHER (*Warningly*). Nobody in this house dast take her faith away, Joe. Strangers might. But not his father, not his brother.

KELLER (*Exasperated*). What do you want me to do? What do you want?

MOTHER. I want you to act like he's coming back. Both of you. Don't think I haven't noticed you since Chris invited her. I won't stand for any nonsense.

KELLER. But, Kate . . .

MOTHER. Because if he's not coming back, then I'll kill myself! Laugh. Laugh at me. (*She points to tree.*) But why did that happen the very night she came back? Laugh, but there are meanings in such things. She goes to sleep in his room and his memorial breaks in pieces. Look at it; look. (*She sits on bench at his left.*) Joe . . .

KELLER. Calm yourself.

MOTHER. Believe with me, Joe. I can't stand all alone.

KELLER. Calm yourself.

MOTHER. Only last week a man turned up in Detroit, missing longer than Larry. You read it yourself.

KELLER. All right, all right, calm yourself.

MOTHER. You above all have got to believe, you . . .

KELLER (*Rises*). Why me above all?

MOTHER. . . . Just don't stop believing . . .

KELLER. What does that mean, me above all? (BERT *comes rushing on from left.*)

BERT. Mr. Keller! Say, Mr. Keller . . . (*Pointing up driveway.*) Tommy just said it again!

KELLER (*Not remembering any of it*). Said what? . . . Who? . . .

BERT. The dirty word.

KELLER. Oh. Well . . .

BERT. Gee, aren't you going to arrest him? I warned him.

MOTHER (*With suddenness*). Stop that, Bert. Go home. (BERT *backs up, as she advances.*) There's no jail here.

KELLER (*As though to say, "Oh-what-the-hell-let-him-believe-there-is."*). Kate . . .

MOTHER (*Turning on* KELLER, *furiously*). There's no jail here! I want you to stop that jail business! (*He turns, shamed, but peeved.*)

BERT (*Past her to* KELLER). He's right across the street.

MOTHER. Go home, Bert. (BERT *turns around and goes up driveway. She is shaken. Her speech is bitten off, extremely urgent.*) I want you to stop that, Joe. That whole jail business!

KELLER (*Alarmed, therefore angered*). Look at you, look at you shaking.

MOTHER (*Trying to control herself, moving about clasping her hands*). I can't help it.

KELLER. What have I got to hide? What the hell is the matter with you, Kate?

MOTHER. I didn't say you had anything to hide, I'm just telling you to stop it; now stop it! (*As* ANN *and* CHRIS *appear on porch.* ANN *is twenty-six, gentle but despite herself capable of holding fast to what she knows.* CHRIS *opens door for her.*)

ANN. Hya, Joe! (*She leads off a general laugh that is not self-conscious because they know one another too well.*)

CHRIS (*Bringing* ANN *down, with an outstretched, chivalric arm*). Take a breath of that air, kid. You never get air like that in New York.

MOTHER (*Genuinely overcome with it*). Annie, where did you get that dress!

ANN. I couldn't resist. I'm taking it right off before I ruin it. (*Swings around.*) How's that for three weeks' salary?

MOTHER (*To* KELLER). Isn't she the most . . . ? (*To* ANN.) It's gorgeous, simply gor . . .

CHRIS (*To* MOTHER). No kidding, now, isn't she the prettiest gal you ever saw?

MOTHER (*Caught short by his obvious admiration, she finds herself reaching out for a glass of water and aspirin in his hand, and . . .*) You gained a little weight, didn't you, darling? (*She gulps pill and drinks.*)

ANN. It comes and goes.

KELLER. Look how nice her legs turned out!

ANN (*She runs to fence, left*). Boy, the poplars got thick, didn't they?

KELLER (*Moves upstage to settee and sits*). Well, it's three years, Annie. We're gettin' old, kid.

MOTHER. How does Mom like New York? (ANN *keeps looking through trees.*)

ANN (*A little hurt*). Why'd they take our hammock away?

KELLER. Oh, no, it broke. Couple of years ago.

MOTHER. What broke? He had one of his light lunches and flopped into it.

ANN (*She laughs and turns back toward* JIM's *yard. . . .*) Oh, excuse me! (JIM *has come to fence and is looking over it. He is smoking a cigar. As she cries out, he comes on around on stage.*)

JIM. How do you do. (*To* CHRIS.) She looks very intelligent!

CHRIS. Ann, this is Jim . . . Doctor Bayliss.

ANN (*Shaking* JIM's *hand*). Oh sure, he writes a lot about you.

JIM. Don't believe it. He likes everybody. In the Battalion he was known as Mother McKeller.

ANN. I can believe it . . . You know——? (*To* MOTHER.) It's so strange seeing him come out of that yard. (*To* CHRIS.) I guess I never grew up. It almost seems that Mom and Pop are in there now. And you and my brother doing Algebra, and Larry trying to copy my home-work. Gosh, those dear dead days beyond recall.

JIM. Well, I hope that doesn't mean you want me to move out?

SUE (*Calling from off left*). Jim, come in here! Mr. Hubbard is on the phone!

JIM. I told you I don't want . . .

SUE (*Commandingly sweet*). Please, dear! Please!!

JIM (*Resigned*). All right, Susie, (*Trailing off.*) all right, all right . . . (*To* ANN.) I've only met you, Ann, but if I may offer you a piece of advice—When you marry, never—even in your mind—never count your husband's money.

SUE (*From off*). Jim?!

JIM. At once! (*Turns and goes left.*) At once. (*He exits left.*)

MOTHER (ANN *is looking at her. She speaks meaningfully*). I told her to take up the guitar. It'd be a common interest for them. (*They laugh.*) Well, he loves the guitar!

ANN (*As though to overcome* MOTHER, *she becomes suddenly*

lively, crosses to KELLER *on settee, sits on his lap).* Let's eat at the shore tonight! Raise some hell around here, like we used to before Larry went!

MOTHER *(Emotionally).* You think of him! You see? *(Triumphantly.)* She thinks of him!

ANN *(With an uncomprehending smile).* What do you mean, Kate?

MOTHER. Nothing. Just that you . . . remember him, he's in your thoughts.

ANN. That's a funny thing to say; how could I help remembering him?

MOTHER *(It is drawing to a head the wrong way for her; she starts anew. She rises and comes to* ANN*).* Did you hang up your things?

ANN. Yeah . . . *(To* CHRIS.*)* Say, you've sure gone in for clothes. I could hardly find room in the closet.

MOTHER. No, don't you remember? That's Larry's room.

ANN. You mean . . . they're Larry's?

MOTHER. Didn't you recognize them?

ANN *(Slowly rising, a little embarrassed).* Well, it never occurred to me that you'd . . . I mean the shoes are all shined.

MOTHER. Yes, dear. *(Slight pause.* ANN *can't stop staring at her.* MOTHER *breaks it by speaking with the relish of gossip, putting her arm around* ANN *and walking stage left with her.)* For so long I've been aching for a nice conversation with you, Annie. Tell me something.

ANN. What?

MOTHER. I don't know. Something nice.

CHRIS *(Wryly).* She means do you go out much?

MOTHER. Oh, shut up.

KELLER. And are any of them serious?

MOTHER *(Laughing, sits in her chair).* Why don't you both choke?

KELLER. Annie, you can't go into a restaurant with that woman any more. In five minutes thirty-nine strange people are sitting at the table telling her their life story.

MOTHER. If I can't ask Annie a personal question . . .

KELLER. Askin' is all right, but don't beat her over the head.

You're beatin' her, you're beatin' her. *(They are laughing.)*

ANN *(To* MOTHER. *Takes pan of beans off stool, puts them on floor under chair and sits).* Don't let them bulldoze you. Ask me anything you like. What do you want to know, Kate? Come on, let's gossip.

MOTHER *(To* CHRIS *and* KELLER*).* She's the only one is got any sense. *(To* ANN.*)* Your mother . . . She's not getting a divorce, heh?

ANN. No, she's calmed down about it now. I think when he gets out they'll probably live together. In New York, of course.

MOTHER. That's fine. Because your father is still . . . I mean he's a decent man after all is said and done.

ANN. I don't care. She can take him back if she likes.

MOTHER. And you? You . . . *(Shakes her head negatively.)* . . . go out much? *(Slight pause.)*

ANN *(Delicately).* You mean am I still waiting for him?

MOTHER. Well, no, I don't expect you to wait for him but . . .

ANN *(Kindly).* But that's what you mean, isn't it?

MOTHER. . . . Well . . . yes.

ANN. Well, I'm not, Kate.

MOTHER *(Faintly).* You're not?

ANN. Isn't it ridiculous? You don't really imagine he's . . . ?

MOTHER. I know, dear, but don't say it's ridiculous, because the papers were full of it; I don't know about New York, but there was half a page about a man missing even longer than Larry, and he turned up from Burma.

CHRIS *(Coming to* ANN*).* He couldn't have wanted to come home very badly, Mom.

MOTHER. Don't be so smart.

CHRIS. You can have a helluva time in Burma.

ANN *(Rises and swings around in back of* CHRIS*).* So I've heard.

CHRIS. Mother, I'll bet you money that you're the only woman in the country who after three years is still . . .

MOTHER. You're sure?

CHRIS. Yes, I am.

MOTHER. Well, if you're sure then you're sure. *(She turns her head away an instant.)* They don't say it on the radio but I'm sure that in the dark at night they're still waiting for their sons.

CHRIS. Mother, you're absolutely——

MOTHER *(Waving him off).* Don't be so damned smart! Now stop it! *(Slight pause.)* There are just a few things you *don't* know. All of you. And I'll tell you one of them, Annie. Deep, deep in your heart you've always been waiting for him.

ANN *(Resolutely).* No, Kate.

MOTHER *(With increasing demand).* But deep in your heart, Annie!

CHRIS. She ought to know, shouldn't she?

MOTHER. Don't let them tell you what to think. Listen to your heart. Only your heart.

ANN. Why does your heart tell you he's alive?

MOTHER. Because he has to be.

ANN. But why, Kate?

MOTHER *(Going to her).* Because certain things have to be, and certain things can never be. Like the sun has to rise, it has to be. That's why there's God. Otherwise anything could happen. But there's God, so certain things can never happen. I would know, Annie—just like I knew the day he *(indicates* CHRIS.*)* went into that terrible battle. Did he write me? Was it in the papers? No, but that morning I couldn't raise my head off the pillow. Ask Joe. Suddenly, I knew. I knew! And he was nearly killed that day. Ann, you *know* I'm right!

ANN *(She stands there in silence, then turns trembling, going upstage).* No, Kate.

MOTHER. I have to have some tea. *(FRANK appears from left, carrying ladder.)*

FRANK. Annie! *(Coming down.)* How are you, gee whiz!

ANN *(Taking his hand).* Why, Frank, you're losing your hair.

KELLER. He's got responsibility.

FRANK. Gee whiz!

KELLER. Without Frank the stars wouldn't know when to come out.

FRANK (*Laughs. To* ANN). You look more womanly. You've matured. You . . .

KELLER. Take it easy, Frank, you're a married man.

ANN (*As they laugh*). You still haberdashering?

FRANK. Why not? Maybe I too can get to be president. How's your brother? Got his degree, I hear.

ANN. Oh, George has his own office now!

FRANK. Don't say! (*Funereally.*) And your dad? Is he . . . ?

ANN (*Abruptly*). Fine. I'll be in to see Lydia.

FRANK (*Sympathetically*). How about it, does Dad expect a parole soon?

ANN (*With growing ill-ease*). I really don't know, I . . .

FRANK (*Staunchly defending her father for her sake*). I mean because I feel, y'know, that if an intelligent man like your father is put in prison, there ought to be a law that says either you execute him, or let him go after a year.

CHRIS (*Interrupting*). Want a hand with that ladder, Frank?

FRANK (*Taking cue*). That's all right, I'll . . . (*Picks up ladder.*) I'll finish the horoscope tonight, Kate. (*Embarrassed.*) See you later, Ann, you look wonderful. (*He exits right. They look at* ANN.)

ANN (*To* CHRIS, *sits slowly on stool*). Haven't they stopped talking about Dad?

CHRIS (*Comes down and sits on arm of chair*). Nobody talks about him any more.

KELLER (*Rises and comes to her*). Gone and forgotten, kid.

ANN. Tell me. Because I don't want to meet anybody on the block if they're going to . . .

CHRIS. I don't want you to worry about it.

ANN (*To* KELLER). Do they still remember the case, Joe? Do they talk about you?

KELLER. The only one still talks about it is my wife.

MOTHER. That's because you keep on playing policeman with the kids. All their parents hear out of you is jail, jail, jail.

KELLER. Actually what happened was that when I got home from the penitentiary the kids got very interested in me. You know kids. I was (*Laughs.*) like the expert on the jail situ-

ation. And as time passed they got it confused and . . . I
ended up a detective. (*Laughs.*)

MOTHER. Except that *they* didn't get it confused. (*To* ANN.)
He hands out police badges from the Post Toasties boxes.
(*They laugh.*)

ANN (*Wondrously at them, happily. She rises and comes to*
KELLER, *putting her arm around his shoulder*). Gosh, it's
wonderful to hear you laughing about it.

CHRIS. Why, what'd you expect?

ANN. The last thing I remember on this block was one word—
"Murderers!" Remember that, Kate? . . . Mrs. Hammond
standing in front of our house and yelling that word . . .
She's still around, I suppose?

MOTHER. They're all still around.

KELLER. Don't listen to her. Every Saturday night the whole
gang is playin' poker in this arbor. All the ones who yelled
murderer takin' my money now.

MOTHER. Don't, Joe, she's a sensitive girl, don't fool her. (*To*
ANN.) They still remember about Dad. It's different with
him—(*Indicates* JOE.)—he was exonerated, your father's
still there. That's why I wasn't so enthusiastic about your
coming. Honestly, I know how sensitive you are, and I told
Chris, I said . . .

KELLER. Listen, you do like I did and you'll be all right. The
day I come home, I got out of my car;—but not in front
of the house . . . on the corner. You should've been here,
Annie, and you too, Chris; you'd-a seen something. Everybody knew I was getting out that day; the porches were
loaded. Picture it now; none of them believed I was innocent. The story was, I pulled a fast one getting myself
exonerated. So I get out of my car, and I walk down the
street. But very slow. And with a smile. The beast! I was
the beast; the guy who sold cracked cylinder heads to the
Army Air Force; the guy who made twenty-one P-40's crash
in Australia. Kid, walkin' down the street that day I was
guilty as hell. Except I wasn't, and there was a court paper
in my pocket to prove I wasn't, and I walked . . . past . . .
the porches. Result? Fourteen months later I had one of

the best shops in the state again, a respected man again; bigger than ever.

CHRIS *(With admiration).* Joe McGuts.

KELLER *(Now with great force).* That's the only way you lick 'em is guts! *(To* ANN.*)* The worst thing you did was to move away from here. You made it tough for your father when he gets out. That's why I tell you, I like to see him move back right on this block.

MOTHER *(Pained).* How could they move back?

KELLER. It ain't gonna end *till* they move back! *(To* ANN.*)* Till people play cards with him again, and talk with him, and smile with him—you play cards with a man you know he can't be a murderer. And the next time you write him I like you to tell him just what I said. *(*ANN *simply stares at him.)* You hear me?

ANN *(Surprised).* Don't you hold anything against him?

KELLER. Annie, I never believed in crucifying people.

ANN *(Mystified).* But he was your partner, he dragged you through the mud . . .

KELLER. Well, he ain't my sweetheart, but you gotta forgive, don't you?

ANN. You, either, Kate? Don't you feel any . . . ?

KELLER *(To* ANN*).* The next time you write Dad . . .

ANN. I don't write him.

KELLER *(Struck).* Well every now and then you . . .

ANN *(A little ashamed, but determined).* No, I've *never* written to him. Neither has my brother. *(To* CHRIS.*)* Say, do you feel this way, too?

CHRIS. He murdered twenty-one pilots.

KELLER. What the hell kinda talk is that?

MOTHER. That's not a thing to say about a man.

ANN. What else can you say? When they took him away I followed him, went to him every visiting day. I was crying all the time. Until the news came about Larry. Then I realized. It's wrong to pity a man like that. Father or no father, there's only one way to look at him. He knowingly shipped out parts that would crash an airplane. And how do you know Larry wasn't one of them?

MOTHER. I was waiting for that. *(Going to her.)* As long as you're here, Annie, I want to ask you never to say that again.

ANN. You surprise me. I thought you'd be mad at him.

MOTHER. What your father did had nothing to do with Larry. Nothing.

ANN. But we can't know that.

MOTHER *(Striving for control)*. As long as you're here!

ANN *(Perplexed)*. But, Kate . . .

MOTHER. Put that out of your head!

KELLER. Because . . .

MOTHER *(Quickly to KELLER)*. That's all, that's enough. *(Places her hand on her head.)* Come inside now, and have some tea with me. *(She turns and goes up steps.)*

KELLER *(To ANN)*. The one thing you . . .

MOTHER *(Sharply)*. He's not dead, so there's no argument! Now come!

KELLER *(Angrily)*. In a minute! (MOTHER *turns and goes into house.)* Now look, Annie . . .

CHRIS. All right, Dad, forget it.

KELLER. No, she dasn't feel that way. Annie . . .

CHRIS. I'm sick of the whole subject, now cut it out.

KELLER. You want her to go on like this? *(To ANN.)* Those cylinder heads went into P-40's only. What's the matter with you? You know Larry never flew a P-40.

CHRIS. So who flew those P-40's, pigs?

KELLER. The man was a fool, but don't make a murderer out of him. You got no sense? Look what it does to her! *(To ANN.)* Listen, you gotta appreciate what was doin' in that shop in the war. The both of you! It was a madhouse. Every half hour the Major callin' for cylinder heads, they were whippin' us with the telephone. The trucks were hauling them away hot, damn near. I mean just try to see it human, see it human. All of a sudden a batch comes out with a crack. That happens, that's the business. A fine, hairline crack. All right, so . . . so he's a little man, your father, always scared of loud voices. What'll the Major say?—Half a day's production shot. . . . What'll I say? You know what I mean? Human. *(He pauses.)* So he takes out his tools and he . . . covers over the cracks. All right . . . that's bad, it's wrong, but that's what a little man does. If I could have gone in that day I'd a told him—junk 'em, Herb, we can afford it. But alone he was afraid. But I know he meant no harm. He believed they'd hold up a hundred percent. That's a mistake, but it ain't murder. You mustn't feel that way about him. You understand me? It ain't right.

ANN (*She regards him a moment*). Joe, let's forget it.

KELLER. Annie, the day the news came about Larry he was in the next cell to mine . . . Dad. And he cried, Annie . . . he cried half the night.

ANN (*Touched*). He shoulda cried all night. (*Slight pause.*)

KELLER (*Almost angered*). Annie, I do not understand why you . . . !

CHRIS (*Breaking in—with nervous urgency*). Are you going to stop it?!

ANN. Don't yell at him. He just wants everybody happy.

KELLER (*Clasps her around waist, smiling*). That's my sentiments. Can you stand steak?

CHRIS. And champagne!

KELLER. Now you're operatin'! I'll call Swanson's for a table! Big time tonight, Annie!

ANN. Can't scare me.

KELLER (*To* CHRIS, *pointing at* ANN). I like that girl. Wrap her up. (*They laugh. Goes up porch.*) You got nice legs, Annie! . . . I want to see everybody drunk tonight. (*Pointing to* CHRIS.) Look at him, he's blushin'! (*He exits, laughing, into house.*)

CHRIS (*Calling after him*). Drink your tea, Casanova. (*He turns to* ANN.) Isn't he a great guy?

ANN. You're the only one I know who loves his parents!

CHRIS. I know. It went out of style, didn't it?

ANN (*With a sudden touch of sadness*). It's all right. It's a good thing. (*She looks about.*) You know? It's lovely here. The air is sweet.

CHRIS (*Hopefully*). You're not sorry you came?

ANN. Not sorry, no. But I'm . . . not going to stay . . .

CHRIS. Why?

ANN. In the first place, your mother as much as told me to go.

CHRIS. Well . . .

ANN. You saw that . . . and then you . . . you've been kind of . . .

CHRIS. What?

ANN. Well . . . kind of embarrassed ever since I got here.

CHRIS. The trouble is I planned on kind of sneaking up on you over a period of a week or so. But they take it for granted that we're all set.

ANN. I knew they would. Your mother anyway.

CHRIS. How did you know?

ANN. From *her* point of view, why else would I come?

CHRIS. Well . . . would you want to? (ANN *studies him.*) I guess you know this is why I asked you to come.

ANN. I guess this is why I came.

CHRIS. Ann, I love you. I love you a great deal. *(Finally.)* I love you. *(Pause. She waits.)* I have no imagination . . . that's all I know to tell you. (ANN, *waiting, ready.*) I'm embarrassing you. I didn't want to tell it to you here. I wanted some place we'd never been; a place where we'd be brand new to each other. . . . You feel it's wrong here, don't you? This yard, this chair? I want you to be ready for me. I don't want to win you away from anything.

ANN *(Putting her arms around him).* Oh, Chris, I've been ready a long, long time!

CHRIS. Then he's gone forever. You're sure.

ANN. I almost got married two years ago.

CHRIS. . . . why didn't you?

ANN. You started to write to me . . . *(Slight pause.)*

CHRIS. You felt something that far back?

ANN. Every day since!

CHRIS. Ann, why didn't you let me know?

ANN. I was waiting for you Chris. Till then you never wrote. And when you did, what did you say? You sure can be ambiguous, you know.

CHRIS *(He looks toward house, then at her, trembling).* Give me a kiss, Ann. Give me a . . . *(They kiss.)* God, I kissed you,

Annie, I kissed Annie. How long, how long I've been waiting to kiss you!

ANN. I'll never forgive you. Why did you wait all these years? All I've done is sit and wonder if I was crazy for thinking of you.

CHRIS. Annie, we're going to live now! I'm going to make you so happy. (*He kisses her, but without their bodies touching.*)

ANN (*A little embarrassed*). Not like that you're not.

CHRIS. I kissed you . . .

ANN. Like Larry's brother. Do it like you, Chris. (*He breaks away from her abruptly.*) What is it, Chris?

CHRIS. Let's drive some place . . . I want to be alone with you.

ANN. No . . . what is it, Chris, your mother?

CHRIS. No . . . nothing like that . . .

ANN. Then what's wrong? . . . Even in your letters, there was something ashamed.

CHRIS. Yes. I suppose I have been. But it's going from me.

ANN. You've got to tell me—

CHRIS. I don't know how to start. (*He takes her hand. He speaks quietly, factually at first.*)

ANN. It wouldn't work this way. (*Slight pause.*)

CHRIS. It's all mixed up with so many other things. . . . You remember, overseas, I was in command of a company?

ANN. Yeah, sure.

CHRIS. Well, I lost them.

ANN. How many?

CHRIS. Just about all.

ANN. Oh, gee!

CHRIS. It takes a little time to toss that off. Because they weren't just men. For instance, one time it'd been raining several days and this kid came to me, and gave me his last pair of dry socks. Put them in my pocket. That's only a little thing . . . but . . . that's the kind of guys I had. They didn't die; they killed themselves for each other. I mean that exactly; a little more selfish and they'd've been here today. And I got an idea—watching them go down. Everything was being destroyed, see, but it seemed to me that one new thing was made. A kind of . . . responsibility. Man for man.

You understand me?—To show that, to bring that on to the earth again like some kind of a monument and everyone would feel it standing there, behind him, and it would make a difference to him. *(Pause.)* And then I came home and it was incredible. I . . . there was no meaning in it here; the whole thing to them was a kind of a—bus accident. I went to work with Dad, and that rat-race again. I felt . . . what you said . . . ashamed somehow. Because nobody was changed at all. It seemed to make suckers out of a lot of guys. I felt wrong to be alive, to open the bank-book, to drive the new car, to see the new refrigerator. I mean you can take those things out of a war, but when you drive that car you've got to know that it came out of the love a man can have for a man, you've got to be a little better because of that. Otherwise what you have is really loot, and there's blood on it. I didn't want to take any of it. And I guess that included you.

ANN. And you still feel that way?

CHRIS. I want you now, Annie.

ANN. Because you mustn't feel that way any more. Because you have a right to whatever you have. Everything, Chris, understand that? To me, too . . . And the money, there's nothing wrong in your money. Your father put hundreds of planes in the air, you should be proud. A man should be paid for that . . .

CHRIS. Oh, Annie, Annie . . . I'm going to make a fortune for you!

KELLER *(Offstage)*. Hello . . . Yes. Sure.

ANN *(Laughing softly)*. What'll I do with a fortune . . . ? *(They kiss. KELLER enters from house.)*

KELLER *(Thumbing toward house)*. Hey, Ann, your brother . . . *(They step apart shyly. KELLER comes down, and wryly . . .)* What is this, Labor Day?

CHRIS *(Waving him away, knowing the kidding will be endless)*. All right, all right . . .

ANN. You shouldn't burst out like that.

KELLER. Well, nobody told me it was Labor Day. *(Looks around.)* Where's the hot dogs?

CHRIS (*Loving it*). All right. You said it once.

KELLER. Well, as long as I know it's Labor Day from now on, I'll wear a bell around my neck.

ANN (*Affectionately*). He's so subtle!

CHRIS. George Bernard Shaw as an elephant.

KELLER. George—hey, you kissed it out of my head—your brother's on the phone.

ANN (*Surprised*). My brother?

KELLER. Yeah, George. Long distance.

ANN. What's the matter, is anything wrong?

KELLER. I don't know, Kate's talking to him. Hurry up, she'll cost him five dollars.

ANN (*She takes a step upstage, then comes down toward* CHRIS). I wonder if we ought to tell your mother yet? I mean I'm not very good in an argument.

CHRIS. We'll wait till tonight. After dinner. Now don't get tense, just leave it to me.

KELLER. What're you telling her?

CHRIS. Go ahead, Ann. (*With misgivings,* ANN *goes up and into house.*) We're getting married, Dad. (KELLER *nods indecisively.*) Well, don't you say anything?

KELLER (*Distracted*). I'm glad, Chris, I'm just . . . George is calling from Columbus.

CHRIS. Columbus!

KELLER. Did Annie tell you he was going to see his father today?

CHRIS. No, I don't think she knew anything about it.

KELLER (*Asking uncomfortably*). Chris! You . . . you think you know her pretty good?

CHRIS (*Hurt and apprehensive*). What kind of a question . . . ?

KELLER. I'm just wondering. All these years George don't go to see his father. Suddenly he goes . . . and she comes here.

CHRIS. Well, what about it?

KELLER. It's crazy, but it comes to my mind. She don't hold nothin' against me, does she?

CHRIS (*Angry*). I don't know what you're talking about.

KELLER (*A little more combatively*). I'm just talkin'. To his last day in court the man blamed it all on me; and this is his daughter. I mean if she was sent here to find out something?

CHRIS *(Angered)*. Why? What is there to find out?

ANN *(On phone, offstage)*. Why are you so excited, George? What happened there?

KELLER. I mean if they want to open up the case again, for the nuisance value, to hurt us?

CHRIS. Dad . . . how could you think that of her? ⎫

ANN *(Still on phone)*. But what did he say to ⎬ *(Together.)*
you, for God's sake? ⎭

KELLER. It couldn't be, heh. You know.

CHRIS. Dad, you amaze me . . .

KELLER *(Breaking in)*. All right, forget it, forget it. *(With great force, moving about.)* I want a clean start for you, Chris. I want a new sign over the plant—Christopher Keller, Incorporated.

CHRIS *(A little uneasily)*. J. O. Keller is good enough.

KELLER. We'll talk about it. I'm going to build you a house, stone, with a driveway from the road. I want you to spread out, Chris, I want you to use what I made for you . . . *(He is close to him now.)* . . . I mean, with joy, Chris, without shame . . . with joy.

CHRIS *(Touched)*. I will, Dad.

KELLER *(With deep emotion)*. . . . Say it to me.

CHRIS. Why?

KELLER. Because sometimes I think you're . . . ashamed of the money.

CHRIS. No, don't feel that.

KELLER. Because it's good money, there's nothing wrong with that money.

CHRIS *(A little frightened)*. Dad, you don't have to tell me this.

KELLER *(With overriding affection and self-confidence now. He grips CHRIS by the back of the neck, and with laughter between his determined jaws)*. Look, Chris, I'll go to work on Mother for you. We'll get her so drunk tonight we'll all get married! *(Steps away, with a wide gesture of his arm.)* There's gonna be a wedding, kid, like there never was seen! Champagne, tuxedoes . . . !

(He breaks off as ANN's *voice comes out loud from the house where she is still talking on phone.)*

ANN. Simply because when you get excited you don't control yourself. . . . (MOTHER *comes out of house.)* Well, what did he tell you for God's sake? *(Pause.)* All right, come then. *(Pause.)* Yes, they'll all be here. Nobody's running away from you. And try to get hold of yourself, will you? *(Pause.)* All right, all right. Goodbye. *(There is a brief pause as* ANN *hangs up receiver, then comes out of kitchen.)*

CHRIS. Something happen?

KELLER. He's coming here?

ANN. On the seven o'clock. He's in Columbus. *(To* MOTHER.*)* I told him it would be all right.

KELLER. Sure, fine! Your father took sick?

ANN *(Mystified).* No, George didn't say he was sick. I . . . *(Shaking it off.)* I don't know, I suppose it's something stupid, you know my brother . . . *(She comes to* CHRIS.*)* Let's go for a drive, or something . . .

CHRIS. Sure. Give me the keys, Dad.

MOTHER. Drive through the park. It's beautiful now.

CHRIS. Come on, Ann. *(To them.)* Be back right away.

ANN *(As she and* CHRIS *exit up driveway).* See you. *(MOTHER comes down toward* KELLER, *her eyes fixed on him.)*

KELLER. Take your time. *(To* MOTHER.*)* What does George want?

MOTHER. He's been in Columbus since this morning with Steve. He's gotta see Annie right away, he says.

KELLER. What for?

MOTHER. I don't know. *(She speaks with warning.)* He's a lawyer now, Joe. George is a lawyer. All these years he never even sent a postcard to Steve. Since he got back from the war, not a postcard.

KELLER. So what?

MOTHER *(Her tension breaking out).* Suddenly he takes an airplane from New York to see him. An airplane!

KELLER. Well? So?

MOTHER *(Trembling).* Why?

KELLER. I don't read minds. Do you?

MOTHER. Why, Joe? What has Steve suddenly got to tell him that he takes an airplane to see him?

KELLER. What do I care what Steve's got to tell him?

MOTHER. You're sure, Joe?

KELLER *(Frightened, but angry)*. Yes, I'm sure.

MOTHER *(She sits stiffly in a chair)*. Be smart now, Joe. The boy is coming. Be smart.

KELLER *(Desperately)*. Once and for all, did you hear what I said? I said I'm sure!

MOTHER *(She nods weakly)*. All right, Joe. *(He straightens up.)* Just . . . be smart. (KELLER, *in hopeless fury, looks at her, turns around, goes up to porch and into house, slamming screen door violently behind him.* MOTHER *sits in chair downstage, stiffly, staring, seeing.)*

Act Two

(As twilight falls, that evening.

On the rise, CHRIS *is discovered at right, sawing the broken-off tree, leaving stump standing alone. He is dressed in good pants, white shoes, but without a shirt. He disappears with tree up the alley when* MOTHER *appears on porch. She comes down and stands watching him. She has on a dressing-gown, carries a tray of grape-juice drink in a pitcher, and glasses with sprigs of mint in them.)*

MOTHER *(Calling up alley).* Did you have to put on good pants to do that? *(She comes downstage and puts tray on table in the arbor. Then looks around uneasily, then feels pitcher for coolness.* CHRIS *enters from alley brushing off his hands.)* You notice there's more light with that thing gone?

CHRIS. Why aren't you dressing?

MOTHER. It's suffocating upstairs. I made a grape drink for Georgie. He always liked grape. Come and have some.

CHRIS *(Impatiently).* Well, come on, get dressed. And what's Dad sleeping so much for? *(He goes to table and pours a glass of juice.)*

MOTHER. He's worried. When he's worried he sleeps. *(Pauses. Looks into his eyes.)* We're dumb, Chris. Dad and I are stupid people. We don't know anything. You've got to protect us.

CHRIS. You're silly; what's there to be afraid of?

MOTHER. To his last day in court Steve never gave up the idea that Dad made him do it. If they're going to open the case again I won't live through it.

CHRIS. George is just a damn fool, Mother. How can you take him seriously?

MOTHER. That family hates us. Maybe even Annie. . . .

CHRIS. Oh, now, Mother . . .

MOTHER. You think just because you like everybody, they like you!

CHRIS. All right, stop working yourself up. Just leave everything to me.

MOTHER. When George goes home tell her to go with him.

CHRIS (*Noncommittally*). Don't worry about Annie.

MOTHER. Steve is her father, too.

CHRIS. Are you going to cut it out? Now, come.

MOTHER (*Going upstage with him*). You don't realize how people can hate, Chris, they can hate so much they'll tear the world to pieces. . . . (ANN, *dressed up, appears on porch.*)

CHRIS. Look! She's dressed already. (*As he and* MOTHER *mount porch.*) I've just got to put on a shirt.

ANN (*In a preoccupied way*). Are you feeling well, Katie?

MOTHER. What's the difference, dear. There are certain people, y'know, the sicker they get the longer they live. (*She goes into house.*)

CHRIS. You look nice.

ANN. We're going to tell her tonight.

CHRIS. Absolutely, don't worry about it.

ANN. I wish we could tell her now. I can't stand scheming. My stomach gets hard.

CHRIS. It's not scheming, we'll just get her in a better mood.

MOTHER (*Offstage, in the house*). Joe, are you going to sleep all day!

ANN (*Laughing*). The only one who's relaxed is your father. He's fast asleep.

CHRIS. I'm relaxed.

ANN. Are you?

CHRIS. Look. (*He holds out his hand and makes it shake.*) Let me know when George gets here. (*He goes into the house. She moves aimlessly, and then is drawn toward tree stump. She goes to it, hesitantly touches broken top in the hush of her thoughts. Offstage* LYDIA *calls,* "Johnny! Come get your supper!" SUE *enters from left, and calls, seeing* ANN.)

SUE. Is my husband . . . ?

ANN *(Turns, startled).* Oh!

SUE. I'm terribly sorry.

ANN. It's all right, I . . . I'm a little silly about the dark.

SUE *(Looks about).* It is getting dark.

ANN. Are you looking for your husband?

SUE. As usual. *(Laughs tiredly.)* He spends so much time here, they'll be charging him rent.

ANN. Nobody was dressed so he drove over to the depot to pick up my brother.

SUE. Oh, your brother's in?

ANN. Yeah, they ought to be here any minute now. Will you have a cold drink?

SUE. I will, thanks. (ANN *goes to table and pours.)* My husband. Too hot to drive me to beach.—Men are like little boys; for the neighbors they'll always cut the grass.

ANN. People like to do things for the Kellers. Been that way since I can remember.

SUE. It's amazing. I guess your brother's coming to give you away, heh?

ANN *(Giving her drink).* I don't know. I suppose.

SUE. You must be all nerved up.

ANN. It's always a problem getting yourself married, isn't it?

SUE. That depends on your shape, of course. I don't see why you should have had a problem.

ANN. I've had chances—

SUE. I'll bet. It's romantic . . . it's very unusual to me, marrying the brother of your sweetheart.

ANN. I don't know. I think it's mostly that whenever I need somebody to tell me the truth I've always thought of Chris. When he tells you something you know it's so. He relaxes me.

SUE. And he's got money. That's important, you know.

ANN. It wouldn't matter to me.

SUE. You'd be surprised. It makes all the difference. I married an interne. On my salary. And that was bad, because as soon as a woman supports a man he owes her something. You can never owe somebody without resenting them. (ANN *laughs.)* That's true, you know.

ANN. Underneath, I think the doctor is very devoted.

SUE. Oh, certainly. But it's bad when a man always sees the bars in front of him. Jim thinks he's in jail all the time.

ANN. Oh . . .

SUE. That's why I've been intending to ask you a small favor, Ann . . . it's something very important to me.

ANN. Certainly, if I can do it.

SUE. You can. When you take up housekeeping, try to find a place away from here.

ANN. Are you fooling?

SUE. I'm very serious. My husband is unhappy with Chris around.

ANN. How is that?

SUE. Jim's a successful doctor. But he's got an idea he'd like to do medical research. Discover things. You see?

ANN. Well, isn't that good?

SUE. Research pays twenty-five dollars a week minus laundering the hair shirt. You've got to give up your life to go into it.

ANN. How does Chris?

SUE *(With growing feeling)*. Chris makes people want to be better than it's possible to be. He does that to people.

ANN. Is that bad?

SUE. My husband has a family, dear. Every time he has a session with Chris he feels as though he's compromising by not giving up everything for research. As though Chris or anybody else isn't compromising. It happens with Jim every couple of years. He meets a man and makes a statue out of him.

ANN. Maybe he's right. I don't mean that Chris is a statue, but . . .

SUE. Now darling, you know he's not right.

ANN. I don't agree with you. Chris . . .

SUE. Let's face it, dear. Chris is working with his father, isn't he? He's taking money out of that business every week in the year.

ANN. What of it?

SUE. You ask me what of it?

ANN. I certainly do ask you. (*She seems about to burst out.*) You oughtn't cast aspersions like that, I'm surprised at you.

SUE. You're surprised at me!

ANN. He'd never take five cents out of that plant if there was anything wrong in it.

SUE. You know that.

ANN. I know it. I resent everything you've said.

SUE (*Moving toward her*). You know what I resent, dear?

ANN. Please, I don't want to argue.

SUE. I resent living next door to the Holy Family. It makes me look like a bum, you understand?

ANN. I can't do anything about that.

SUE. Who is he to ruin a man's life? Everybody knows Joe pulled a fast one to get out of jail.

ANN. That's not true!

SUE. Then why don't you go out and talk to people? Go on, talk to them. There's not a person on the block who doesn't know the truth.

ANN. That's a lie. People come here all the time for cards and . . .

SUE. So what? They give him credit for being smart. I do, too, I've got nothing against Joe. But if Chris wants people to put on the hair shirt let him take off his broadcloth. He's driving my husband crazy with that phony idealism of his, and I'm at the end of my rope on it! (CHRIS *enters on porch, wearing shirt and tie now. She turns quickly, hearing. With a smile.*) Hello, darling. How's Mother?

CHRIS. I thought George came.

SUE. No, it was just us.

CHRIS (*Coming down to them*). Susie, do me a favor, heh? Go up to Mother and see if you can calm her. She's all worked up.

SUE. She still doesn't know about you two?

CHRIS (*Laughs a little*). Well, she senses it, I guess. You know my mother.

SUE (*Going up to porch*). Oh, yeah, she's psychic.

CHRIS. Maybe there's something in the medicine chest.

SUE. I'll give her one of everything. (*On porch.*) Don't worry about Kate; couple of drinks, dance her around a little . . . she'll love Ann. *(To* ANN.*)* Because you're the female version of him. (CHRIS *laughs.)* Don't be alarmed, I said version. *(She goes into house.)*

CHRIS. Interesting woman, isn't she?

ANN. Yeah, she's very interesting.

CHRIS. She's a great nurse, you know, she . . .

ANN *(In tension, but trying to control it).* Are you still doing that?

CHRIS *(Sensing something wrong, but still smiling).* Doing what?

ANN. As soon as you get to know somebody you find a distinction for them. How do you know she's a great nurse?

CHRIS. What's the matter, Ann?

ANN. The woman hates you. She despises you!

CHRIS. Hey . . . what's hit you?

ANN. Gee, Chris . . .

CHRIS. What happened here?

ANN. You never . . . Why didn't you tell me?

CHRIS. Tell you what?

ANN. She says they think Joe is guilty.

CHRIS. What difference does it make what they think?

ANN. I don't care what they think, I just don't understand why you took the trouble to deny it. You said it was all forgotten.

CHRIS. I didn't want you to feel there was anything wrong in you coming here, that's all. I know a lot of people think my father was guilty, and I assumed there might be some question in your mind.

ANN. But I never once said I suspected him.

CHRIS. Nobody says it.

ANN. Chris, I know how much you love him, but it could never . . .

CHRIS. Do you think I could forgive him if he'd done that thing?

ANN. I'm not here out of a blue sky, Chris. I turned my back on my father, if there's anything wrong here now . . .

CHRIS. I know that, Ann.

ANN. George is coming from Dad, and I don't think it's with a blessing.

CHRIS. He's welcome here. You've got nothing to fear from George.

ANN. Tell me that . . . just tell me that.

CHRIS. The man is innocent, Ann. Remember he was falsely accused once and it put him through hell. How would you behave if you were faced with the same thing again? Annie, believe me, there's nothing wrong for you here, believe me, kid.

ANN. All right, Chris, all right. (*They embrace as* KELLER *appears quietly on porch.* ANN *simply studies him.*)

KELLER. Every time I come out here it looks like Playland!

(*They break and laugh in embarrassment.*)

CHRIS. I thought you were going to shave?

KELLER (*Sitting on bench*). In a minute. I just woke up, I can't see nothin'.

ANN. You look shaved.

KELLER. Oh, no. (*Massages his jaw.*) Gotta be extra special tonight. Big night, Annie. So how's it feel to be a married woman?

ANN (*Laughs*). I don't know, yet.

KELLER (*To* CHRIS). What's the matter, you slippin'? (*He takes a little box of apples from under the bench as they talk.*)

CHRIS. The great roué!

KELLER. What is that, roué?

CHRIS. It's French.

KELLER. Don't talk dirty. (*They laugh.*)

CHRIS (*To* ANN). You ever meet a bigger ignoramus?

KELLER. Well, somebody's got to make a living.

ANN (*As they laugh*). That's telling him.

KELLER. I don't know, everybody's gettin' so Goddam educated in this country there'll be nobody to take away the garbage. (*They laugh.*) It's gettin' so the only dumb ones left are the bosses.

ANN. You're not so dumb, Joe.

KELLER. I know, but you go into our plant, for instance. I got so many lieutenants, majors and colonels that I'm ashamed to ask somebody to sweep the floor. I gotta be careful I'll insult somebody. No kiddin'. It's a tragedy: you stand on the street today and spit, you're gonna hit a college man.

CHRIS. Well, don't spit.

KELLER (*Breaks apple in half, passing it to* ANN *and* CHRIS). I mean to say, it's comin' to a pass. (*He takes a breath.*) I been thinkin', Annie . . . your brother, George. I been thinkin' about your brother George. When he comes I like you to brooch something to him.

CHRIS. Broach.

KELLER. What's the matter with brooch?

CHRIS (*Smiling*). It's not English.

KELLER. When I went to night school it was brooch.

ANN (*Laughing*). Well, in day school it's broach.

KELLER. Don't surround me, will you? Seriously, Ann . . . You say he's not well. George, I been thinkin', why should he knock himself out in New York with that cut-throat competition, when I got so many friends here; I'm very friendly with some big lawyers in town. I could set George up here.

ANN. That's awfully nice of you, Joe.

KELLER. No, kid, it ain't nice of me. I want you to understand me. I'm thinking of Chris. (*Slight pause.*) See . . . this is what I mean. You get older, you want to feel that you . . . accomplished something. My only accomplishment is my son. I ain't brainy. That's all I accomplished. Now, a year, eighteen months, your father'll be a free man. Who is he going to come to Annie? His baby. You. He'll come, old, mad, into your house.

ANN. That can't matter any more, Joe.

KELLER. I don't want that hate to come between us. (*Gestures between* CHRIS *and himself.*)

ANN. I can only tell you that that could never happen.

KELLER. You're in love now, Annie, but believe me, I'm older than you and I know—a daughter is a daughter, and a father is a father. And it could happen. (*He pauses.*) I like you and George to go to him in prison and tell him. . . .

"Dad, Joe wants to bring you into the business when you get out."

ANN (*Surprised, even shocked*). You'd have him as a partner?

KELLER. No, no partner. A good job. (*Pause. He sees she is shocked, a little mystified. He gets up, speaks more nervously.*) I want him to know, Annie . . . while he's sitting there I want him to know that when he gets out he's got a place waitin' for him. It'll take his bitterness away. To know you got a place . . . it sweetens you.

ANN. Joe, you owe him nothing.

KELLER. I owe him a good kick in the teeth, but he's your father. . . .

CHRIS. Then kick him in the teeth! I don't want him in the plant, so that's that! You understand? And besides, don't talk about him like that. People misunderstand you!

KELLER. And I don't understand why she has to crucify the man.

CHRIS. Well it's her father, if she feels . . .

KELLER. No, no. . . .

CHRIS (*Almost angrily*). What's it to you? Why . . . ?

KELLER (*A commanding outburst in his high nervousness*). A father is a father! (*As though the outburst had revealed him, he looks about, wanting to retract it. His hand goes to his cheek.*) I better . . . I better shave. (*He turns and a smile is on his face. To ANN.*) I didn't mean to yell at you, Annie.

ANN. Let's forget the whole thing, Joe.

KELLER. Right. (*To CHRIS.*) She's likable.

CHRIS (*A little peeved at the man's stupidity*). Shave, will you?

KELLER. Right again.

(*As he turns to porch LYDIA comes hurrying from her house, right.*)

LYDIA. I forgot all about it . . . (*Seeing CHRIS and ANN.*) Hya. (*To JOE.*) I promised to fix Kate's hair for tonight. Did she comb it yet?

KELLER. Always a smile, hey, Lydia?

LYDIA. Sure, why not?

KELLER *(Going up on porch).* Come on up and comb my Katie's hair. *(*LYDIA *goes up on porch.)* She's got a big night, make her beautiful.

LYDIA. I will.

KELLER *(He holds door open for her and she goes into kitchen. To* CHRIS *and* ANN*).* Hey, that could be a song. *(He sings softly.)*

"Come on up and comb my Katie's hair . . .

Oh, come on up, 'cause she's my lady fair——"

(To ANN.*)* How's that for one year of night school? *(He continues singing as he goes into kitchen.)*

"Oh, come on up, come on up, and comb my lady's hair——"

*(*JIM BAYLISS *rounds corner of driveway, walking rapidly.* JIM *crosses to* CHRIS, *motions him up and pulls him down to stage left, excitedly.* KELLER *stands just inside kitchen door, watching them.)*

CHRIS. What's the matter? Where is he?

JIM. Where's your mother?

CHRIS. Upstairs, dressing.

ANN *(Crossing to them rapidly).* What happened to George?

JIM. I asked him to wait in the car. Listen to me now. Can you take some advice? *(They wait.)* Don't bring him in here.

ANN. Why?

JIM. Kate is in bad shape, you can't explode this in front of her.

ANN. Explode what?

JIM. You know why he's here, don't try to kid it away. There's blood in his eye; drive him somewhere and talk to him alone.

*(*ANN *turns to go up drive, takes a couple of steps, sees* KELLER *and stops. He goes quietly on into house.)*

CHRIS *(Shaken, and therefore angered).* Don't be an old lady.

JIM. He's come to take her home. What does that mean? *(To*

ANN.) You know what that means. Fight it out with him some place else.

ANN (*She comes back down toward* CHRIS). I'll drive . . . him somewhere.

CHRIS (*Goes to her*). No.

JIM. Will you stop being an idiot?

CHRIS. Nobody's afraid of him here. Cut that out! (*He starts for driveway, but is brought up short by* GEORGE, *who enters there.* GEORGE *is* CHRIS' *age, but a paler man, now on the edge of his self-restraint. He speaks quietly, as though afraid to find himself screaming. An instant's hesitation and* CHRIS *steps up to him, hand extended, smiling.*) Helluva way to do; what're you sitting out there for?

GEORGE. Doctor said your mother isn't well, I . . .

CHRIS. So what? She'd want to see you, wouldn't she? We've been waiting for you all afternoon. (*He puts his hand on* GEORGE's *arm, but* GEORGE *pulls away, coming across toward* ANN.)

ANN (*Touching his collar*). This is filthy, didn't you bring another shirt? (GEORGE *breaks away from her, and moves down and left, examining the yard. Door opens, and he turns rapidly, thinking it is* KATE, *but it's* SUE. *She looks at him, he turns away and moves on left, to fence. He looks over it at his former home.* SUE *comes down stage.*)

SUE (*Annoyed*). How about the beach, Jim?

JIM. Oh, it's too hot to drive.

SUE. How'd you get to the station—Zeppelin?

CHRIS. This is Mrs. Bayliss, George. (*Calling, as* GEORGE *pays no attention, staring at house off left.*) George! (GEORGE *turns.*) Mrs. Bayliss.

SUE. How do you do.

GEORGE (*Removing his hat*). You're the people who bought our house, aren't you?

SUE. That's right. Come and see what we did with it before you leave.

GEORGE (*He walks down and away from her*). I liked it the way it was.

SUE (*After a brief pause*). He's frank, isn't he?

JIM (*Pulling her off left*). See you later. . . . Take it easy, fella. (*They exit, left.*)

CHRIS (*Calling after them*). Thanks for driving him! (*Turning to* GEORGE.) How about some grape juice? Mother made it especially for you.

GEORGE (*With forced appreciation*). Good old Kate, remembered my grape juice.

CHRIS. You drank enough of it in this house. How've you been, George?—Sit down.

GEORGE (*He keeps moving*). It takes me a minute. (*Looking around.*) It seems impossible.

CHRIS. What?

GEORGE. I'm back here.

CHRIS. Say, you've gotten a little nervous, haven't you?

GEORGE. Yeah, toward the end of the day. What're you, big executive now?

CHRIS. Just kind of medium. How's the law?

GEORGE. I don't know. When I was studying in the hospital it seemed sensible, but outside there doesn't seem to be much of a law. The trees got thick, didn't they? (*Points to stump.*) What's that?

CHRIS. Blew down last night. We had it there for Larry. You know.

GEORGE. Why, afraid you'll forget him?

CHRIS (*Starts for* GEORGE). Kind of a remark is that?

ANN (*Breaking in, putting a restraining hand on* CHRIS). When did you start wearing a hat?

GEORGE (*Discovers hat in his hand*). Today. From now on I decided to look like a lawyer, anyway. (*He holds it up to her.*) Don't you recognize it?

ANN. Why? Where . . . ?

GEORGE. Your father's . . . he asked me to wear it.

ANN. . . . How is he?

GEORGE. He got smaller.

ANN. Smaller?

GEORGE. Yeah, little. (*Holds out his hand to measure.*) He's a little man. That's what happens to suckers, you know. It's good I went to him in time—another year there'd be nothing left but his smell.

CHRIS. What's the matter, George, what's the trouble?

GEORGE. The trouble? The trouble is when you make suckers out of people once, you shouldn't try to do it twice.

CHRIS. What does that mean?

GEORGE *(To* ANN*).* You're not married yet, are you?

ANN. George, will you sit down and stop—?

GEORGE. Are you married yet?

ANN. No, I'm not married yet.

GEORGE. You're not going to marry him.

ANN. Why am I not going to marry him?

GEORGE. Because his father destroyed your family.

CHRIS. Now look, George . . .

GEORGE. Cut it short, Chris. Tell her to come home with me. Let's not argue, you know what I've got to say.

CHRIS. George, you don't want to be the voice of God, do you?

GEORGE. I'm . . .

CHRIS. That's been your trouble all your life, George, you dive into things. What kind of a statement is that to make? You're a big boy now.

GEORGE. I'm a big boy now.

CHRIS. Don't come bulling in here. If you've got something to say, be civilized about it.

GEORGE. Don't civilize me!

ANN. Shhh!

CHRIS *(Ready to hit him).* Are you going to talk like a grown man or aren't you?

ANN *(Quickly, to forestall an outburst).* Sit down, dear. Don't be angry, what's the matter? *(He allows her to seat him, looking at her.)* Now what happened? You kissed me when I left, now you . . .

GEORGE *(Breathlessly).* My life turned upside down since then. I couldn't go back to work when you left. I wanted to go to Dad and tell him you were going to be married. It seemed impossible not to tell him. He loved you so much . . . *(He pauses.)* Annie . . . we did a terrible thing. We can never be forgiven. Not even to send him a card at Christmas. I didn't

see him once since I got home from the war! Annie, you
don't know what was done to that man. You don't know
what happened.

ANN *(Afraid)*. Of course I know.

GEORGE. You can't know, you wouldn't be here. Dad came to
work that day. The night foreman came to him and showed
him the cylinder heads . . . they were coming out of the
process with defects. There was something wrong with the
process. So Dad went directly to the phone and called here
and told Joe to come down right away. But the morning
passed. No sign of Joe. So Dad called again. By this time he
had over a hundred defectives. The Army was screaming
for stuff and Dad didn't have anything to ship. So Joe told
him . . . on the phone he told him to weld, cover up the
cracks in any way he could, and ship them out.

CHRIS. Are you through now?

GEORGE *(Surging up at him)*. I'm not through now! *(Back to
ANN.)* Dad was afraid. He wanted Joe there if he was going
to do it. But Joe can't come down . . . he's sick. Sick! He
suddenly gets the flu! Suddenly! But he promised to take
responsibility. Do you understand what I'm saying? On the
telephone you can't have responsibility! In a court you can
always deny a phone call and that's exactly what he did.
They knew he was a liar the first time, but in the appeal
they believed that rotten lie and now Joe is a big shot and
your father is the patsy. *(He gets up.)* Now what're you going to do? Eat his food, sleep in his bed? Answer me; what're
you going to do?

CHRIS. What're you going to do, George?

GEORGE. He's too smart for me, I can't prove a phone call.

CHRIS. Then how dare you come in here with that rot?

ANN. George, the court . . .

GEORGE. The court didn't know your father! But you know
him. You know in your heart Joe did it.

CHRIS *(Whirling him around)*. Lower your voice or I'll throw
you out of here!

GEORGE. She knows. She knows.

CHRIS *(To ANN)*. Get him out of here, Ann. Get him out of here.

ANN. George, I know everything you've said. Dad told that whole thing in court, and they . . .

GEORGE (*Almost a scream*). The court did not know him, Annie!

ANN. Shhh!— But he'll say anything, George. You know how quick he can lie.

GEORGE (*Turning to* CHRIS, *with deliberation*). I'll ask you something, and look me in the eye when you answer me.

CHRIS. I'll look you in the eye.

GEORGE. You know your father . . .

CHRIS. I know him well.

GEORGE. And he's the kind of boss to let a hundred and twenty-one cylinder heads be repaired and shipped out of his shop without even knowing about it?

CHRIS. He's that kind of boss.

GEORGE. And that's the same Joe Keller who never left his shop without first going around to see that all the lights were out.

CHRIS (*With growing anger*). The same Joe Keller.

GEORGE. The same man who knows how many minutes a day his workers spend in the toilet.

CHRIS. The same man.

GEORGE. And my father, that frightened mouse who'd never buy a shirt without somebody along—that man would dare do such a thing on his own?

CHRIS. On his own. And because he's a frightened mouse this is another thing he'd do;—throw the blame on somebody else because he's not man enough to take it himself. He tried it in court but it didn't work, but with a fool like you it works!

GEORGE. Oh, Chris, you're a liar to yourself!

ANN (*Deeply shaken*). Don't talk like that!

CHRIS (*Sits facing* GEORGE). Tell me, George. What happened? The court record was good enough for you all these years, why isn't it good now? Why did you believe it all these years?

GEORGE (*After a slight pause*). Because you believed it. . . . That's the truth, Chris. I believed everything, because I thought you did. But today I heard it from his mouth. From his mouth it's altogether different than the record. Anyone who knows him, and knows your father, will believe it from his mouth. Your Dad took everything we have. I can't beat that. But she's one item he's not going to grab. *(He turns to* ANN.) Get your things. Everything they have is covered with blood. You're not the kind of a girl who can live with that. Get your things.

CHRIS. Ann . . . you're not going to believe that, are you?

ANN *(She goes to him).* You know it's not true, don't you?

GEORGE. How can he tell you? It's his father. *(To* CHRIS.) None of these things ever even cross your mind?

CHRIS. Yes, they crossed my mind. Anything can cross your mind!

GEORGE. *He knows,* Annie. He knows!

CHRIS. The Voice of God!

GEORGE. Then why isn't your name on the business? Explain that to her!

CHRIS. What the hell has that got to do with . . . ?

GEORGE. Annie, why isn't his name on it?

CHRIS. Even when I don't own it!

GEORGE. Who're you kidding? Who gets it when he dies? *(To* ANN.) Open your eyes, you know the both of them, isn't that the first thing they'd do, the way they love each other? — J. O. Keller & Son? *(Pause.* ANN *looks from him to* CHRIS.) I'll settle it. Do you want to settle it, or are you afraid to?

CHRIS. . . . What do you mean?

GEORGE. Let me go up and talk to your father. In ten minutes you'll have the answer. Or are you afraid of the answer?

CHRIS. I'm not afraid of the answer. I know the answer. But my mother isn't well and I don't want a fight here now.

GEORGE. Let me go to him.

CHRIS. You're not going to start a fight here now.

GEORGE *(To* ANN). What more do you want!!! *(There is a sound of footsteps in the house.)*

ANN *(Turns her head suddenly toward the house).* Someone's coming.

CHRIS. *(To* GEORGE, *quietly).* You won't say anything now.

ANN. You'll go soon. I'll call a cab.

GEORGE. You're coming with me.

ANN. And don't mention marriage, because we haven't told her yet.

GEORGE. You're coming with me.

ANN. You understand? Don't . . . George, you're not going to start anything now! *(She hears footsteps)*. Shsh! *(MOTHER enters on porch. She is dressed almost formally, her hair is fixed. They are all turned toward her. On seeing GEORGE she raises both hands, comes down toward him.)*

MOTHER. Georgie, Georgie.

GEORGE *(He has always liked her)*. Hello, Kate.

MOTHER *(She cups his face in her hands)*. They made an old man out of you. *(Touches his hair.)* Look, you're gray.

GEORGE *(Her pity, open and unabashed, reaches into him, and he smiles sadly)*. I know, I . . .

MOTHER. I told you when you went away, don't try for medals.

GEORGE *(He laughs, tiredly)*. I didn't try, Kate. They made it very easy for me.

MOTHER *(Actually angry)*. Go on. You're all alike. *(To ANN.)* Look at him, why did you say he's fine? He looks like a ghost.

GEORGE *(Relishing her solicitude)*. I feel all right.

MOTHER. I'm sick to look at you. What's the matter with your mother, why don't she feed you?

ANN. He just hasn't any appetite.

MOTHER. If he ate in my house he'd have an appetite. *(To ANN.)* I pity your husband! *(To GEORGE.)* Sit down. I'll make you a sandwich.

GEORGE *(Sits with an embarrassed laugh)*. I'm really not hungry.

MOTHER. Honest to God, it breaks my heart to see what happened to all the children. How we worked and planned for you, and you end up no better than us.

GEORGE *(With deep feeling for her)*. You . . . you haven't changed at all, you know that, Kate?

MOTHER. None of us changed, Georgie. We all love you. Joe was just talking about the day you were born and the water got shut off. People were carrying basins from a block away

—a stranger would have thought the whole neighborhood was on fire! *(They laugh. She sees the juice. To* ANN.*)* Why didn't you give him some juice!

ANN *(Defensively).* I offered it to him.

MOTHER *(Scoffingly).* You offered it to him! *(Thrusting glass into* GEORGE'S *hand.) Give* it to him! *(To* GEORGE, *who is laughing.)* And now you're going to sit here and drink some juice . . . and look like something!

GEORGE *(Sitting).* Kate, I feel hungry already.

CHRIS *(Proudly).* She could turn Mahatma Gandhi into a heavy-weight!

MOTHER *(To* CHRIS, *with great energy).* Listen, to hell with the restaurant! I got a ham in the icebox, and frozen straw-berries, and avocados, and . . .

ANN. Swell, I'll help you!

GEORGE. The train leaves at eight-thirty, Ann.

MOTHER *(To* ANN*).* You're leaving?

CHRIS. No, Mother, she's not . . .

ANN *(Breaking through it, going to* GEORGE*).* You hardly got here; give yourself a chance to get acquainted again.

CHRIS. Sure, you don't even know us any more.

MOTHER. Well, Chris, if they can't stay, don't . . .

CHRIS. No, it's just a question of George, Mother, he planned on . . .

GEORGE *(He gets up politely, nicely, for* KATE'S *sake).* Now wait a minute, Chris . . .

CHRIS *(Smiling and full of command, cutting him off).* If you want to go, I'll drive you to the station now, but if you're staying, no arguments while you're here.

MOTHER *(At last confessing the tension).* Why should he argue? *(She goes to him, and with desperation and compassion, stroking his hair.)* Georgie and us have no argument. How could we have an argument, Georgie? We all got hit by the same lightning, how can you . . . ? Did you see what hap-pened to Larry's tree, Georgie? *(She has taken his arm, and unwillingly he moves across stage with her.)* Imagine? While I was dreaming of him in the middle of the night, the wind came along and . . . (LYDIA *enters on porch. As soon as she sees him.*)

LYDIA. Hey, Georgie! Georgie! Georgie! Georgie! Georgie! (*She comes down to him eagerly. She has a flowered hat in her hand, which* KATE *takes from her as she goes to* GEORGE.)

GEORGE (*They shake hands eagerly, warmly*). Hello, Laughy. What'd you do, grow?

LYDIA. I'm a big girl now.

MOTHER (*Taking hat from her*). Look what she can do to a hat!

ANN (*To* LYDIA, *admiring the hat*). Did you make that?

MOTHER. In ten minutes! (*She puts it on.*)

LYDIA (*Fixing it on her head*). I only rearranged it.

GEORGE. You still make your own clothes?

CHRIS (*To* MOTHER). Ain't she classy! All she needs now is a Russian wolfhound.

MOTHER (*Moving her head from left to right*). It feels like somebody is sitting on my head.

ANN. No, it's beautiful, Kate.

MOTHER (*Kisses* LYDIA—*to* GEORGE). She's a genius! You should've married her. (*They laugh.*) This one can feed you!

LYDIA (*Strangely embarrassed*). Oh, stop that, Kate.

GEORGE (*To* LYDIA). Didn't I hear you had a baby?

MOTHER. You don't hear so good. She's got three babies.

GEORGE (*A little hurt by it—to* LYDIA). No kidding, three?

LYDIA. Yeah, it was one, two, three— You've been away a long time, Georgie.

GEORGE. I'm beginning to realize.

MOTHER (*To* CHRIS *and* GEORGE). The trouble with you kids is you *think* too much.

LYDIA. Well, we think, too.

MOTHER. Yes, but not all the time.

GEORGE (*With almost obvious envy*). They never took Frank, heh?

LYDIA (*A little apologetically*). No, he was always one year ahead of the draft.

MOTHER. It's amazing. When they were calling boys twenty-seven Frank was just twenty-eight, when they made it twenty-eight he was just twenty-nine. That's why he took up astrology. It's all in when you were born, it just goes to show.

CHRIS. What does it go to show?

MOTHER *(To* CHRIS*)*. Don't be so intelligent. Some superstitions are very nice! *(To* LYDIA*.)* Did he finish Larry's horoscope?

LYDIA. I'll ask him now, I'm going in. *(To* GEORGE, *a little sadly, almost embarrassed.)* Would you like to see my babies? Come on.

GEORGE. I don't think so, Lydia.

LYDIA *(Understanding)*. All right. Good luck to you, George.

GEORGE. Thanks. And to you . . . And Frank. *(She smiles at him, turns and goes off right to her house.* GEORGE *stands staring after her.)*

LYDIA *(As she runs off)*. Oh, Frank!

MOTHER *(Reading his thoughts)*. She got pretty, heh?

GEORGE *(Sadly)*. Very pretty.

MOTHER *(As a reprimand)*. She's beautiful, you damned fool!

GEORGE *(Looks around longingly; and softly, with a catch in his throat)*. She makes it seem so nice around here.

MOTHER *(Shaking her finger at him)*. Look what happened to you because you wouldn't listen to me! I told you to marry that girl and stay out of the war!

GEORGE *(Laughs at himself)*. She used to laugh too much.

MOTHER. And you didn't laugh enough. While you were getting mad about Fascism, Frank was getting into her bed.

GEORGE *(To* CHRIS*)*. He won the war, Frank.

CHRIS. All the battles.

MOTHER *(In pursuit of this mood)*. The day they started the draft, Georgie, I told you you loved that girl.

CHRIS *(Laughs)*. And truer love hath no man!

MOTHER. I'm smarter than any of you.

GEORGE *(Laughing)*. She's wonderful!

MOTHER. And now you're going to listen to me, George. You had big principles, Eagle Scouts the three of you; so now I got a tree, and this one, *(Indicating* CHRIS.*)* when the weather gets bad he can't stand on his feet; and that big dope *(Pointing to* LYDIA's *house.)* next door who never reads anything but Andy Gump has three children and his house paid off. Stop being a philosopher, and look after yourself. Like Joe was just saying—you move back here, he'll help you get set, and I'll find you a girl and put a smile on your face.

GEORGE. Joe? Joe wants me here?

ANN (*Eagerly*). He asked me to tell you, and I think it's a good idea.

MOTHER. Certainly. Why must you make believe you hate us? Is that another principle?—that you have to hate us? You don't hate us, George, I know you, you can't fool me, I diapered you. (*Suddenly to* ANN.) You remember Mr. Marcy's daughter?

ANN (*Laughing, to* GEORGE). She's got you hooked already!

(GEORGE *laughs, is excited.*)

MOTHER. You look her over, George; you'll see she's the most beautiful . . .

CHRIS. She's got warts, George.

MOTHER (*To* CHRIS). She hasn't got warts! (*To* GEORGE.) So the girl has a little beauty mark on her chin . . .

CHRIS. And two on her nose.

MOTHER. You remember. Her father's the retired police inspector.

CHRIS. Sergeant, George.

MOTHER. He's a very kind man!

CHRIS. He looks like a gorilla.

MOTHER (*To* GEORGE). He never shot anybody. (*They all burst out laughing, as* KELLER *appears in doorway.* GEORGE *rises abruptly, stares at* KELLER, *who comes rapidly down to him.*)

KELLER (*The laughter stops. With strained joviality*). Well! Look who's here! (*Extending his hand.*) Georgie, good to see ya.

GEORGE (*Shakes hands—somberly*). How're you, Joe?

KELLER. So-so. Gettin' old. You comin' out to dinner with us?

GEORGE. No, got to be back in New York.

ANN. I'll call a cab for you. (*She goes up into the house.*)

KELLER. Too bad you can't stay, George. Sit down. *(To MOTHER.)* He looks fine.

MOTHER. He looks terrible.

KELLER. That's what I said, you look terrible, George. *(They laugh.)* I wear the pants and she beats me with the belt.

GEORGE. I saw your factory on the way from the station. It looks like General Motors.

KELLER. I wish it was General Motors, but it ain't. Sit down, George. Sit down. *(Takes cigar out of his pocket.)* So you finally went to see your father, I hear?

GEORGE. Yes, this morning. What kind of stuff do you make now?

KELLER. Oh, little of everything. Pressure cookers, an assembly for washing machines. Got a nice, flexible plant now. So how'd you find Dad? Feel all right?

GEORGE *(Searching KELLER, he speaks indecisively)*. No, he's not well, Joe.

KELLER *(Lighting his cigar)*. Not his heart again, is it?

GEORGE. It's everything, Joe. It's his soul.

KELLER *(Blowing out smoke)*. Uh huh—

CHRIS. How about seeing what they did with your house?

KELLER. Leave him be.

GEORGE *(To CHRIS, indicating KELLER)*. I'd like to talk to him.

KELLER. Sure, he just got here. That's the way they do, George. A little man makes a mistake and they hang him by the thumbs; the big ones become ambassadors. I wish you'd-a told me you were going to see Dad.

GEORGE *(Studying him)*. I didn't know you were interested.

KELLER. In a way, I am. I would like him to know, George, that as far as I'm concerned, any time he wants, he's got a place with me. I would like him to know that.

GEORGE. He hates your guts, Joe. Don't you know that?

KELLER. I imagined it. But that can change, too.

MOTHER. Steve was never like that.

GEORGE. He's like that now. He'd like to take every man who made money in the war and put him up against a wall.

CHRIS. He'll need a lot of bullets.

GEORGE. And he'd better not get any.

KELLER. That's a sad thing to hear.

GEORGE (*With bitterness dominant*). Why? What'd you expect him to think of you?

KELLER (*The force of his nature rising, but under control*). I'm sad to see he hasn't changed. As long as I know him, twenty-five years, the man never learned how to take the blame. You know that, George.

GEORGE (*He does*). Well, I . . .

KELLER. But you do know it. Because the way you come in here you don't look like you remember it. I mean like in 1937 when we had the shop on Flood Street. And he damn near blew us all up with that heater he left burning for two days without water. He wouldn't admit that was his fault, either. I had to fire a mechanic to save his face. You remember that.

GEORGE. Yes, but . . .

KELLER. I'm just mentioning it, George. Because this is just another one of a lot of things. Like when he gave Frank that money to invest in oil stock.

GEORGE (*Distressed*). I know that, I . . .

KELLER (*Driving in, but restrained*). But it's good to remember those things, kid. The way he cursed Frank because the stock went down. Was that Frank's fault? To listen to him Frank was a swindler. And all the man did was give him a bad tip.

GEORGE (*Gets up, moves away*). I know those things . . .

KELLER. Then remember them, remember them. (ANN *comes out of house.*) There are certain men in the world who rather see everybody hung before they'll take blame. You understand me, George? (*They stand facing each other,* GEORGE *trying to judge him.*)

ANN (*Coming downstage*). The cab's on its way. Would you like to wash?

MOTHER (*With the thrust of hope*). Why must he go? Make the midnight, George.

KELLER. Sure, you'll have dinner with us!

ANN. How about it? Why not? We're eating at the lake, we could have a swell time.

GEORGE (*Long pause, as he looks at* ANN, CHRIS, KELLER, *then back to her*). All right.

MOTHER. Now you're talking.

CHRIS. I've got a shirt that'll go right with that suit.

MOTHER. Size fifteen and a half, right, George?

GEORGE. Is Lydia . . . ? I mean—Frank and Lydia coming?

MOTHER. I'll get you a date that'll make her look like a . . . (*She starts upstage.*)

GEORGE (*Laughs*). No, I don't want a date.

CHRIS. I know somebody just for you! Charlotte Tanner! (*He starts for the house.*)

KELLER. Call Charlotte, that's right.

MOTHER. Sure, call her up. (CHRIS *goes into house.*)

ANN. You go up and pick out a shirt and tie.

GEORGE (*He stops, looks around at them and the place*). I never felt at home anywhere but here. I feel so . . . (*He nearly laughs, and turns away from them.*) Kate, you look so young, you know? You didn't change at all. It . . . rings an old bell. (*Turns to* KELLER.) You too, Joe, you're amazingly the same. The whole atmosphere is.

KELLER. Say, I ain't got time to get sick.

MOTHER. He hasn't been laid up in fifteen years. . . .

KELLER. Except my flu during the war.

MOTHER. Huhh?

KELLER. My flu, when I was sick during . . . the war.

MOTHER. Well, sure . . . (*To* GEORGE.) I meant except for that flu. (GEORGE *stands perfectly still.*) Well, it slipped my mind, don't look at me that way. He wanted to go to the shop but he couldn't lift himself off the bed. I thought he had pneumonia.

GEORGE. Why did you say he's never . . . ?

KELLER. I know how you feel, kid, I'll never forgive myself. If I could've gone in that day I'd never allow Dad to touch those heads.

GEORGE. She said you've never been sick.

MOTHER. I said he was sick, George.

GEORGE (*Going to* ANN). Ann, didn't you hear her say . . . ?

MOTHER. Do you remember every time you were sick?

GEORGE. I'd remember pneumonia. Especially if I got it just the day my partner was going to patch up cylinder heads . . . What happened that day, Joe?

FRANK *(Enters briskly from driveway, holding* LARRY's *horoscope in his hand. He comes to* KATE*).* Kate! Kate!

MOTHER. Frank, did you see George?

FRANK *(Extending his hand).* Lydia told me, I'm glad to . . . you'll have to pardon me. *(Pulling* MOTHER *over right.)* I've got something amazing for you, Kate, I finished Larry's horoscope.

MOTHER. You'd be interested in this, George. It's wonderful the way he can understand the . . .

CHRIS *(Entering from house).* George, the girl's on the phone . . .

MOTHER *(Desperately).* He finished Larry's horoscope!

CHRIS. Frank, can't you pick a better time than this?

FRANK. The greatest men who ever lived believed in the stars!

CHRIS. Stop filling her head with that junk!

FRANK. Is it junk to feel that there's a greater power than ourselves? I've studied the stars of his life! I won't argue with you, I'm telling you. Somewhere in this world your brother is alive!

MOTHER *(Instantly to* CHRIS*).* Why isn't it possible?

CHRIS. Because it's insane.

FRANK. Just a minute now. I'll tell you something and you can do as you please. Just let me say it. He was supposed to have died on November twenty-fifth. But November twenty-fifth was his favorable day.

CHRIS. Mother!

MOTHER. Listen to him!

FRANK. It was a day when everything good was shining on him, the kind of day he should've married on. You can laugh at a lot of it, I can understand you laughing. But the odds are a million to one that a man won't die on his favorable day. That's known, that's known, Chris!

MOTHER. Why isn't it possible, why isn't it possible, Chris!

GEORGE *(To* ANN*).* Don't you understand what she's saying? She just told you to go. What are you waiting for now?

CHRIS. Nobody can tell her to go. *(A car horn is heard.)*

MOTHER *(To* FRANK*)*. Thank you, darling, for your trouble. Will you tell him to wait, Frank?

FRANK *(As he goes)*. Sure thing.

MOTHER *(Calling out)*. They'll be right out, driver!

CHRIS. She's not leaving, Mother.

GEORGE. You heard her say it, he's never been sick!

MOTHER. He misunderstood me, Chris! *(*CHRIS *looks at her, struck.)*

GEORGE *(To* ANN*)*. He simply told your father to kill pilots, and covered himself in bed!

CHRIS. You'd better answer him, Annie. Answer him.

MOTHER. I packed your bag, darling . . .

CHRIS. What?

MOTHER. I packed your bag. All you've got to do is close it.

ANN. I'm not closing anything. He asked me here and I'm staying till he tells me to go. *(To* GEORGE.*)* Till Chris tells me!

CHRIS. That's all! Now get out of here, George!

MOTHER *(To* CHRIS*)*. But if that's how he feels . . .

CHRIS. That's all, nothing more till Christ comes, about the case or Larry as long as I'm here! *(To* ANN.*)* Now get out of here, George!

GEORGE *(To* ANN*)*. You tell me. I want to hear you tell me.

ANN. Go, George! *(They disappear up the driveway,* ANN *saying "Don't take it that way, Georgie! Please don't take it that way.")*

*(*CHRIS *turns to his mother.)*

CHRIS. What do you mean, you packed her bag? How dare you pack her bag?

MOTHER. Chris . . .

CHRIS. How dare you pack her bag?

MOTHER. She doesn't belong here.

CHRIS. Then I don't belong here.

MOTHER. She's Larry's girl.

CHRIS. And I'm his brother and he's dead, and I'm marrying his girl.

MOTHER. Never, never in this world!

KELLER. You lost your mind?

MOTHER. You have nothing to say!

KELLER *(Cruelly)*. I got plenty to say. Three and a half years you been talking like a maniac—

MOTHER *(She smashes him across the face)*. Nothing. You have nothing to say. Now I say. He's coming back, and everybody has got to wait.

CHRIS. Mother, Mother . . .

MOTHER. Wait, wait . . .

CHRIS. How long? How long?

MOTHER *(Rolling out of her)*. Till he comes; forever and ever till he comes!

CHRIS *(As an ultimatum)*. Mother, I'm going ahead with it.

MOTHER. Chris, I've never said no to you in my life, now I say no!

CHRIS. You'll never let him go till I do it.

MOTHER. I'll never let him go and you'll never let him go . . . !

CHRIS. I've let him go. I've let him go a long . . .

MOTHER *(With no less force, but turning from him)*. Then let your father go. *(Pause.* CHRIS *stands transfixed.)*

KELLER. She's out of her mind.

MOTHER. Altogether! *(To* CHRIS, *but not facing them.)* Your brother's alive, darling, because if he's dead, your father killed him. Do you understand me now? As long as you live, that boy is alive. God does not let a son be killed by his father. Now you see, don't you? Now you see. *(Beyond control, she hurries up and into house.)*

KELLER *(*CHRIS *has not moved. He speaks insinuatingly, questioningly)*. She's out of her mind.

CHRIS *(A broken whisper)*. Then . . . you did it?

KELLER *(The beginning of plea in his voice)*. He never flew a P-40—

CHRIS *(Struck. Deadly)*. But the others.

KELLER *(Insistently)*. She's out of her mind. *(He takes a step toward* CHRIS, *pleadingly.)*

CHRIS *(Unyielding)*. Dad . . . you did it?

KELLER. He never flew a P-40, what's the matter with you?

CHRIS (*Still asking, and saying*). Then you did it. To the others.

(*Both hold their voices down.*)

KELLER (*Afraid of him, his deadly insistence*). What's the matter with you? What the hell is the matter with you?

CHRIS (*Quietly, incredibly*). How could you do that? How?

KELLER. What's the matter with you?

CHRIS. Dad . . . Dad, you killed twenty-one men!

KELLER. What, killed?

CHRIS. You killed them, you murdered them.

KELLER (*As though throwing his whole nature open before CHRIS*). How could I kill anybody?

CHRIS. Dad! Dad!

KELLER (*Trying to hush him*). I didn't kill anybody!

CHRIS. Then explain it to me. What did you do? Explain it to me or I'll tear you to pieces!

KELLER (*Horrified at his overwhelming fury*). Don't Chris, don't . . .

CHRIS. I want to know what you did, now what did you do? You had a hundred and twenty cracked engine-heads, now what did you do?

KELLER. If you're going to hang me then I . . .

CHRIS. I'm listening, God Almighty, I'm listening!

KELLER (*Their movements now are those of subtle pursuit and escape. KELLER keeps a step out of CHRIS' range as he talks*). You're a boy, what could I do! I'm in business, a man is in business; a hundred and twenty cracked, you're out of business; you got a process, the process don't work you're out of business; you don't know how to operate, your stuff is no good; they close you up, they tear up your contracts, what the hell's it to them? You lay forty years into a business and they knock you out in five minutes, what could I do, let them take forty years, let them take my life away? (*His voice cracking.*) I never thought they'd install them. I swear to God. I thought they'd stop 'em before anybody took off.

CHRIS. Then why'd you ship them out?

KELLER. By the time they could spot them I thought I'd have

the process going again, and I could show them they needed me and they'd let it go by. But weeks passed and I got no kick-back, so I was going to tell them.

CHRIS. Then why didn't you tell them?

KELLER. It was too late. The paper, it was all over the front page, twenty-one went down, it was too late. They came with handcuffs into the shop, what could I do? *(He sits on bench at center.)* Chris . . . Chris, I did it for you, it was a chance and I took it for you. I'm sixty-one years old, when would I have another chance to make something for you? Sixty-one years old you don't get another chance, do ya?

CHRIS. You even knew they wouldn't hold up in the air.

KELLER. I didn't say that . . .

CHRIS. But you were going to warn them not to use them . . .

KELLER. But that don't mean . . .

CHRIS. It means you knew they'd crash.

KELLER. It don't mean that.

CHRIS. Then you *thought* they'd crash.

KELLER. I was afraid maybe . . .

CHRIS. You were afraid maybe! God in heaven, what kind of a man are you? Kids were hanging in the air by those heads. You knew that!

KELLER. For you, a business for you!

CHRIS *(With burning fury)*. For me! Where do you live, where have you come from? For me!—I was dying every day and you were killing my boys and you did it for me? What the hell do you think I was thinking of, the goddam business? Is that as far as your mind can see, the business? What is that, the world—the business? What the hell do you mean, you did it for me? Don't you have a country? Don't you live in the world? What the hell are you? You're not even an animal, no animal kills his own, what are you? What must I do to you? I ought to tear the tongue out of your mouth, what must I do? *(With his fist he pounds down upon his father's shoulder. He stumbles away, covering his face as he weeps.)* What must I do, Jesus God, what must I do?

KELLER. Chris . . . My Chris . . .

Act Three

(Two o'clock the following morning, MOTHER is discovered on the rise, rocking ceaselessly in a chair, staring at her thoughts. It is an intense, slight, sort of rocking. A light shows from upstairs bedroom, lower floor windows being dark. The moon is strong and casts its bluish light.

Presently JIM, dressed in jacket and hat, appears from the left, and seeing her, goes up beside her.)

JIM. Any news?

MOTHER. No news.

JIM *(Gently).* You can't sit up all night, dear, why don't you go to bed?

MOTHER. I'm waiting for Chris. Don't worry about me, Jim, I'm perfectly all right.

JIM. But it's almost two o'clock.

MOTHER. I can't sleep. *(Slight pause.)* You had an emergency?

JIM *(Tiredly).* Somebody had a headache and thought he was dying. *(Slight pause.)* Half of my patients are quite mad. Nobody realizes how many people are walking around loose, and they're cracked as coconuts. Money. Money-money-money-money. You say it long enough it doesn't mean anything. *(She smiles, makes a silent laugh.)* Oh, how I'd love to be around when that happens!

MOTHER *(Shakes her head).* You're so childish, Jim! Sometimes you are.

JIM *(Looks at her a moment).* Kate. *(Pause.)* What happened?

KATE. I told you. He had an argument with Joe. Then he got in the car and drove away.

JIM. What kind of an argument?

255

MOTHER. An argument, Joe . . . he was crying like a child, before.

JIM. They argued about Ann?

MOTHER *(Slight hesitation).* No, not Ann. Imagine? *(Indicates lighted window above.)* She hasn't come out of that room since he left. All night in that room.

JIM *(Looks at window, then at her).* What'd Joe do, tell him?

MOTHER *(She stops rocking).* Tell him what?

JIM. Don't be afraid, Kate, I know. I've always known.

MOTHER. How?

JIM. It occurred to me a long time ago.

MOTHER. I always had the feeling that in the back of his head, Chris . . . almost knew. I didn't think it would be such a shock.

JIM *(Gets up).* Chris would never know how to live with a thing like that. It takes a certain talent . . . for lying. You have it, and I do. But not him.

MOTHER. What do you mean . . . he's not coming back?

JIM. Oh, no, he'll come back. We all come back, Kate. These private little revolutions always die. The compromise is always made. In a peculiar way. Frank is right—every man does have a star. The star is one's honesty. And you spend your life groping for it, but once it's out it never lights again. I don't think he went very far. He probably just wanted to be alone to watch his star go out.

MOTHER. Just as long as he comes back.

JIM. I wish he wouldn't, Kate. One year I simply took off, went to New Orleans; for two months I lived on bananas and milk, and studied a certain disease. It was beautiful. And then she came, and she cried. And I went back home with her. And now I live in the usual darkness; I can't find myself; it's even hard sometimes to remember the kind of man I wanted to be. I'm a good husband; Chris is a good son— he'll come back. (KELLER *comes out on porch in dressing-gown and slippers. He goes upstage—to alley.* JIM *goes to him.)*

JIM. I have a feeling he's in the park. I'll look around for him.

Put her to bed, Joe; this is no good for what she's got. (JIM *exits up driveway.*)

KELLER (*Coming down*). What does he want here?

MOTHER. His friend is not home.

KELLER (*His voice is husky. Comes down to her*). I don't like him mixing in so much.

MOTHER. It's too late, Joe. He knows.

KELLER (*Apprehensively*). How does he know?

MOTHER. He guessed a long time ago.

KELLER. I don't like that.

MOTHER (*Laughs dangerously, quietly into the line*). What you don't like . . .

KELLER. Yeah, what I don't like.

MOTHER. You can't bull yourself through this one, Joe, you better be smart now. This thing—this thing is not over yet.

KELLER (*Indicating lighted window above*). And what is she doing up there? She don't come out of the room.

MOTHER. I don't know, what is she doing? Sit down, stop being mad. You want to live? You better figure out your life.

KELLER. She don't know, does she?

MOTHER. She saw Chris storming out of here. It's one and one —she knows how to add.

KELLER. Maybe I ought to talk to her?

MOTHER. Don't ask me, Joe.

KELLER (*Almost an outburst*). Then who do I ask? But I don't think she'll do anything about it.

MOTHER. You're asking me again.

KELLER. I'm askin' you. What am I, a stranger? I thought I had a family here. What happened to my family?

MOTHER. You've got a family. I'm simply telling you that I have no strength to think any more.

KELLER. You have no strength. The minute there's trouble you have no strength.

MOTHER. Joe, you're doing the same thing again; all your life whenever there's trouble you yell at me and you think that settles it.

KELLER. Then what do I do? Tell me, talk to me, what do I do?

MOTHER. Joe . . . I've been thinking this way. If he comes back . . .

KELLER. What do you mean "if"? . . . he's comin' back!

MOTHER. I think if you sit him down and you . . . explain yourself. I mean you ought to make it clear to him that you know you did a terrible thing. (*Not looking into his eyes.*) I mean if he saw that you realize what you did. You see?

KELLER. What ice does that cut?

MOTHER (*A little fearfully*). I mean if you told him that you want to pay for what you did.

KELLER (*Sensing . . . quietly*). How can I pay?

MOTHER. Tell him . . . you're willing to go to prison. (*Pause.*)

KELLER (*Struck, amazed*). I'm willing to . . . ?

MOTHER (*Quickly*). You wouldn't go, he wouldn't ask you to go. But if you told him you wanted to, if he could feel that you wanted to pay, maybe he would forgive you.

KELLER. He would forgive me! For what?

MOTHER. Joe, you know what I mean.

KELLER. I don't know what you mean! You wanted money, so I made money. What must I be forgiven? You wanted money, didn't you?

MOTHER. I didn't want it that way.

KELLER. I didn't want it that way, either! What difference is it what you want? I spoiled the both of you. I should've put him out when he was ten like I was put out, and made him earn his keep. Then he'd know how a buck is made in this world. Forgiven! I could live on a quarter a day myself, but I got a family so I . . .

MOTHER. Joe, Joe . . . it don't excuse it that you did it for the family.

KELLER. It's got to excuse it!

MOTHER. There's something bigger than the family to him.

KELLER. Nothin' is bigger!

MOTHER. There is to him.

KELLER. There's nothin' he could do that I wouldn't forgive. Because he's my son. Because I'm his father and he's my son.

MOTHER. Joe, I tell you . . .

KELLER. Nothin's bigger than that. And you're goin' to tell him, you understand? I'm his father and he's my son, and if there's something bigger than that I'll put a bullet in my head!

MOTHER. You stop that!

KELLER. You heard me. Now you know what to tell him. *(Pause. He moves from her—halts.)* But he wouldn't put me away though . . . He wouldn't do that . . . Would he?

MOTHER. He loved you, Joe, you broke his heart.

KELLER. But to put me away . . .

MOTHER. I don't know. I'm beginning to think we don't really know him. They say in the war he was such a killer. Here he was always afraid of mice. I don't know him. I don't know what he'll do.

KELLER. Goddamn, if Larry was alive he wouldn't act like this. He understood the way the world is made. He listened to me. To him the world had a forty-foot front, it ended at the building line. This one, everything bothers him. You make a deal, overcharge two cents, and his hair falls out. He don't understand money. Too easy, it came too easy. Yes sir. Larry. That was a boy we lost. Larry. Larry. *(He slumps on chair in front of her.)* What am I gonna do, Kate . . .

MOTHER. Joe, Joe, please . . . you'll be all right, nothing is going to happen . . .

KELLER *(Desperately, lost)*. For you, Kate, for both of you, that's all I ever lived for . . .

MOTHER. I know, darling, I know . . . *(ANN enters from house. They say nothing, waiting for her to speak.)*

ANN. Why do you stay up? I'll tell you when he comes.

KELLER *(Rises, goes to her)*. You didn't eat supper, did you? *(To MOTHER.)* Why didn't you make her eat something?

MOTHER. Sure, I'll . . .

ANN. Never mind, Kate, I'm all right. *(They are unable to speak to each other.)* There's something I want to tell you. *(She starts, then halts.)* I'm not going to do anything about it. . . .

MOTHER. She's a good girl! *(To KELLER.)* You see? She's a . . .

ANN. I'll do nothing about Joe, but you're going to do something for me. (*Directly to* MOTHER.) You made Chris feel guilty with me. Whether you wanted to or not, you've crippled him in front of me. I'd like you to tell him that Larry is dead and that you know it. You understand me? I'm not going out of here alone. There's no life for me that way. I want you to set him free. And then I promise you, everything will end, and we'll go away, and that's all.

KELLER. You'll do that. You'll tell him.

ANN. I know what I'm asking, Kate. You had two sons. But you've only got one now.

KELLER. You'll tell him . . .

ANN. And you've got to say it to him so he knows you mean it.

MOTHER. My dear, if the boy was dead, it wouldn't depend on my words to make Chris know it. . . . The night he gets into your bed, his heart will dry up. Because he knows and you know. To his dying day he'll wait for his brother! No, my dear, no such thing. You're going in the morning, and you're going alone. That's your life, that's your lonely life.

(*She goes to porch, and starts in.*)

ANN. Larry is dead, Kate.

MOTHER (*She stops*). Don't speak to me.

ANN. I said he's dead. I know! He crashed off the coast of China November twenty-fifth! His engine didn't fail him. But he died. I know . . .

MOTHER. How did he die? You're lying to me. If you know, how did he die?

ANN. I loved him. You know I loved him. Would I have looked at anyone else if I wasn't sure? That's enough for you.

MOTHER (*Moving on her*). What's enough for me? What're you talking about? (*She grasps* ANN's *wrists.*)

ANN. You're hurting my wrists.

MOTHER. What are you talking about! (*Pause. She stares at* ANN *a moment, then turns and goes to* KELLER.)

ANN. Joe, go in the house . . .

KELLER. Why should I . . .

ANN. Please go.

KELLER. Lemme know when he comes. (KELLER *goes into house.*)

MOTHER (*She sees* ANN *take a letter from her pocket*). What's that?

ANN. Sit down . . . (MOTHER *moves left to chair, but does not sit.*) First you've got to understand. When I came, I didn't have any idea that Joe . . . I had nothing against him or you. I came to get married. I hoped . . . So I didn't bring this to hurt you. I thought I'd show it to you only if there was no other way to settle Larry in your mind.

MOTHER. Larry? (*Snatches letter from* ANN's *hand.*)

ANN. He wrote it to me just before he—(MOTHER *opens and begins to read letter.*) I'm not trying to hurt you, Kate. You're making me do this, now remember you're—— Remember. I've been so lonely, Kate . . . I can't leave here alone again. (*A long, low moan comes from* MOTHER's *throat as she reads.*) You made me show it to you. You wouldn't believe me. I told you a hundred times, why wouldn't you believe me!

MOTHER. Oh, my God . . .

ANN (*With pity and fear*). Kate, please, please . . .

MOTHER. My God, my God . . .

ANN. Kate, dear, I'm so sorry . . . I'm so sorry. (CHRIS *enters from driveway. He seems exhausted.*)

CHRIS. What's the matter . . . ?

ANN. Where were you? . . . you're all perspired. (MOTHER *doesn't move.*) Where were you?

CHRIS. Just drove around a little. I thought you'd be gone.

ANN. Where do I go? I have nowhere to go.

CHRIS (*To* MOTHER). Where's Dad?

ANN. Inside lying down.

CHRIS. Sit down, both of you. I'll say what there is to say.

MOTHER. I didn't hear the car . . .

CHRIS. I left it in the garage.

MOTHER. Jim is out looking for you.

CHRIS. Mother . . . I'm going away. There are a couple of firms in Cleveland, I think I can get a place. I mean, I'm going away for good. (*To* ANN *alone.*) I know what you're thinking Annie. It's true. I'm yellow. I was made yellow in this house because I suspected my father and I did nothing about it, but if I knew that night when I came home what I know now, he'd be in the district attorney's office by this time, and I'd have brought him there. Now if I look at him, all I'm able to do is cry.

MOTHER. What are you talking about? What else can you do?

CHRIS. I could jail him! I could jail him, if I were human any more. But I'm like everybody else now. I'm practical now. You made me practical.

MOTHER. But you have to be.

CHRIS. The cats in that alley are practical, the bums who ran away when we were fighting were practical. Only the dead ones weren't practical. But now I'm practical, and I spit on myself. I'm going away. I'm going now.

ANN (*Goes up to stop him*). I'm coming with you. . . .

CHRIS. No, Ann.

ANN. Chris, I don't ask you to do anything about Joe.

CHRIS. You do, you do . . .

ANN. I swear I never will.

CHRIS. In your heart you always will.

ANN. Then do what you have to do!

CHRIS. Do what? What is there to do? I've looked all night for a reason to make him suffer.

ANN. There's reason, there's reason!

CHRIS. What? Do I raise the dead when I put him behind bars? Then what'll I do it for? We used to shoot a man who acted like a dog, but honor was real there, you were protecting something. But here? This is the land of the great big dogs, you don't love a man here, you eat him! That's the principle; the only one we live by—it just happened to kill a few people this time, that's all. The world's that way, how can I take it out on him? What sense does that make? This is a zoo, a zoo!

ANN (*To* MOTHER). You know what he's got to do! Tell him!

MOTHER. Let him go.

ANN. I won't let him go. You'll tell him what he's got to do . . .

MOTHER. Annie!

ANN. Then I will! *(KELLER enters from house. CHRIS sees him, goes down right near arbor.)*

KELLER. What's the matter with you? I want to talk to you.

CHRIS. I've got nothing to say to you.

KELLER *(Taking his arm).* I want to talk to you!

CHRIS *(Pulling violently away from him).* Don't do that, Dad. I'm going to hurt you if you do that. There's nothing to say, so say it quick.

KELLER. Exactly what's the matter? What's the matter? You got too much money? Is that what bothers you?

CHRIS *(With an edge of sarcasm).* It bothers me.

KELLER. If you can't get used to it, then throw it away. You hear me? Take every cent and give it to charity, throw it in the sewer. Does that settle it? In the sewer, that's all. You think I'm kidding? I'm tellin' you what to do, if it's dirty then burn it. It's your money, that's not my money. I'm a dead man, I'm an old dead man, nothing's mine. Well, talk to me!—what do you want to do!

CHRIS. It's not what I want to do. It's what you want to do.

KELLER. What should I want to do? *(CHRIS is silent.)* Jail? You want me to go to jail? If you want me to go, say so! Is that where I belong?—then tell me so! *(Slight pause.)* What's the matter, why can't you tell me? *(Furiously.)* You say everything else to me, say that! *(Slight pause.)* I'll tell you why you can't say it. Because you know I don't belong there. Because you know! *(With growing emphasis and passion, and a persistent tone of desperation.)* Who worked for nothin' in that war? When they work for nothin', I'll work for nothin'. Did they ship a gun or a truck outa Detroit before they got their price? Is that clean? It's dollars and cents, nickels and dimes; war and peace, it's nickels and dimes, what's clean? Half the goddamn country is gotta go if I go! That's why you can't tell me.

CHRIS. That's exactly why.

KELLER. Then . . . why am *I* bad?

CHRIS. *I* know you're no worse than most men but I thought you were better. I never saw you as a man. I saw you as my father. *(Almost breaking.)* I can't look at you this way, I can't look at myself! (*He turns away unable to face* KELLER. ANN *goes quickly to* MOTHER, *takes letter from her and starts for* CHRIS. MOTHER *instantly rushes to intercept her.*)

MOTHER. Give me that!

ANN. He's going to read it! (*She thrusts letter into* CHRIS' *hand.*) Larry. He wrote it to me the day he died. . . .

KELLER. Larry!?

MOTHER. Chris, it's not for you. (*He starts to read.*) Joe . . . go away . . .

KELLER (*Mystified, frightened*). Why'd she say, Larry, what . . . ?

MOTHER (*She desperately pushes him toward alley, glancing at* CHRIS). Go to the street Joe, go to the street! (*She comes down beside* KELLER.) Don't, Chris . . . (*Pleading from her whole soul.*) Don't tell him . . .

CHRIS (*Quietly*). Three and one half years . . . talking, talking. Now you tell me what you must do. . . . This is how he died, now tell me where you belong.

KELLER (*Pleading*). Chris, a man can't be a Jesus in this world!

CHRIS. I know all about the world. I know the whole crap story. Now listen to this, and tell me what a man's got to be! (*Reads.* "My dear Ann: . . ." You listening? He wrote this the day he died. Listen, don't cry . . . listen! "My dear Ann: It is impossible to put down the things I feel. But I've got to tell you something. Yesterday they flew in a load of papers from the States and I read about Dad and your father being convicted. I can't express myself. I can't tell you how I feel—I can't bear to live any more. Last night I circled the base for twenty minutes before I could bring myself in. How could he have done that? Every day three or four men never come back and he sits back there doing business. . . . I don't know how to tell you what I feel . . . I can't face anybody . . . I'm going out on a mission in a few minutes. They'll probably report me missing. If they do, I want you to know that you mustn't wait for me. I tell you, Ann, if I had him here now I could kill him—" (KELLER *grabs letter from* CHRIS' *hand and reads it. After a long pause.)* Now blame the world. Do you understand that letter?

KELLER *(He speaks almost inaudibly).* I think I do. Get the car, I'll put on my jacket. *(He turns and starts slowly for the house.* MOTHER *rushes to intercept him.)*

MOTHER. Why are you going? You'll sleep, why are you going?

KELLER. I can't sleep here. I'll feel better if I go.

MOTHER. You're so foolish. Larry was your son too, wasn't he? You know he'd never tell you to do this.

KELLER *(Looking at letter in his hand).* Then what is this if it isn't telling me? Sure, he was my son. But I think to him they were all my sons. And I guess they were, I guess they were. I'll be right down. *(Exits into house.)*

MOTHER *(To* CHRIS, *with determination).* You're not going to take him!

CHRIS. I'm taking him.

MOTHER. It's up to you, if you tell him to stay he'll stay. Go and tell him!

CHRIS. Nobody could stop him now.

MOTHER. You'll stop him! How long will he live in prison?— are you trying to kill him?

CHRIS *(Holding out letter).* I thought you read this!

MOTHER *(Of Larry, the letter).* The war is over! Didn't you hear? ——it's over!

CHRIS. Then what was Larry to you? A stone that fell into the water? It's not enough for him to be sorry. Larry didn't kill himself to make you and Dad sorry.

MOTHER. What more can we be!

CHRIS. You can be better! Once and for all you can know there's a universe of people outside and you're responsible to it, and unless you know that you threw away your son because that's why he died.

(A shot is heard in the house. They stand frozen for a brief second. CHRIS *starts for porch, pauses at step, turns to* ANN.)

CHRIS. Find Jim! *(He goes on into the house and* ANN *runs up driveway.* MOTHER *stands alone, transfixed.)*

MOTHER *(Softly, almost moaning).* Joe . . . Joe . . . Joe . . . Joe . . . (CHRIS *comes out of house, down to* MOTHER's *arms.)*

CHRIS *(almost crying).* Mother, I didn't mean to . . .

MOTHER. Don't dear. Don't take it on yourself. Forget now. Live. (CHRIS *stirs as if to answer.)* Shhh . . . *(She puts his arms down gently and moves towards porch.)* Shhh . . . *(As she reaches porch steps she begins sobbing, as the curtain falls.)*